"To Spare No Pains"

Zebulon Montgomery Pike and His 1806–1807 Southwest Expedition

Pikes Peak Regional History Symposium
Sponsored by
Special Collections, Pikes Peak Library District
Friends of the Pikes Peak Library District
Pikes Peak Library District Foundation

In Partnership With
Colorado Springs Pioneers Museum
Pikes Peak Community College
Western Museum of Mining and Industry
McAllister House Museum
San Luis Museum
Santa Fe Trail Association, Zebulon M. Pike Expedition

Endorsed by
Colorado Humanities

Project Director
Chris Nicholl

Pikes Peak Regional History
Symposium Committee
Chris Nicholl, Co-Chair
Calvin P. Otto, Co-Chair
Steve Antonuccio
Tim Blevins
Aaron Callicut
David Carroll
Beverly Diehl
Dolores Fowler
Barbara Gately
Lynn A. Gilfillan-Morton
Carol Kennis
Michael Olsen
Kathy Sturdevant
Dee Vazquez

"To Spare No Pains"

Zebulon Montgomery Pike and His 1806–1807 Southwest Expedition

A Bicentennial Commemoration

Edited by
Tim Blevins, Matt Mayberry, Chris Nicholl,
Calvin P. Otto & Nancy Thaler

Published by

PIKES PEAK LIBRARY DISTRICT

with the

COLORADO SPRINGS PIONEERS MUSEUM

"To Spare No Pains": Zebulon Montgomery Pike and His 1806–1807 Southwest Expedition, A Bicentennial Commemoration

"How Lost was Zebulon Pike?" by Donald Jackson reprinted courtesy of American Heritage Inc. 1965.

"Enemies & Friends: Zebulon Montgomery Pike & Facundo Melgares in the Struggle for Control of the Louisiana Purchase" by Leo Oliva and "Zebulon Pike & American Popular Culture, or, Has Pike Peaked?" by Michael L. Olsen previously appeared in *Kansas History: A Journal of the Central Plains*, Vol. 29, No. 1.

"The Pike Centennial Celebration 1906" by Edwin A. and Nancy E. Bathke previously appeared in the *Denver Westerner's Brand Book*, Vol. 28.

Publisher's Cataloging-in-Publication Data

"To spare no pains" : Zebulon Montgomery Pike and his 1806–1807 Southwest expedition, a bicentennial commemoration / edited by Tim Blevins, Matt Mayberry, Chris Nicholl, Calvin P. Otto & Nancy Thaler. — 1st ed.
    p. cm. (Regional history series)
 Includes bibliographical references and index.
 LCCN 2006940244
 ISBN 978-1-56735-224-5
 1. Pike, Zebulon Montgomery, 1779–1813 — Travel — Southwest, New.
 2. Southwest, New — Discovery and exploration. 3. Burr Conspiracy, 1805–1807. 4. Pikes Peak (Colo.) 5. Rocky Mountains — Discovery and exploration. I. Blevins, Tim, ed. II. Mayberry, Matt, ed. III. Nicholl, Chris, ed. IV. Series.

F592
917.8042 — dc22

About Pikes Peak Library District

Pikes Peak Library District (PPLD) is a nationally recognized system of public libraries serving a population of more than 500,000 in El Paso County, Colorado. With twelve facilities and two bookmobiles, PPLD responds to the unique needs of individual neighborhoods and the community at large. PPLD has an employee base of four hundred full and part-time staff, and utilizes roughly twelve hundred volunteers. It strives to reach all members of the community, providing free and equitable access to information and an avenue for personal and community enrichment.

PPLD is rated ninth among library systems its size in the country. Volume of circulations, number of visits, and hours of access contribute to the ranking. PPLD is also recognized for its commitment to diversity, its quality programming, and its excellent customer service.

Regional History Series

Currently In Print

The Colorado Labor Wars: Cripple Creek 1903–1904,
A Centennial Commemoration

Forthcoming

Doctor at Timberline

Extraordinary Women of the Rocky Mountain West

Legends, Labors & Loves: William Jackson Palmer, 1836–1909

Regional History Series
Editorial Committee

Tim Blevins
Chris Nicholl
Calvin P. Otto

Principal Series Consultant
Calvin P. Otto

Acknowledgments

The Editorial Committee is grateful to the many people whose dedication to preserving our regional history made the Zebulon Montgomery Pike symposium and this book possible. Matt Mayberry and the staff of the Colorado Springs Pioneers Museum did a wonderful job bringing the Pike Bicentennial to life. The entire staff of Pikes Peak Library District's Special Collections contributed to the symposium event, this book, and related projects. Nancy Thaler is to be credited for her expert design and editorial work, and Nina Kuberski's skill at digitizing images for this book is unmatched. The Editorial Committee also extends its appreciation to Dee Fowler, PPLD Foundations Director, Dee Vazquez, Community Relations Officer, her staff, and Steve Antonuccio, Multimedia Center and Production Studio Manager and his staff for video recording these lectures.

The Editorial Committee

This publication was made possible by private funds.

Cover and Book Design
Nancy Thaler

For purchasing information, contact:

Clausen Books
2131 North Weber Street
Colorado Springs, Colorado 80907
tel: (719) 471-5884, toll free: (888)-412-7717
http://www.clausenbooks.com

CONTENTS

Zebulon Montgomery Pike, engraving based on the painting by Charles Willson Peale. *From Special Collections, Pikes Peak Library District.*

FOREWORD

Pikes Peak Library District's third annual Pikes Peak Regional History Symposium, *"To Spare No Pains": Zebulon Montgomery Pike & His 1806 – 1807 Expedition, A Bicentennial Symposium*, mustered the talents of exceptional Pike scholars who presented a captivating look back at Pike's Southwest Expedition and how the twelve-month exploration during his brief thirty-four-year life impacts our community and nation today.

Our much-appreciated Symposium partner, Colorado Springs Pioneers Museum, under the leadership of Matt Mayberry, guided the community's participation in recognition of Lieutenant Pike's travels through our region. Matt negotiated the temporary return of selected Pike documents to the region for the first time in two hundred years. He welcomed citizens of all ages to include their postcard messages in the 2006 time capsule to be read by those commemorating the future tercentennial of Pike's expedition. The capsule is now sealed under a fourteen-ton boulder in Antlers Park. The Museum's bicentennial celebration events piqued interest in this symposium and drew crowds to many other commemorative events in 2006. Matt himself kicked off the Symposium with an incredible keynote address.

Matt's stirring talk set the stage for a day of thought-provoking presentations that dissected what we know – and what we *thought* we knew – about Pike's trek through our Colorado plains and mountains. The focus was not on disputing the events so well documented in Pike's journals and later analyzed by notable historians, however. Rather, each scholar offered a view of these historic events through a different lens. Each contributed to a better, more holistic understanding of the influences and circumstances acting on the participants of Pike's Southwest Expedition.

Presenters at the June 3, 2006, Symposium included professional historians and history teachers, a retired cardiac surgeon and wilderness medicine expert, a park ranger, an attorney, a Colorado National Guard officer, and an archivist. This book, *"To Spare No Pains": Zebulon Montgomery Pike & His 1806 – 1807 Southwest Expedition, A Bicentennial Commemoration,* contains the written work resulting from each presenter's research on the Expedition events, the politics of the time, and the popular use of Pike and his legacy in cultural and commercial endeavors. We also include herein Donald Jackson's erudite article, "How Lost was Zebulon Pike?," papers presented at the Pioneer Museum's Speakers Series, the entertaining interpretive script for the Symposium's historical puppet program and an enlightening introduction by historian, writer, and musician Mark L. Gardner. Finally, you can experience the 1906 Pike Centennial Commemoration events, as told by Edwin and Nancy Bathke, and Katie Davis Gardner's article on the art inspired by our Peak's dominating presence.

I invite you to join in the commemoration of Zebulon Montgomery Pike's expedition and to read this book from cover to cover. Your reward will be a new understanding of both a complex man and of the formative years of our nation's expansion. These are also just great stories—read and enjoy!

Paula J. Miller
Executive Director
Pikes Peak Library District

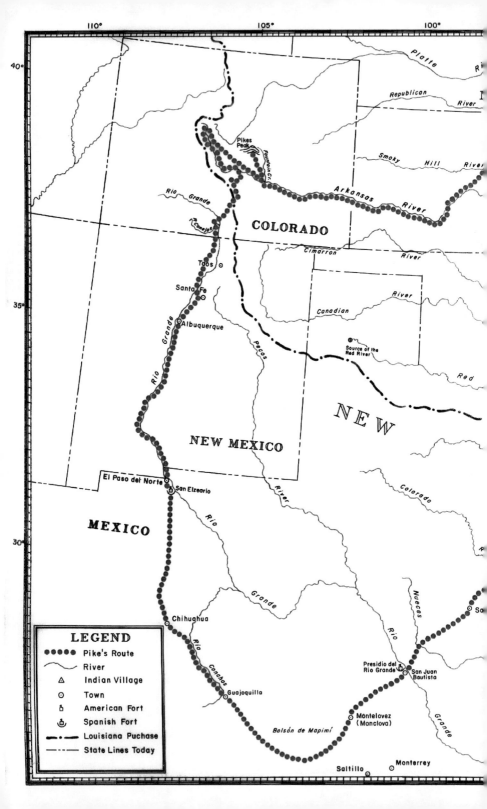

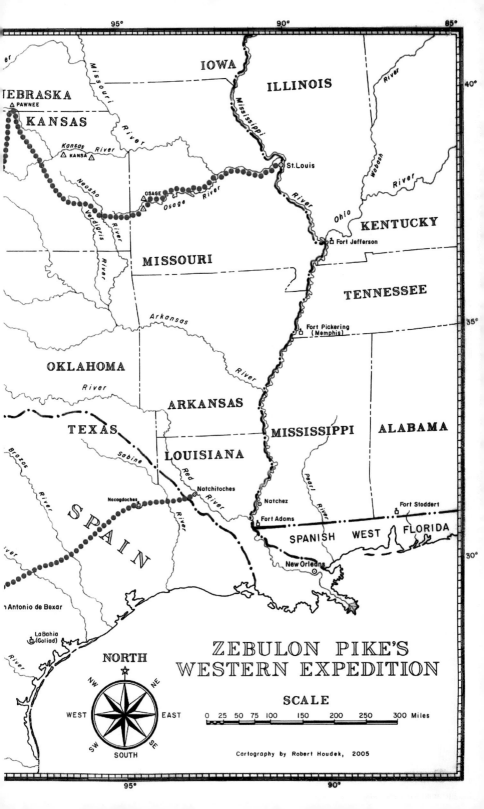

ZEBULON PIKE'S
WESTERN EXPEDITION

SCALE

0 25 50 75 100   150   200   250   300 Miles

Cartography by Robert Houdek, 2005

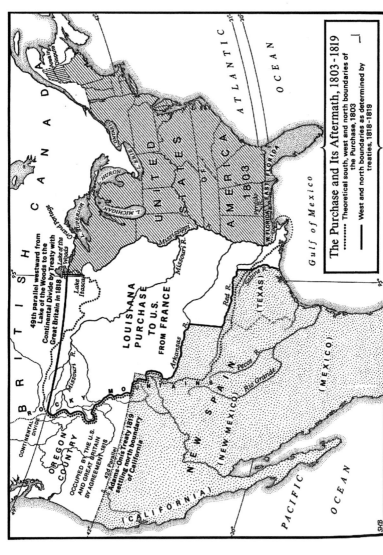

The Purchase and Its Aftermath, 1803-1819
·········· Theoretical south, west and north boundaries of the Purchase, 1803
———— West and north boundaries as determined by treaties, 1818-1819

From *So Vast and Beautiful a Land: Louisiana and the Purchase* by Marshall Sprague, Boston, Little, Brown and Co., 1974.

Introduction

Mark L. Gardner

In November of 1818, a large advertisement in *The Ohio Repository* of Canton undoubtedly piqued the interest of readers, perhaps even causing some excitement. The advertisement announced the opening of a "New Museum of Wax-Work" at Samuel Patton's Inn. At the top of the list of "characters" to be "represented in Wax, in the first style of excellence" were George Washington, followed by Andrew Jackson, "the hero of New Orleans." Listed third was Brigadier General Zebulon M. Pike, who had received a fatal wound during his overwhelming victory at the Battle of York, Ontario, Canada, just five years previous. Pike, whose wax form was "represented as being supported by his surgeon in his dying moments," was listed above such luminaries as James Madison, the Duke of York, and the ever-beguiling Sleeping Beauty.[1]

A national hero in 1818, Zebulon Pike's ultimate sacrifice for his country is little known or remembered by the majority of Americans today. However, because of a milestone of time important only to the living, his name has graced the pages of newspapers across America once again. Two hundred years ago, Zebulon Pike led a small exploring party west/southwest from present-day Missouri across a territory then largely unknown to a young United States. As part of that grueling expedition, Pike would attempt and fail to climb a majestic peak on the Front Range of the Rocky Mountains, a peak that now bears his name (famously one might add). Later apprehended by Spanish soldiers in the San Luis Valley, Pike and his men would receive a stunning firsthand view of New Spain — again, a mysterious and foreign region to Americans at the time — as his party was escorted back to U.S. soil in 1807.

The ramifications of Pike's Southwestern expedition were, in every sense of the word, immense. His revelations concerning Spanish settlements, military strength, natural resources, Indian tribes, and, most importantly, commerce, cast a bright beam of light on a world that opportunistic Americans believed ripe for trade and, eventually, the taking. Robert L. Duffus, in his classic history of the Santa Fe Trail, provides us with a breathless, if somewhat romanticized, explanation of the dramatic impact of

Pike's printed report of 1810:

> After Pike's narrative was published, New Mexico had
> for American adventurers something of the appeal
> that the golden cities of Cibola and Quivira had had
> for the Spanish pioneers. Only this gold was real. Pike
> described no land of dreams. He gave statistics. He
> mentioned the fact that high grade imported cloth sold
> in Santa Fe for between $20 and $25 a yard, linen for
> $4 a yard and other dry goods in proportion. . . . Pike
> stirred men's imaginations. He made them restless to
> be up and going. His prairies and his mountains called
> to them as the sea calls to predestined sailors.[2]

Pike's published account, complete with beautifully engraved
and detailed maps, became the impetus for both the important
Santa Fe trade and, in turn, U.S. territorial expansion into what
is today's American Southwest. Although the U.S. conquest of
northern Mexico would not physically occur until Stephen Watts
Kearny's Army of the West marched down the Santa Fe Trail
in the summer of 1846, that conquest, that tangible upshot of
America's then-obsession with a fatalistic ideal called Manifest
Destiny, began with Zebulon Montgomery Pike.

It was because of Zebulon Pike's significance to Western
history, not to mention the prominence of his name in regional
geography, and, of course, the happy circumstance of the
bicentennial, that Pike and his 1806–1807 Southwestern expedition
was chosen as the subject of a major exhibition and lecture series
at the Colorado Springs Pioneers Museum and the theme for the
Pikes Peak Library District's third annual Pikes Peak Regional
History Symposium. The several speakers for both the symposium
and the lecture series composed a variety of backgrounds (Ph. D'd
historians, a medical doctor, a lieutenant in the Colorado National
Guard, museum professionals, and others), and they covered a
wide array of topics related to Pike, as will be seen in the thought-
provoking papers that follow this introduction. As a whole, the
symposium and lecture series sought to explore Pike's legacy and
to somehow "get to know," get closer to the man who left such a
significant stamp on this region we call the West.

Pike the man, the father, the husband; his character, passions, loves, hates, fears, ideals, can be rather elusive. How does one *really* get to know a person who's been dead for almost two centuries? Fortunately, we do have Pike's own writings, which offer a number of revealing insights.[3] And, in addition to the observations and findings of the scholars represented in this volume, there are a very few descriptions left by Pike's contemporaries. The best, in my opinion, was recorded by Major Amos Holton, who served under Pike during the War of 1812. Holton vividly remembered an intimate campfire scene in the province of Quebec, Canada. It was well after midnight in late November 1812. A sharp night engagement had been fought with a superior force of British soldiers and Indians, and Pike, then a colonel, gathered around him Holton and one or two "favorite subordinates." "The scene was well suited to the contemplative and sublimated soul of Pike," Holton wrote.

It was a moment for calm and solemn reflection and musing . . . He would speak for some time in a glowing and elevated strain of moralizing; then pause awhile, and appear to be wrapped in profound thought—and then pour fourth another continuous strain of just sentiment and sublime eloquence, seldom equaled. — The occasional interruptions from the wind, which, at brief intervals, rose and fell, and sent its moaning voice through the bending tree-tops, was a circumstance rather in correspondence and harmony with the others; and instead of diminishing, seemed to lend additional interest and solemnity to the scene.—He dwelt on the relative duties of man, as a member of society, in different situations, at considerable length; and all his remarks were pertinent and well applied and many of them forcible and thrilling. Abstraction from self or disinterestedness, public spirit, and a chivalrous patriotism, were his favorite themes; and he spoke with peculiar force and feeling of the duty of dying for one's country, in defense of a just and righteous cause—and the rewards that must be in reserve for all such, beyond the grave. He referred with enthusiasm, to the glorious examples of the Royal Gustavus Adolphus, and of General Wolfe and Desaix, who had fallen on the field of battle, in the embrace of victory—regarding theirs as an enviable fate; and expressing a fervent hope that such might be his. He repeated some poetical effusions, tasteful and appropriate to the occasion—imbued with patriotic sentiment, and rich in sublime and original thought.—And thus we spent four or five of the last hours of that eventful night.[4]

Six months later, Pike's yearning for a patriotic death would be realized—thus his portrayal in wax in 1818 as one of the heroic and famous. Interestingly, names not found in that curious wax museum announcement are those of Meriwether Lewis and William Clark. Yet for the last century or so, Pike's seemingly waxen legacy has melted under the supernova that Lewis and Clark and their Corps of Discovery have become in American popular culture. Why? It is a question that has been asked often during the Pike Bicentennial.[5] There are at least three reasons, perhaps more.

First, Pike's expedition, although having its own fair share of obstacles and physical trials and tribulations, did not have the same cast of characters as the Corps of Discovery. There was no Sacagawea or a York for Pike. The Lewis and Clark expedition offers something that truly every American—man, woman, and child—can marvel at or relate to in some way. Second, as already noted, Pike's glorious death at the moment of victory for his country has been largely forgotten, as has the large majority of our military heroes dating before the Civil War. Consequently, Pike is remembered primarily as an early explorer of the West, and within that category he is considered by the uninformed to have been a failure. He failed to climb Pikes Peak; got lost, mistaking the Rio Grande for the Red River; and, to add insult to injury, was gathered up by the none-too-pleased Spanish and escorted back to U.S. territory. Third, Pike has often been linked with the Aaron Burr conspiracy through his rapscallion commanding officer, General James Wilkinson, which has raised questions as to the true intent of Pike's Southwestern expedition in the first place.

For all of the above reasons, then, as interest in the frontier West flourished in the twentieth century, Pike became somewhat of a historical footnote. It is a trend that, regrettably, is likely to continue. By and large, the Pike Bicentennial has proven to be a regional phenomenon, with most of the commemorative events occurring in Colorado. Unquestionably, the shining highlights of those events were the vastly popular Pioneers Museum bicentennial exhibits and lecture series and the filled-to-capacity Zebulon Pike Symposium. The Pikes Peak Library District, the Pioneers Museum, and also their partners and sponsors, are to be commended for making the following papers available in printed form. They certainly reveal new facts about Pike, his expedition, and his legacy, and amply demonstrate that there is still much more to learn.

What I most hope that readers of these papers will come away with, though, is the knowledge that Zebulon Pike was anything but a failure. The true measure of an explorer is this: Is he open to what's around him—new discoveries, new knowledge, new worlds? Is he flexible enough to alter an original goal, idea, or *mission*? When Pike strayed into Spanish territory and found himself under the escort of Spanish soldiers through northern New Spain, he kept his wits about him. At that time, a second, unwritten, mission presented itself to the ambitious young lieutenant, one of reconnaissance of foreign soil about which there was much interest in the United States, and the information Pike so carefully—and discreetly—gathered and brought back was of tremendous value to both the American government and its citizens.

In 1966, Pike scholar Donald Jackson wrote that "An explorer . . . is involved with filling in the blank spaces on maps. To use a convenient Jeffersonian phrase, he is on a 'tour of discovery.' Pike's draftsmanship was inept, and his readings of latitude and longitude were often wide of the mark, but he filled in blanks."[6]

A fitting tribute to Pike is that there will by no means be a blank space next to the 14,110-foot peak he admired but never climbed. On our maps, America's most famous mountain will always bear the name Pikes Peak. And as for this modest volume you hold in your hands, the scholars whose works are published here have admirably filled in several blanks in the story of Zebulon Montgomery Pike and his Southwestern expedition.

Mark L. Gardner is a professional historian, author, and musician with a broad range of publications—both popular and scholarly—focusing on the American West. He has written several interpretive histories for National Park Service historic sites, including Little Bighorn Battlefield, Fort Laramie, the Santa Fe Trail, and Bent's Old Fort. He has also written biographies of frontier icons George Armstrong Custer (2005) and Geronimo (2006). He lives with his family in Cascade, Colorado.

Notes

1. *The Ohio Repository*, Canton, Ohio, November 27, 1818. Admission to the wax museum was 25 cents, half price for children.

2. R. L. Duffus, *The Santa Fe Trail* (New York: Longmans, Green and Co., 1930), 53.

3. Pike's one and only book is *An Account of Expeditions to the Sources of the Mississippi, and Through the Western Parts of Louisiana, to the Sources of the Arkansaw, Kans, La Platte, and Pierre Juan, Rivers...* (Philadelphia: C. & A. Conrad & Co., 1810). This publication, along with all the known letters written by Pike and his contemporaries relating to his two expeditions in Louisiana Territory, appear in Donald Jackson's seminal *The Journals of Zebulon Montgomery Pike, with Letters and Related Documents* (Norman: University of Oklahoma Press, 1966). Sadly, the Jackson edition of Pike's journals is long out of print, and its publisher, the University of Oklahoma Press, chose not to reprint the hefty two-volume set for the Pike Bicentennial. However, the University of New Mexico Press did reprint an older edition of Pike's Southwestern journals for the bicentennial, which included a new introduction by this writer. That work is *The Southwestern Journals of Zebulon Pike, 1806-1807*, ed. Stephen Harding Hart and Archer Butler Hulbert (Albuquerque: University of New Mexico Press, 2006).

4. Holton's account is an excerpt from his planned biography of Pike. Unfortunately, it appears that Holton's manuscript was never completed, or it least it never saw publication. This excerpt originally appeared in the Columbus, Ohio, *Democratic Monthly Magazine and Western Review* and was reprinted in the Wellsburg, Pennsylvania, *Tioga Eagle* of July 31, 1844.

5. See Ed Quillen, "Footnotes to Lewis and Clark," *Denver Post*, August 29, 2006.

6. Jackson, ed., *The Journals of Zebulon Montgomery Pike*, 1:451.

Zebulon Pike & the Exploration of the Southwest

Matt Mayberry

NOTE: This is an edited transcript of the keynote speech given by Matt Mayberry at the Pikes Peak Regional History Symposium on June 3, 2006, "To Spare No Pains: Zebulon Montgomery Pike and His 1806-1807 Expedition."

I'm honored to provide the opening remarks to this book. There is a great deal of excellent research that will be presented in these pages. I will provide the overview, the general survey of what Zebulon Montgomery Pike's Southwestern expedition was all about; but I will also introduce a few topics that you will read about in depth later, and I think when you finish this book you will understand what "to spare no pains" means.

That phrase from Pike's journals describes what he was trying to do here in the West: it describes his personality and many of the challenges that he faced. I will point out when that quote comes up in the journals and what it means, because that concept of doing whatever it took to achieve his mission is of major importance to our region. Pike's willingness 'to spare no pains' set us on the road to becoming what we are today.

The work that has been done on Pike is decidedly less thorough than that of the other major western explorers of the time, Meriwether Lewis and William Clark. During the recent commemoration of the Lewis and Clark Bicentennial one could hardly avoid those explorers — but not Zebulon Montgomery Pike. Even though we see Pike and the phrase "Pikes Peak" everywhere, we don't really understand the man behind the name; and so what we're going to try to do in this book is to introduce you to what he did, what he tried to accomplish, and some of the challenges he faced. I also hope to suggest some of the reasons why his legacy is less well established than that of Lewis and Clark. Hopefully, through this process, I will encourage readers to think more about who he was and how he has influenced our existence.

If you were to compare how many books there are on Lewis and Clark and how many on Pike the difference would be readily apparent: Lewis and Clark could fill libraries, Pike would fill bookshelves. But much of the work that has been done is by local scholars, in particular Donald Jackson. Dr. Jackson's research is the foundation for the exhibits and programs created by the Colorado Springs Pioneers Museum for the bicentennial. In the 1960s Jackson served as editor for the definitive work of Pike source materials, simply called *The Journals of Zebulon Montgomery Pike*. Jackson died in 1987, but nothing has yet supplanted this authoritative two-volume set. In addition to Donald Jackson, Steven Hart and A. B. Hulbert produced an edition of the *Southwestern Journals* in the 1930s, which has recently been re-released by the University of New Mexico with additional scholarship provided by Mark Gardner, who is also represented in this book. Colorado College professors Frank Tucker and Harvey Carter also produced works for the sesquicentennial of the Pike expedition fifty years ago. It seems only natural that so much of this work would be produced right here at the base of Pikes Peak.

I bring up Donald Jackson not only because his was the main scholarship that was used in our work but because he produced the key quote that has been remembered about Zebulon Pike. This quote, which is the first sentence in his introduction to the journals, accurately describes both the upside and the challenges of the man: "Nothing Pike tried to do was easy and most of his luck was bad." That has, unfortunately, been his legacy, but it's certainly accurate and it fits Pike's experience from the time he was born until his untimely death at the age of 34.

Who was Zebulon Montgomery Pike? Pike was born in 1779, a fortuitous year for the region that would later bear his name. That year another party of explorers came through the Pikes Peak region. The group was under the command of Juan Bautista de Anza, a Spanish Colonial military officer dispatched from Santa Fe. Anza, with the guidance and support of the Ute people, led some three hundred cavalry soldiers through the San Luis Valley, into South Park, and down Ute Pass. They traveled through present-day Woodland Park, Manitou and Old Colorado City, and further south into the Pueblo area and beyond. They were searching for Comanche who'd been raiding the Spanish settlements surrounding Santa Fe. That search ended in a decisive battle between the Spanish and

Comanche. What a coincidence that the man for whom Pikes Peak is named was born the same year as other explorers from another nation were also in the area trying to determine what was here.

There is only one known portrait of Pike, painted by Charles Willson Peale in 1808, the year after Pike returned from the West. Peale was the first curator of the first museum in the United States. He was also a renowned artist who painted portraits of all of the key figures of his time. The fact that Peale painted Pike tells you something of Pike's importance among his contemporaries.

Pike was the son of another Zebulon Pike. The elder Pike was a career military officer who only made the rank of major. Pike tried hard to distinguish himself from his father, most notably by signing his letters "Z. M." His father was occasionally referred to as "old, lame and addled," and Pike wanted to do anything he could to get out from under that shadow and to make a name for himself. As one historian described it, "he felt very strongly a spur of fame." He wanted to prove himself.

To do so he studied military tactics, taught himself French and Spanish, followed scientific advances, and generally sought excellence in every position that he held. He even gained fame for the very lowly, tedious task of paymaster in a frontier fort. These efforts would prove valuable in the West. His job, like that of Lewis and Clark, was to expand American empire and to develop our interests in the West. All of their efforts throughout their journeys—their diligent note-taking, their specimen collecting, mapmaking, and interactions with Indians—were aimed at the goal of furthering the nation's military, commercial and scientific knowledge.

He nurtured any contact he could find, even writing a letter to his father begging him to send names of people who might help advance his career. While seeking to enhance his reputation, Pike was constantly seeking to hitch his wagon to a star. In this effort, though, Pike was, as Jackson points out, "more ambitious than he was prudent and more trusting than cautious." Unfortunately, he hitched his wagon to one particular star which influenced the rest of his life and his legacy—General James Wilkinson.

John Hutchins has written an excellent paper on General Wilkinson which appears later in this book, so I will just touch on the subject here. General James Wilkinson was the commanding officer of the United States military and the governor of Louisiana Territory. He was a powerful figure at the time and a good man to know if you wanted to advance your career. But working for General Wilkinson was a far cry from dealing directly with the President as did Lewis and Clark. I can picture in my mind Meriwether Lewis and Thomas Jefferson on the White House floor with a map rolled out, trying to figure out where they were going and what they would see. Lewis and Clark had many connections with Thomas Jefferson—they came from the same part of Virginia and the same social class. Jefferson provided them with the finest instruction and equipment. Pike grew up in New Jersey and on the frontier with none of the same advantages. He was significantly removed from that seat of power.

Wilkinson was involved in several nefarious plots, many of which still aren't clearly understood to this day, including his involvement with Aaron Burr. Today Aaron Burr is most famous for one thing—killing Alexander Hamilton in a duel in 1805. Beyond that though, Burr was involved in what would become known as the Burr-Wilkinson Conspiracy. Their conspiratorial interests lay in the West, but because the documentation didn't survive, nobody knows the ultimate goal of that effort. It may have been to separate the West from the United States and create a new western empire with Burr and Wilkinson at its head. It may have been to foment revolution in Mexico and to throw out the Spanish. It may have been to open trade with Mexico. It may have also had something to do with the Port of New Orleans. It's largely a mystery. The one thing we do know is that Wilkinson was involved, and since Pike worked for Wilkinson he was always tainted by that relationship.

We also know that Wilkinson served as Agent Number 13, a secret agent for the Spanish, paid to provide Spain with information about what was going on in the West. As territorial governor he was certainly in a position to know these secrets, but documents indicate that even the Spanish were frustrated with their relationship with Wilkinson and his ability to be forthright. In the end though, the information that Wilkinson provided to the Spanish would have a deep impact on Pike's experiences as he traveled west.

It's not really clear how Wilkinson and Pike met. Wilkinson probably had some interaction with career officer Major Zebulon Pike. It has been suggested that Wilkinson may have had business dealings with the family of Clarissa Pike—the younger Pike's wife. It may have been that Meriwether Lewis met Pike in some remote frontier outpost and later recommended him to Wilkinson.

One thing that many people forget is that Pike led two expeditions—in fact, he always thought he led three expeditions—and he always felt as if he got short shrift compared to Lewis and Clark. Lewis and Clark led one. Pike led three: first, the Mississippi River expedition; second, the Southwestern expedition; and the third, in Pike's mind, was his involuntary guided tour of Mexico, from which he finally returned in June 1807.

For those of us in the West the first expedition is of little significance except, perhaps, as a training mission. Pike left St. Louis in August 1805 and returned the following year. He was young and had few resources available to him. Unlike Lewis and Clark's, his men were not hand-selected for their skills but rather ordered to participate. Pike needed training to prepare him for his trip out west, and so I think that's the value of this expedition.

General Wilkinson composed the orders for this mission, though they may have sounded as though they came from the President. They certainly reflected the spirit of Jeffersonian exploration. Pike's job was to explore and map the upper reaches of the Mississippi River and return before winter set in.

He was to secure land for new forts. To do this he arranged the purchase of 155,000 acres for what would ultimately become Fort Snelling at the site of St. Paul, Minnesota. Instead of returning before winter arrived, he decided to continue exploring, meeting with British trappers who were working in the area, spreading the word of the new boundaries of the U.S. territory, and literally planting the flag there. In Wilkinson's words, Pike "stretched his orders a bit" by extending his stay.

"More ambitious than prudent" — perhaps that describes what Pike was doing when he decided to winter over in Minnesota.

The trip proved Pike to be earnest and brave, though sometimes inept and perhaps a little lacking in caution. Those qualities accompanied him out west.

Immediately upon returning from the Mississippi River trip, Pike was handed — or actually sat down and wrote out — orders as they were read by General Wilkinson for another expedition. This one would send him west to feel out the southwestern portion of the Louisiana Purchase. His job was to figure out what was out there, to interact with the nations within and around the borders, and to return home with that information. Again, the orders suggested that they were driven by Jeffersonian ideals of scientific exploration and mapping, though there were hints that Wilkinson had more nefarious goals in mind. These shadowy goals have always created problems for Pike.

He was to begin by escorting home a large group of Osage Indians who had been kidnapped by another band of American Indians, the Potawatomie. In order to keep peace between the various nations in the new American territory, the United States had ransomed them back with goods and materials. Pike's first task was to make sure that those Osage Indians returned home to their village in western Missouri. Then, he was to interact with several bands of American Indians — the Kansas and the Pawnee nations specifically — to try to forge peace between them. He was then to strike up communication with the Comanche, the most powerful nation in this part of the country. Finally, he was to explore the headwaters of the Arkansas and to return home by way of the Red River. This task would undoubtedly bring him to the very edges of American territory and perhaps beyond. As with the Minnesota expedition, he was to return home before winter set in. The orders and the ambitious timeline betray an absolute ignorance of the American West and the geography that he would encounter. This ignorance, along with Pike's own self-assurance and determination, would nearly lead to disaster.

His party included a total of twenty-three American soldiers and civilians who he lovingly referred to as the "damn'd rascels." Additionally, he would escort the fifty-one ransomed

Osage men, women and children as well as eight elders from various nations who had visited Philadelphia and Washington D.C. to meet with the Jefferson administration.

The Lewis and Clark expedition was built for speed. They had well-equipped, hand-picked men along with lots of boats, knowledge and experience. Pike's expedition was anything but. At times in Pike's journals you can feel his frustration at how slow they were moving because they had so many people to care for. Pike remarked one morning very sarcastically, "we finally traveled at a decent hour." Imagine family vacations when you can never quite get everything ready to go: that's the feeling that I had in reading those journal entries from the first portion of the trip.

Pike's expedition started near St. Louis on July 15, 1806. Again, their mission was to get from there to the Colorado Rockies and back before the snow flew, and again, betrayed a real ignorance of the west's geography.

Pike went a short way up the Mississippi River, then connected to the Osage River and traveled into western Missouri to the villages of the Osage. It took them nearly two months for this portion of the journey, and it was already September when they arrived. By then, most of the people in his charge had returned to their villages.

As you read the journals and see the days fly by, you get a feeling that things are not going to go well. And then another ominous sign came around, and again, it had to do with the difference between Lewis and Clark and Pike.

Lewis and Clark took with them a Newfoundland dog named Seaman—a great dog that traveled all the way from St. Louis to the Pacific Ocean and back, surviving even while they were eating their horses.

Pike's journals also indicate that he took at least two dogs with him. Unfortunately, as was Pike's wont, they didn't have as much success. According to the journal entry on July 31, just two weeks after they left St. Louis, "I this day lost my dog . . .and the misfortune was the greater as we had no other dog that would bring anything out of the water." It ran off and never returned. The second dog met a worse fate. On October 20, while in the middle of Kansas, they came across a tree along the Arkansas River. In order to build the morale of his men, Pike set up a shooting competition. He used the tree as the target and promised the winner a new tent and boots. Unfortunately, while they were aiming at the tree, one of the weapons apparently misfired and killed the dog. So, again, if you believed in omens, you might be wondering what was to come.

Pike then made an overland march from the Osage villages into Kansas, across the Republican River, and into south-central Nebraska. Near the present-day site of Red Cloud, Nebraska, Pike established a two-week encampment with the Pawnee in order to negotiate peace between them and the surrounding American Indian nations.

Often what captures our current-day imagination is the vision of Pike standing near Pikes Peak or traveling through southeast Colorado. I'm going to present a different vision for you, because I think of that encampment—that moment in time—as the most critical moment in the expedition. It's the one that is most telling and has the most echoes throughout American history.

We know that Wilkinson was a spy for the Spanish and was providing them with information. He told the Spanish that Lewis and Clark were traveling through Louisiana Territory, and the Spanish sent out an expedition to try to find them, either to capture them or escort them back to U.S. territory. That expedition was led by a Spanish soldier named Facundo Melgares, and had traveled to the site of the Pawnee encampment only weeks before Pike arrived. As he traveled further west Pike, in fact, often followed in the path of the Melgares expedition.

So here is the vision: three nations coming together— intersecting at one point near Red Cloud, Nebraska. The Spanish had been there and had left banners and flags and other items for the Pawnee nation. A large group of horse-mounted Spanish soldiers must have been a very impressive sight coming into the Pawnee village with their armor gleaming and banners waving. Several weeks later Pike walked into camp, with only twenty-three tired and foot-sore men—not nearly as impressive an image as the Spanish provided. So the setting became this: there were the Pawnee people with their own banners. The Spanish flag was flying over the Pawnee camp as Pike and his men came in. At that point, Pike tried to negotiate with the Pawnee people to take down the flag—having a Spanish flag flying over American territory was offensive to the very patriotic Pike—so he began the sensitive negotiation with them to take down that flag and to put up the American flag. That one moment in time is a precursor to the West's history for the next two hundred years and the complex issues of land ownership, American Indian rights, and border disputes with Spain and with Mexico. There are many echoes that come through that one moment on the Pike expedition.

There was yet another moment of tension in the Pawnee village, a potential clash that could have turned into tragedy. As Pike's men prepared to head west, the Pawnee threatened them in an attempted to block their path. Though vastly outnumbered, Pike stood his ground. On October 1, Pike wrote about this interaction in his journals:

> He [the Pawnee Chief] must know that we are warriors of our great American father and we're not women to be turned back by words. And that I should therefore proceed. He could attempt to stop me, but we were men, well-armed, and would sell our lives at a dear rate to his nation. That we knew our great father would send our warriors there to gather our bones and revenge our deaths on his people.

What an interesting moment where Pike almost seemed to be daring the Pawnee into a conflict. It is hard to overlook the visions of glory portrayed in the words of our young, idealistic, and ambitious Pike. His threats, however, seemed to work and he managed to defuse the situation.

During his two-week interaction with the Pawnee, Pike traded for horses. Now mounted, they traveled south from the Pawnee village and reached the Arkansas River. At this point, the orders were to split the command. Some of the men were to explore the southern reaches of that river, the rest were to continue traveling west. It turned out that six men under the leadership of General Wilkinson's son, Lieutenant James Wilkinson, traveled down the river. Before splitting up, the men rested, hunted buffalo and built canoes. Finally all was ready and Lieutenant Wilkinson set the canoes in the Arkansas River. They got in the boats, went about a hundred yards downstream and there was not enough water to keep going, and so there was the rather ignominious sight of men having to pick up and carry their canoes downstream until there was enough water to float their boats.

For the rest of Pike's party, their journey now seemed rather mundane. They kept moving west, hunting buffalo, and remarking on what they saw during the day, but as they entered Colorado, things started to get more interesting. On November 11, 1806, Pike entered Colorado and noted in his journal: "finding the impossibility of performing the voyage in the time proposed, I determined to spare no pains to accomplish every object even should I be obliged to spend another winter in the desert." Just like the previous year, he couldn't quite get everything done before winter set in so he was going to forge ahead. He couldn't allow himself to return without accomplishing all of his tasks.

So, he decided to forge on. Several days later, on November 15, he spotted the "small blue cloud" on the horizon, and he wrote that his men gave three cheers to what they called the "Mexican Mountains."

While the mountains gave them hope that their mission was nearly done, it was also during this period that we begin to see the impact of the environment on the expedition. On November 18, the men killed seventeen buffaloes and packed out nine hundred pounds of meat. They were living very well and eating lots of meat every day. Pike said that the prairie was covered with buffalo, and he was amazed at the vast herds. Strangely enough though, their horses were overworked and didn't have enough forage on the short grass prairie. The day after this successful hunt, the first of Pike's horses died. Pike began to understand the unique nature of the western landscape, and this understanding helped to create the concept of the Great American Desert. This idea, first proposed by Pike and later supported by Stephen Long and other explorers, was that the West was too dry to support American settlement. Pike's report about the aridity of the West still echoes in our history. It influenced the timing and extent of western settlement. While today the Great American Desert is sniffed at as a myth, it still seems relevant given our recurring, modern-day droughts. We keep pushing at the desert and the desert keeps pushing back at us.

When I began researching Pike, one of my first questions was why did he try to climb the mountain? At first I thought that he climbed it because it was there, but Pike's journal gives us a different answer about why he risked his life to climb that mountain.

By the time he reached the site of Pueblo, where the Arkansas River and Fountain Creek came together, the expedition consisted of sixteen men. Twelve of them stayed in a small fortification, while the other four, including Pike, Dr. John Robinson and two privates, decided to climb the peak. In the journals he stated that he wanted to get up onto what he called "Highest Peak" or "Grand Mountain" so he could survey the surroundings below him in order to figure out where the rivers were flowing and where he should go. Pike left the encampment at Pueblo at 1:00 in the afternoon, thinking that they would reach the base of the mountain that evening. Four days later they were still not there.

John Patrick Michael Murphy has done great research on what route Pike took, and he's got me convinced that the highest point Pike reached was the top of Mt. Rosa. He arrived there with John Robinson, who was ultimately responsible for naming Pikes Peak, and the two other soldiers. Once there, they decided that getting to the top of the mountain was impossible. One of the enduring myths about the expedition is that Pike thought no one would ever climb that mountain. That statement doesn't give a true sense of the challenges he faced. In his journal entry, Pike noted that no one could have survived that climb equipped the way they were, dressed in those summer uniforms, in that season of the year. So, after forty-eight hours of bitter cold and snow and without food, Pike's party turned back to rejoin the rest of the men. That was the extent of Pike's Pikes Peak adventure. I doubt that he ever imagined anyone would pay attention to this lost weekend.

Pike went back to Pueblo and gathered his men. They continued up the Arkansas to the present-day site of Cañon City, and then had to figure out which way the river actually went. They started up the Royal Gorge, but soon turned back thinking they were following the wrong stream. They followed another tributary that led toward Cripple Creek and when that petered out Pike thought that he had reached the headwaters of the Arkansas. From there, they continued into South Park and crossed over Trout Creek Pass. The view from the pass showed the Collegiate Range in the background and a river at the base of the mountains. Pike assumed this was the Red River, just where he thought it should be. He headed down towards the river and explored a little bit and decided that it was indeed the headwaters of the Red River, and so they continued on south.

Winter was a difficult time to travel, and they were critically short of food and supplies. They passed many days without anything to eat, but celebrated Christmas Day feasting on four buffalo. While they were still a long way from home, tired and hungry, they felt that the journey's end was in sight.

From the site of Salida where they had Christmas, they continued back down what they believed to be the Red River and once again came to the Royal Gorge. At that moment you can sense Pike's shock as he realized his error. Far from being on the Red River, he had made a big circle and never left the vicinity of the Arkansas. Pike didn't know where he was or how to find the Red River. He noted in his journal that the West's geography absolutely baffled him. He was running out of supplies, and he had no earthly idea where to get more. He decided to strike off across country in order to find the Red River. He went south across the Wet Mountains, and then across the Sangre de Cristos into the San Luis Valley. From the top of the sand dunes they saw another river, and again, he believed it to be the Red River. They continued down into the San Luis Valley and set up a stockade near Alamosa.

By this time it was late February, and the central goal of the expedition was now survival. They were trying to regain their strength and waiting for spring to arrive so they could sail down river to an American settlement.

On February 27, a group of one hundred Spanish soldiers came into camp. Pike wrote in his journal that he asked the Spanish soldier, "What? Is this not the Red River? Is this not American territory?" The Spanish officer informed him that it was indeed the Rio Grande, and they were undoubtedly in

Spanish territory. Pike took down his flag and he and his men, escorted by the Spanish soldiers, continued south, first to Santa Fe and then to Chihuahua, the territorial capital. In June 1807 the men were finally escorted back into American territory, and an expedition that had been projected to take three or four months had lasted just two weeks shy of a year.

There were some important results of the expedition. Most notably, it was the first projection of United States authority into that portion of the Louisiana territory. Pike's job was to explore and to feel out the edges of Spanish territory. At the time we were in a cold war with Spain, and another critical aspect of his job was to make sure it did not become a shooting war. In this he succeeded.

He published his journals, beating Lewis and Clark into publication by four years. He created the concept of the Great American Desert, one that has stayed with us right up to the present day. Was the West a "Garden of Eden" or was it a dry, barren desert? That was the idea that Pike was trying to test. Unfortunately, by the time Pike returned, the Burr–Wilkinson Conspiracy had blown up, and Pike, tainted by his relationship with Wilkinson, never received acclaim like Lewis and Clark.

There are many challenges to Pike's legacy, and chief among these is that he didn't work for the President. All of the rumors about Pike being a spy have to do with Pike's relationship with the known spy, Wilkinson. I think if you sat Pike down right here in front of us and asked "were you a spy, sir?" he would say that he absolutely was. He was a good, loyal officer and spied for his country.

He continued to serve his country, ultimately rising to the rank of brigadier general. He died young and heroically during the War of 1812. In many ways he achieved the fame he had chased for so long. Unfortunately, his untimely death meant he couldn't support his own legacy. He couldn't continue to promote what he had done in the West. His story was never able to compete with that of Lewis and Clark. What's more, he hasn't yet had a storyteller like Lewis and Clark. He needs someone like a Stephen Ambrose, who produced the widely read Lewis and Clark chronicle *Undaunted Courage*. Pike needs and deserves a dramatic, authentic, narrative account of his tireless journey.

Pike's memory throughout the years has changed somewhat. For the centennial, one hundred years ago, I believe Pike was a symbol of a frontier that had disappeared. In the 1890s the frontier was declared closed. There was no wide-open expanse of territory left for us to settle, and I think Pike was seen at that time as the symbol of a lost era in the American West. But Coloradoans have always connected with Pike in a very different way, so we had a party in 1906. We tried to build a statue to honor Pike. We had a plaster model made that was intended to raise money to complete the sculpture; unfortunately, we couldn't raise the money and the plaster model melted away. Again, Pike's luck. We did raise enough money to create a monument in Antlers Park.

How do we see Pike today? How has Pike's meaning changed? Is his story one of international relations? Is it a story of political intrigue? Is it a story of romance and human drama? Is the expedition about espionage? Hopefully by the end of this book, you'll be able to answer those questions in your own mind. Enjoy the journey.

Matt Mayberry is the Director of the Colorado Springs Pioneers Museum. In 2006, he curated the exhibit *Pike's World: Exploration and Empire in the Greater Southwest,* which was one of three major exhibits mounted by the Museum to commemorate the Pike bicentennial. He holds an M.A. in history from the University of Colorado and is a former elected member of the governing council of the American Association for State and Local History. His publications include "Reforging the Golden Spike: The U.S. Gold Mining Industry During World War II" published in *Colorado History* magazine in 2005.

How Lost was Zebulon Pike?

Donald Jackson

In the deepening snows of a high mountain valley, about where Salida, Colorado, now stands, a band of sixteen men were gathered on the day before Christmas, 1806. Earlier they had been separated into straggling parties to forage and explore, but now they were united. Earlier they had been wretchedly hungry, but now they were so fortunate as to kill several buffalo cows. The timely appearance of these animals at a meaningful season must have seemed providential to the young leader of the band, but he was not a man to dwell for long upon such notions in the journal he was keeping.

"We now again found ourselves all assembled together on Christmas Eve," wrote Zebulon Pike, "and appeared generally to be content, although all the refreshment we had to celebrate that day with, was buffalo meat, without salt, or any other thing whatever."

Pike was in a far worse situation than he realized. Although he thought he was on the headwaters of the Red River, he actually was some three hundred miles to the northwest, high up the Arkansas; and before discovering his error he would spend agonizing days along the frozen river bed and in the bottom of an incredible canyon now called the Royal Gorge. His men— some of whom had cut up their blankets to wrap around their feet—had every reason to believe that they were now to start for the more moderate climes of home. Yet they still were to face an ordeal of hunger and cold in the Wet Mountain Valley that would leave some of them forever maimed. Certainly neither Pike nor his men could have foreseen that they were about to mistake still another river for the Red, and that within a few weeks they would all be prisoners of the Spanish government in Mexico.

Could Pike have known that these misadventures would occur, it is altogether likely that he would have chosen to go on, for he was not easily deterred by disappointment and physical discomfort. But it would have distressed him greatly to know that even at that moment, back in the East, many of his countrymen were questioning the very aim of his expedition. Although Pike was officially performing a notable chore in the national interest, he soon would face the allegation that secretly his mission was a private one, somehow linked with the Aaron Burr conspiracy. Burr had been accused of plotting hostile inroads into the Spanish Southwest, and even of trying to divide the Union by separating the western states and territories. For at least a while, Pike's reputation as an explorer would depend less upon his own skill and courage than upon the turn of events at home.

At the age of twenty-seven, Zebulon Pike was a man to whom reputation meant nearly everything. He believed that he would find it, and glory besides, in the United States Army. He would not duplicate the drab career of his father, Major Zebulon Pike, whose lifetime of military service had left him poor, lame, and occasionally addled. Even young Pike's own early years in the service, spent routinely in the Ohio and Mississippi valleys, had not quelled his zeal. He attacked every assignment with enthusiasm, studied military tactics and taught himself French and Spanish, and kept a ready eye on the promotion lists sent out by the Secretary of War.

But making it alone in those times was very difficult for a young officer of modest background; it required all the help a young man could find, including the favors of influential men in the army and the government. Pike knew this. "Send me inclosed some letters . . . to any friends of Influence you may have," he once wrote his father, "as I have Schemes in view that require every exertion in my power to accomplish."

Such a man is a born protégé, waiting for a patron. Pike was lucky enough to come under the patronage of the one man in the world with whom it seemed that he could prosper most, the commanding general of the United States Army. In 1805, when Pike was still a first lieutenant whose most important previous assignment had been that of regimental paymaster, he was picked by this general for an expedition up the Mississippi that sent his career into a steep ascent. From that day until his death in the War of 1812, Pike's heart, hand, and sword were dedicated to the service of Brigadier General James Wilkinson.

Saying that Wilkinson was profoundly a knave puts the historian in no danger of losing perspective; the general's misdeeds throughout decades spent in public office, ranging from petty chicanery to treason, are now well documented. To some he was a charming gallant, but he impressed others as too cocksure and pompous: Washington Irving felt that had he not become a general he would have made "an admirable trumpeter." He had been made a brigadier general during the Revolution, had engaged in various civilian enterprises in Kentucky, then had returned to military life. Upon the death of General Anthony Wayne in 1796, he found himself the ranking general of the army. He was to serve in this status until his failure to take Montreal during the War of 1812 cost him his command. Not until years after his death was it proved that he had taken an oath of allegiance to Spain and had received an annual pension from that country during his service at the head of the United States Army.

The sheer magnitude of Wilkinson's shoddy undertakings is one of the marvels of his time; another is the ease with which he duped such men as Thomas Jefferson and repeatedly escaped disclosure and punishment. It would have been impossible, however, for Wilkinson to serve so long as the commanding general of the army if he had been *completely* a charlatan. He ran the military affairs of his country, including many problems of a lengthening frontier, not brilliantly but at least not disastrously. He had a keen interest in geography and natural history, and like most other Americans he was eager to know just what the United States had acquired in 1803 in the vast tract of land called the Louisiana Purchase. Lewis and Clark were already in the Northwest, encouraged by Jefferson's intense and highly personal interest in their success, when Wilkinson was appointed as governor of the territory of Louisiana in 1805. Upon reaching his headquarters in St. Louis, Wilkinson began at once to carry out Jefferson's wishes in regard to further exploration.

But was Wilkinson interested in what lay to the west for his country's sake or because he had private schemes to develop? Here was a large part of the general's secret of success: his private designs so often overlapped those of the country that they could be easily concealed and implemented.

Neither Pike's expedition up the Mississippi in 1805–1806 nor his second to the West in 1806–1807 was specifically authorized by Jefferson. But Wilkinson kept the President and Secretary of War Henry Dearborn fully informed of Pike's progress, and both expeditions were later approved.

About the Mississippi River expedition there was no air of mystery and no suspicion of scandal. Pike was sent by Wilkinson to explore the headwaters of the Mississippi, to purchase sites from the Indians for future military posts, and to assert both to Indians and to Canadian traders the authority of the United States over the lands it had recently acquired. He was also to bring some influential chiefs back to St. Louis for talks with Wilkinson. Leaving St. Louis in August in a single keelboat with twenty men, Pike worked his way to the vicinity of Little Falls, Minnesota, by the onset of winter. Here he built a stockade for the protection of his party, then pushed on with a few men — traveling on foot and by dog sled to visit various fur-trading establishments. The uppermost point of his journey was Cass Lake in northern Minnesota.

Pike returned to St. Louis in April. He had not found the ultimate source of the Mississippi but had come within a few miles of it. In carrying out the rest of his mission he was only moderately successful. The success of the venture, however, must be judged not on the basis of Wilkinson's extravagant expectations, but on what might have been expected from a small party with an inexperienced leader. The trip seasoned Pike and his men for their more substantial foray into the West, and it produced a notable map and journal.

Upon his return, Pike found that Wilkinson was already planning to send him on a second expedition. Some Osage prisoners taken from the Potawatomis, and a few junketing Osage chiefs, needed to be escorted to their homes in what is now western Missouri. Also, a party of Kansas Indians had recently come down and asked for help in making peace with the Pawnees in the Kansas-Nebraska area. Wilkinson wanted, furthermore, to establish contact with the Comanches farther to the west, because their close association with the Spanish made them seem a dangerous threat to the frontier. And, finally, there was the ever-present need to know what the Spanish themselves were doing along the poorly defined western border of the Louisiana Purchase.

In 1806 almost every American citizen expected a war with Spain, which had not reacted happily to France's sale of Louisiana to the United States. The Secretary of War had instructed Wilkinson to engage in intelligence operations, using army officers disguised as traders if necessary, to find out what Spain was up to, and to get an idea of the terrain "to the west of Louisiana." The Secretary had even hinted that a military expedition against Mexico might become necessary. Some of the government's apprehensions about the Spanish had originated with Wilkinson himself, and even though they were now merely being fed back to the general, the official concern gave Wilkinson a freer rein.

It would soon develop that Wilkinson and Aaron Burr had been planning a coup in the West. Was it a traitorous movement to separate the western states and territories from the Union, or merely a plot to conduct filibustering operations against Spanish-dominated Mexico? The question is still disputed by historians. In either case, the expedition to the Spanish borderlands would serve Wilkinson well. His orders to Pike instructed him to explore the headwaters of the Arkansas and Red Rivers, which were presumed to lie just within the western limits of the Louisiana Purchase. When he had completed his reconnaissance he was to descend the Red to Natchitoches. In a separate letter Wilkinson told the young explorer, "you must indeed be extremely guarded with respect to the Spaniards — neither alarm nor offend them unnecessarily."

After some delay because his Osage charges were ill in St. Louis, Pike got his entourage moving on July 15, 1806. The main portion of his command was an assortment of eighteen enlisted men from the First Infantry Regiment, most of whom had been with Pike on his earlier expedition. "A Dam'd set of Rascels," he called them, "but very proper for such expeditions as I am engaged in."

Besides the enlisted soldiers, three other men accompanied Pike. His second in command was Lieutenant James B. Wilkinson, the general's son. The lieutenant was largely untried, though he had earlier led an unsuccessful Missouri

River expedition attempting to reach the mouth of the Platte. His new assignment was to accompany Pike through what is now Missouri and Kansas, as far as the Great Bend of the Arkansas River, then to return down that river and provide the government with a detailed chart and topographic description of the route.

Accompanying the group as interpreter was Baronet Vasquez, usually called Barney by his American friends. He was a young resident of St. Louis, fluent in both French and Spanish, at home among the Indians, and accustomed to living in the wilds. The most mysterious person in the command, a man whose complex motives are still not entirely clear, was Dr. John H. Robinson. He had lately moved west to St. Louis, where he was serving as acting army surgeon, and when he learned of the expedition he is said to have entreated Wilkinson repeatedly for permission to go along as a volunteer.

In the sultriest days of a Midwestern summer, the soldiers and Indians moved up the mosquito-ridden Missouri. The supplies and most of the soldiers were in boats, and the Indians kept to the shore—afoot and on horseback. They left the Missouri for the smaller, more tortuous channel of the Osage River—part of what is now the Lake of the Ozarks—and had reached the two villages of the Osages in western Missouri by August 20. Here the Osage prisoners and chiefs were returned to their people; the party rested, counseled, tried with some success to recruit horses, and then moved on.

Now the expedition veered to the northwest, traveling diagonally across Kansas toward a band of Pawnees then living on he Republican River. The exact spot has long been disputed by Kansans and Nebraskans, since the river flows close to the border between the two states for several miles and there are remains of Pawnee villages on both sides of the line. Kansans were sufficiently convinced that Pike raised the flag over *their* soil to erect a monument near Republic in 1901. But Pike's tables of course and distance, and his manuscript map of the route, plainly show that he was above the boundary, near Red Cloud, Nebraska.

There, in the very center of the Louisiana Purchase, he talked the Pawnee chiefs into hauling down their Spanish flag and running up the Stars and Stripes. His success in persuading them to do so was all the more satisfying to Pike because the village had recently been visited by a contingent of Spanish cavalry. The glitter and dash of the Spanish horsemen, some three hundred of them, no doubt made a strange contrast to Pike's ill-equipped little command. But Pike was a dogged negotiator if not a gifted one, and the King's ensign came down, at least temporarily. The explorer noted in his journal: "I did not wish to embarrass them . . . for fear that the Spaniards might return there in force again, I returned them their flag, but with an injunction that it should never be hoisted again during our stay."

After making a tenuous peace between some Kansas chiefs and the Pawnees, and trying in vain to get some of the Pawnee men to lead him to the Comanches, Pike set out again. He had two chores remaining: he must try to find and proselyte the Comanches, and he must explore the sources of the Arkansas and the Red Rivers.

By this time Pike had sent a letter to the general — carried by special messenger — which was to become the theme of every discussion of Pike's motives for years to come. On July 22 he had written:

> With respect to the Ietans [Comanches], the Genl. may rest assured I shall use every precaution previous to trusting them — but as to the mode of conduct to be pursued toward the Spaniards I feel more at a loss; as my Instructions lead me into the Country of the Ietans — part of which is no Doubt claimed by Spain — although the Boundary's between Louisiana & N. Mexico have never yet been defined — in consequence of which should I rencounter a [Spanish] party . . . in the vicinity of St. Afee [Santa Fe] — I have thought it would be good policy to give them to understand that we were bound to join our Troops near Natchitoches but had been uncertain aboute the Head Waters of the Rivers over which we passed — but that now, if the [Spanish] Commandt. [at Santa Fe] desired we would pay him a visit of politeness — either by Deputation, or the whole party — but if he refused; signify our intention of pursuing our Direct rout to the posts below — *this if*

acceded to would gratify our most sanguine expectations;
but if not [would] . . . secure us an unmolested retreate
to Natchitoches. But if the Spanish jealousy, and the
instigation of traters, should induce them to make
us prisoners of war—(in time of peace) I trust to the
magnanimity of our Country for our liberation—and a
Due reward to their opposers for the Insult, & indignity,
offer'd their National Honor.

The phrase italicized here for emphasis was not included in
the version of the letter published in the 1810 edition of Pike's
journals: it appears only in his retained copy, captured with him
and kept by the Spanish. Discovery of this version makes some
things quite clear: Pike was eager for firsthand information about
the territory around Santa Fe, he had discussed the matter with
Wilkinson before his departure, and he would not mind being
apprehended by Spanish soldiers in order to gain his objective.
Furthermore, this prior understanding—not spelled out in the
general's written orders—was a point sufficiently sensitive to
call for deletion of the passage before publication.

Actually the letter tells us little about Pike's basic mission
that we have not seen elsewhere. Certainly he was collecting
information—all he could get by any means—but again the
question of motive is crucial. Was he working for Wilkinson,
and maybe for Aaron Burr, or did he believe that he was only
making an important reconnaissance of a country with which
his government might soon be at war?

A more perplexing aspect of the letter is Pike's scheme to
explain his presence to the Spanish by claiming to be "uncertain
aboute the Head Waters of the Rivers." Within a few months
he would be making a claim to Joachín del Real Alencaster,
governor of New Mexico, which sounded very much like this.
To discover how Pike got into the position of seeming to have
predicted his own loss of direction, we must trail him into
country more rugged than any he had ever seen.

Beginning October 7, Pike made a trail southward across
Kansas. He crossed the Solomon, the Saline, and the Smoky Hill,
all typically small prairie rivers lazing through the grasslands,
then approached the Arkansas by way of the swampy Cheyenne

Bottoms and struck that river at the Great Bend. At this point Lieutenant Wilkinson left the party with a small detachment and began to descend the Arkansas, grumbling as he left that Pike had not given him a fair share of the food, equipment and ammunition. He was to complete his mission successfully (though three of his five men deserted in the last stages of the descent), and his findings were later incorporated into Pike's published maps and journals.

Pike and the fifteen others started up the Arkansas on October 28, after watching the lieutenant shove off, and soon found themselves traveling almost due west. Before long they began to scan the horizon for a trace of the Rockies. They were meticulous about following the trail of the Spanish troops who had preceded them, for the chopped-up turf left by the horses' hoofs, and the dozens of cold campfires, offered an excellent guide to — and perhaps through — the mountains. It makes sense that Pike did not try to catch up with the Spanish; he had much work to do before getting involved with them.

By November 11 he was beginning to see that he could not perform his entire mission as quickly as he and General Wilkinson had supposed. But he had survived the previous winter in Minnesota, and this may have encouraged a bold decision: "I determined to spare no pains to accomplish every object even should it oblige me to spend another winter, in the desert." He and his men were wearing cotton uniforms, and they carried no equipment suitable for the snows of the Rockies.

The land was rising now as they entered eastern Colorado. At a point near the junction of the Purgatoire River and the Arkansas, Pike thought he could see mountains on the horizon. He and Dr. Robinson studied the low, blue formation for a while and were sure. "When our small party arrived on the hill," he wrote, "they with one accord gave three *cheers* to the *Mexican mountains*."

A roving band of Pawnees appeared on November 22, about sixty men who had been out hunting for Comanches. They were bent on thievery as they surrounded Pike's men, and it required a good deal of sternness, plus the usual dispensation of presents, to shake them loose and send them on their way.

The expedition reached the site of Pueblo, Colorado, on November 23. Pike had now become fascinated with the great blue peak rising to his right. It was off his course, but he thought he could hike to it in a single day and from its summit make topographic observations of the surrounding area. He was soon to learn that sometimes mountains only *look* close. Early the next day he directed his men in building a small log fortification, and then set out for the mountain with Dr. Robinson and two soldiers.

The four started up Fountain Creek, a branch of the Arkansas that appeared to lead directly to the peak, but they soon abandoned the stream when it seemed to bear too far north (although it would eventually have led them to their goal). They headed northwest across terrain scarred by lightly timbered ridges, but by nightfall were still far from the great mountain that later would bear Pike's name. The next day they reached a formation of lesser peaks that lay between them and the big one. All that day and next they climbed, and at last reached a high point from which they could see how futile their efforts had been. Still more subsidiary prominences lay between them and the highest mountain. They were in deep snow, in those abominable cotton uniforms, and game was scarce. "The summit of the Grand Peak, which was entirely bare of vegetation and covered with snow," Pike wrote, "now appeared at the distance of 15 or 16 miles from us, and as high again as what we had ascended, and would have taken a whole day's march to have arrived at its base, when I believe no human being could have ascended to its pinacal."

Disappointed, they descended to the prairie and returned to camp. Pike's comments about the difficulty of climbing the mountain can be interpreted in two ways. He may have meant that the peak, which he estimated at more than eighteen thousand feet (it actually is a little over fourteen thousand), could never be climbed by anyone. Or he could have meant that no one in his situation, cold and hungry and so far from camp, could have made it to the top. Modern tourists who drive to the summit on a good roadway, and who find there a merchant dispensing hamburgers, milk shakes, and souvenirs, usually assume that Pike actually climbed Pikes Peak.

The next significant stop was on the present site of Cañon City. Here Pike made one of those crucial decisions that shaped the future of his expedition. He had been following the Arkansas for many days, past several forks, and now he found that it forked again. One branch seemed to reach into the very heart of the mountains, between steep cliffs (the Royal Gorge), and the other veered northward through easier country. This branch, now called Four-Mile Creek, is a sizable affluent of the Arkansas which rises high in the north, at the extremity of the Arkansas River watershed. Pike and Dr. Robinson explored both branches for a short distance. Apparently they did not believe that a main branch would extend very far into the surprising canyon from which the Arkansas actually issues. An added argument for following the north fork was the indication that a party of horsemen had recently ascended it. Whether the horsemen were Spanish troops or a band of Comanches, Pike now wanted to get in touch with them, for he was beginning to feel quite uneasy about his location. In his words,

> We are determined to pursue them, as ... the geography of the country, had turned out to be so different from our expectation; we were some what at a loss which course to pursue, unless we attempted to cross the snow cap'd mountains, to the south east of us which was almost impossible.

The expedition followed north along Four-Mile Creek for two days and then chose its western fork. But the branch finally dwindled—and so did the hoof-marked trail they had been tracing. The party then headed straight north. Pike was leading his men toward a high plateau that would later become known as South Park; and there he was surprised to find, on December 12, a river flowing to the east. "Must it not be the head waters of the river Platte?" he wrote in his journal. He was correct; he had found the south fork of the South Platte.

Pike now became convinced that he must head southwest once more and contrive to find the Red River. He had lost the Spanish trail completely and seemed to believe that he had somehow passed above all possible sources of the Arkansas—

which actually rises a little further north, near what later became Leadville. His principal map, and indeed the contemporary map that any sensible explorer would have been delighted to have, was one left in Washington in 1804 by Baron Alexander von Humboldt, the great German naturalist, as one result of a year spent in Mexico. It had been handed down to Pike at the instigation of Wilkinson, and was a remarkable early portrayal of Mexico and the North American Southwest. But among its many departures from actuality was its handling of the Red River. Humboldt showed this stream rising in the Rocky Mountains, near Santa Fe, when in truth it rises on the plains of northwestern Texas. Pike thought that he could find it by proceeding southwest across the towering ranges.

Abandoning the South Platte, Pike made now for a low pass in the mountains, now called Trout Creek Pass and traversed by U.S. Highway 24. His crossing of the pass was not difficult, even in winter—he was still east of the Continental Divide—and when he reached the western foot he made a discovery which sent a shout of joy through the whole command. At a spot just below the present location of Buena Vista, Colorado, they came upon what they assumed was the Red River. It was their highway to home, they thought, for it would lead them to the broad reaches of the Mississippi.

Actually, they were back on the Arkansas, some seventy miles upstream of where they had left it a fortnight earlier. Pike marched northward with two men to probe somewhat deeper into the sources of the river, and sent the rest of his party downstream with urgent instructions to forage for game. The date was December 21; the snow was deep, and the command was short of food, clothing, and ammunition. Pike and his two partners ascended the river to the Twin Lakes region south of Leadville. Here he decided that his "Red River" had nearly played out. Hungry, cold, and separated from his men, he easily convinced himself that he could see the approximate head of the stream where it disappeared into the distant mountains; and, in fact, he was now not far from the source of the Arkansas. He turned back, and on the broadening valley floor where the town of Salida would later appear, beside the carcasses of the buffalo cows which may have saved their lives, he and his men spent Christmas in 1806.

Now they started down the river, seeking a convenient place to await better weather, build boats, and make more side trips before descending to civilization. They worked their way down the valley between towering white peaks, past the present sites of Coaldale, Cotopaxi, and Parkdale. The river was frozen solidly enough to support horses—a fact indicating an extraordinarily low temperature—but Pike had great difficulty moving the animals down the narrow channel among the many rocks impacted in the ice.

> Had frequently to cross the river on the ice, horses falling down, we were obliged to pull them over on the ice. . . . We had great difficulty in getting our horses along, some of the poor animals having nearly killed themselves falling on the ice . . . one horse fell down the precipice, and bruised himself so miserably, that I conceived it mercy to cause the poor animal to be shot. Many others were nearly killed with falls received . . .

Pike was no literary man. Even with an unusual imagination and a flair for words, both of which qualities he lacked, he could hardly have done justice in his journal to the monstrous cleft in the earth which he and his men were entering as they unknowingly approached, once again, the site of Cañon City. He reported that they "encamped at the entrance of the most perpendicular precipices on both sides, through which the river ran and our course lay." So much for the Royal Gorge. Neither Pike nor any of the several parties into which he had divided his men actually descended the whole length of the canyon. Pike traveled about halfway before climbing out.

And now, of course, they had come full circle. Surely in anguish, when he reached the place where the Arkansas left the mountains and recognized it as their old camp, Pike crossed out "Red River" and penned in the word "Arkansaw."

He had brought his men through a considerable hell, but all was not lost. According to his views of geography, reinforced by Baron von Humboldt's map, he could still find the head of the Red River by working his way through the "white, snow-cap'd Mountains, very high" that lay to the southwest—the Sangre de Cristos. Clearly, it would be a cruel journey.

Because the horses were bruised, exhausted, and sick, Pike now decided to attack the mountains on foot, carrying packs and leaving the horses behind to recuperate. A small stockade was built on the north bank of the Arkansas, within the present limits of Cañon City, and Interpreter Vasquez and Private Patrick Smith were detailed to stay with the horses until sent for.

The fourteen-man party left the new stockade on January 14, 1807, and headed up a branch of the Arkansas, now called Grape Creek, which came from the south and offered great promise of a route into the mountains. Three days later Pike stood looking across a valley that was to be the scene of his greatest ordeal of cold and hunger, the Wet Mountain Valley. It is a pleasant enough place in fair weather, and today the yellow school buses speed down the middle of it to gather up the ranchers' children; but Pike was entering it with inadequate food and clothing, and he had the bad luck to reach it just before a severe snowstorm.

Where Pike entered the valley there is little vegetation. To find firewood and the shelter of trees, the expedition marched west, to the opposite side of the slope, on January 17. When they camped that night, nine of the men had frozen feet. Two of the victims were Pike's hunters, so called because of their proficiency in obtaining game, and the party spent a hungry night.

Pike wrote in his journal the next day:

18th January, Sunday.—We started two of the men least injured [to hunt]; the doctor and myself, who fortunately were untouched by the frost, also went out to hunt something to preserve existence, near evening we wounded a buffalo with three balls, but had the mortification to see him run off notwithstanding. We concluded it was useless to go home to add to the general gloom, and went amongst some rocks where we encamped and sat up all night; from the intense cold it was impossible to sleep. Hungry and without cover.

The next day, Pike and Dr. Robinson found and killed a buffalo. They slaughtered it hastily, loaded themselves with meat, and arrived at the camp after midnight. Their men had not eaten for four days.

It now appeared that Privates John Sparks and Thomas Dougherty had been too badly frostbitten to continue. Pike decided to leave them, with some of his supplies, and march on. "I furnished the two poor lads who were to remain with ammunition, made use of every argument in my power to encourage them to have fortitude to resist their fate, and gave them assurance on my sending relief as soon as possible. We parted, but not without tears."

Pike knew that the heights of the Sangre de Cristo range were insurmountable to men so ill-equipped and hungry. He was determined to continue southeast along the base of the range until he encountered a pass. But after marching for a couple of days more, he found his food situation again serious. The snow was waist deep, making hunting almost impossible, and in any case it appeared that the buffalo had quit the valley. He wrote: "I determined to attempt the traverse of the mountain, in which we persevered until the snow became so deep that it was impossible to proceed; when I again turned my face to the plain, and for the first time in the voyage found myself discouraged." Dr. Robinson killed a buffalo the next day, but by this time Private Hugh Menaugh had "froze and gave oute" and had to be left temporarily behind.

A pass now presented itself, and Pike lost no time in entering it. In two days of marching it led him across the Sangre de Cristos and down into the San Luis Valley. At the western foot of the pass he found that unique collection of dunes that has now become the Great Sand Dunes National Monument, and coursing down the middle of the valley was the river then commonly called the Rio del Norte and now named the Rio Grande.

Pike, however, was now lost again. Mistakenly jubilant, he wrote in his tables of course and distance for January 30: "To ye Banks of Red River."

To find logs for a stockade and for building the boats he needed to descend the "Red River," Pike took his men a few miles up a western tributary, the Conejos. Across the stream from a curiously isolated and barren hill, conveniently located for a sentinel's post, they began to construct a small fortification — built of cottonwood logs and surrounded by a moat into which was diverted the water of the Conejos. They were about twelve miles southeast of what today is Alamosa, Colorado. As soon as Pike could get a flagstaff in the ground he unwittingly began to fly the American flag on the soil of His Most Catholic Majesty, the King of Spain.

There is a mistaken belief that Pike would have knowingly trespassed, even if he had actually found the Red River, once he crossed to the far side. But, although the boundary of the Louisiana Purchase was in dispute, the United States laid a firm claim to the Red River and all its waters.

The next episode in the tale belongs to Dr. Robinson. We have seen him thus far as a man with a good shooting eye, but he must have served Pike in other important ways. In a letter to a congressman, Pike later described him as "the right arm of the expedition." The medical ethics of a physician who leaves three men exhausted and freezing in the mountains, while he pushes on with the healthy ones, is open to question; but Dr. Robinson had something on his mind. Armed with a document that gave him authority to collect a debt from an expatriate American near Santa Fe who owed a merchant in Kaskaskia, Illinois, the doctor set out on foot in the direction of the Spanish settlements. He told Pike that he did not plan to identify himself as a member of the expedition, and that he would return in plenty of time to descend the river when the stragglers had been collected and the boats constructed.

When he reached Santa Fe, Dr. Robinson told Governor Alencaster that he had recently separated from a party of hunters and had come to collect a sum from one Baptiste Lalande. The governor immediately reported the incident to his superior, Commandant-General Nemesio Salcedo, in Chihuahua, and he also sent out patrols in the hope of apprehending some of the doctor's companions. Later, when the doctor was taken to Chihuahua, he asked General Salcedo for political asylum. He said he wanted to become a Spanish subject and a convert to Catholicism, and that he would repay the Spanish for their indulgence by exploring the lands lying to the north. He asked the General not to betray his wishes to Pike, who had befriended him. Apparently the Spanish officials were suspicious, for he was not allowed to stay.

Pike, meanwhile, sent two relief parties back for the men and horses he had left behind. The detachment dispatched to recover his three crippled soldiers returned with Hugh Menaugh, the only one able to travel. The other two, Sparks and Dougherty, sent Pike bits of their gangrenous toe bones in a kind of macabre supplication not to be abandoned. "Little did they know my heart," wrote Pike, "if they could suspect me of conduct so ungenerous."

Now one of the patrols sent out from Santa Fe found Pike's stockade; on February 26 he was informed by a young Spanish officer that he was encamped on a branch of the Rio Grande. He was surprised, but not ready to argue: "I immediately ordered my flag to be taken down and rolled up, feeling how sensibly I had committed myself, in entering their territory, and was conscious that they must have positive orders to take me in."

After arranging to collect the stragglers, the Spanish patrol escorted Pike's party to Santa Fe. Here his papers were confiscated, and after some questioning he was sent on to Chihuahua. Neither he nor his men were mistreated, but the members of the expedition were now permanently separated. Pike and a few of his men were back in United States territory by June 30, 1807, having been escorted to the border by their captors. Five of the men, for reasons not altogether clear, were detained two years longer, and Sergeant William E. Meek, after killing Private Theodore Miller in a drunken scuffle, was held for fourteen years.

From here on, the Pike story becomes mainly a wrangle between Spanish and United States officials over the boundary violation, and a long debate in the United States over Pike's intentions. General Salcedo was reprimanded by his government after releasing Pike, for the King and his ministers felt that the exploring party should have been imprisoned until the United States acknowledged the incursion as a border violation. The officials in Spain somehow never corrected their original, erroneous impression that Pike was apprehended in Texas, near San Antonio, which would have placed him much farther into avowedly Spanish territory.

Pike's return to his country received little notice, for by that time General Wilkinson had charged Aaron Burr with treason and the whole populace was caught up in the electrifying drama. Burr's trial was in progress at Richmond when Pike got back. The Burr story is a complex one, but to consider it in connection with Pike we need to distill only two conclusions: first, that Burr's operation seems to have been primarily a planned movement against the Spanish colonies in North America, especially Mexico, and was predicated upon an expected war with Spain; second, that General Wilkinson was surely a co-planner if not an originator of the scheme. The general later found it advisable to extricate himself—in the face of failure—by denouncing Burr.

Almost certainly Pike was not a party to the Aaron Burr movement. His vigorous denials, upon returning from the West, seem to have sprung from a genuine ignorance of the Burr-Wilkinson plan. There is no evidence that he knew of the conspiracy until he read of it in the *Gacetas de Mexico* while in that country.

It is not quite accurate to say that Pike planned to be "captured" by the Spanish. Perhaps it is better to say that he hoped to fall in with a Spanish party and get a chance to visit Santa Fe. Long before he had arrived in the area, word had somehow reached Chihuahua that his expedition was on the way. It is quite possible that Wilkinson himself had originated the message. On the other hand, the Spanish were also quick to learn of the Lewis and Clark expedition and of an abortive American exploration up the Red River, during the same period. Salcedo's orders were to terminate all such expeditions into disputed territory. It would have been most ingenuous of Pike to suppose that Dr. Robinson's visit to Santa Fe would not alert the Spanish garrison there. Yet it does not seem likely that he foresaw his own detention and the loss of his papers.

Besides the lingering suspicion that Pike was in league with Burr and Wilkinson, another charge has lived on—the charge that Pike was never really lost. Historians who build too solidly upon Pike's letter to Wilkinson written in July 1806, have a difficult task. They must show that Pike—who traveled with defective maps and no true mental image of western geography—conducted an elaborate campaign to convince the Spanish that he was lost. According to this theory, we must believe that Pike knew there was no Red River as far west as the Rockies, despite the information he had from such authorities as Baron von Humboldt; that when he and his men were freezing and starving in the Wet Mountain Valley he was engaging in deliberate subterfuge; and that when he was confronted by a Spanish officer and was told he was encamped on the west side of the Rio Grande, his plea of ignorance was a long-planned lie. Given the faulty knowledge of the West that Pike possessed, the thing is impossible.

Pike published his letter to Wilkinson (with that significant deletion) for all the world to see. To him it was not a damaging letter, for it only projected a plan to *pretend* he was lost if the need should arise. When the time came he actually *was* lost. And, to one who had undergone those awful days along the base of the Sangre de Cristos, the difference was substantial. Apparently Pike thought that the reading public would believe so, too. Among the papers the Spanish took from Pike was a notebook filled with sketch maps, accompanied by his faithfully made tables of course and distance. These remained in the archives of Mexico for a century before their rediscovery in 1907; later representations by the American government caused them to be transferred to the National Archives in Washington. The documents show the attempt of an earnest and brave but sometimes inept explorer to make a useful record of his travels. When he found that he had mistaken the Arkansas for the Red River, he corrected his maps and tables. Later, when he learned from the Spanish that he was again mistaken, he deleted in one instance the words "Red River" and wrote "Rio del Nord."

Pike's erratic ramblings, his journal entries, and the evidence revealed by his manuscript maps leave little doubt that he was truly lost—not once, but twice.

When Pike was encamped at the Pawnee village, early in the course of the expedition, word reached him that Meriwether Lewis and William Clark had returned safely from their journey to the Pacific. They had gone up the Missouri, crossed the

Rockies, and descended the Columbia. In Pike's correspondence he referred often to Lewis and Clark, sometimes jealously, for he ardently hoped to rank with them as an explorer. His achievement does not quite measure up to theirs, although there is little doubt that he was their equal in courage and endurance. Together, the two undertakings were of vital importance, representing the first extensive probing of the new Louisiana Purchase. Pike's *An Account of Expeditions to the Sources of the Mississippi, and Through the Western Parts of Louisiana*, published in Philadelphia in 1810, was rich in information and became required reading for those whose eyes were turned to the new lands. Along with his "Dam'd set of Rascels," Pike had found a place high on the roster of notable explorers who first revealed the American West.

Donald Jackson was editor at the University of Illinois Press from 1948 to 1966, and was later associate director of the press from 1966 to 1968. He was professor of history at the University of Virginia, and editor of *The Papers of George Washington*. Among his many scholarly works, Jackson edited the *Letters of the Lewis and Clark Expedition* (1962) and *The Journals of Zebulon Montgomery Pike* (1966), and wrote *Thomas Jefferson & the Stony Mountains: Exploring the West from Monticello* (1981) and *Valley Men: Speculative Account of the Arkansas Expedition of 1807* (1983). Jackson died in Colorado Springs on December 9, 1987.

Zebulon Montgomery Pike & American Science

John L. Allen

On the evening of April 18, 1804, two of the world's greatest scientific minds met at "the President's House" in Washington City. Based on a long-standing invitation arising from their frequent correspondence over the preceding fifteen years, Baron Alexander von Humboldt, the scion of one of the oldest aristocratic families in Central Europe, joined Thomas Jefferson, founder of American liberty and champion of the common man, for an elegant dinner accompanied by the best French wines. It would appear to have been an unlikely combination of quite different minds—the young Prussian aristocrat tied firmly to the traditions of the Old World and the elderly author of the Declaration of Independence, prime mover in breaking away from Old World traditions. But on things scientific, these two men thought remarkably alike.

We know next to nothing of their conversation on the evening of April 18 as they enjoyed what Jefferson referred to as an "agreeable" meal. Indeed, we know little of their other exchanges over the next three weeks while von Humboldt was Jefferson's house guest in the capital city of the new American republic. What we do know is that conversation between these two intellectual giants must have been fascinating and wide-ranging and almost certainly included information on von Humboldt's recent "tour" in South and Central America. The great German geographer/explorer presented Jefferson with a *tableau statistique* giving population and other data on New Spain, and quite probably relayed what information he could on how the Spanish viewed their border with the new American territory of Louisiana.

Von Humboldt had with him a manuscript map of the "Internal Provinces of New Spain" that, upon its publication in Europe, would become the first widely-available map of Spanish possessions in North America. He did not present Jefferson a copy of this map as it was not yet prepared for publication. But he loaned the map to Jefferson's Secretary of the Treasury, Albert Gallatin, with the instructions that it was not to be copied. Gallatin, who had been active in acquiring cartographic data for Meriwether Lewis and William Clark, complied with von Humboldt's request and returned the maps to the German baron before von Humboldt left the United States. It is inconceivable that Jefferson would not have seen the map as well. And, as we shall see later, it is also quite probable that, despite von Humboldt's directions, a copy of the map was made and ended up in the possession of General James Wilkinson, the commander of Zebulon Montgomery Pike and the sponsor of Pike's explorations into the borderlands of the United States and New Spain.

Whatever else might have transpired between von Humboldt and Jefferson during the European savant's stay in Washington must be left entirely to the imagination. But a meeting between perhaps the two most important savants or natural philosophers of their day (the word "scientist" had not yet come into European languages) cannot have been inconsequential. These men helped shape the process of changing scientific thought that we call "the Enlightenment."

Born out of French rationalism of the eighteenth century, the Enlightenment was nothing less than a new approach to inquiry about the natural and cultural world. Prior to the 1700s, the explanations of nearly all natural phenomena had been framed primarily in religious terms and nearly all questions about the natural world answered in terms of divine origin. But astronomical science developed a new view of a heliocentric universe in which the world moved about the sun rather than the older geocentric understanding, and physical science began to explain the movement of sun, earth, and other celestial bodies in terms of the laws of gravity and motion.

Based on these new understandings, those who inquired into the workings of the world now sought the answers to questions in quantifiable natural laws rather than religion. Scientific inquiry moved from the clerical realm to the secular. With the emergence of this new approach to science, the nature of exploration also changed—and, given that von Humboldt had just returned from what was a quintessential Enlightenment exploration, we can expect that this new mode of exploration formed the core of his and Jefferson's conversations.

Pre-Enlightenment exploration was largely commercial and imperial, driven by a need to seek new sources of raw materials and new markets for European products, and by a desire on the part of European countries to develop more colonial empires. There was some leavening of the commercial and imperial objectives of exploration by the missionary impulse that accompanied some European national explorations. In general, however, the religious motivation for exploration was significantly less important than either the commercial or imperial objectives. And with the change in the view of the world and its workings represented by the Enlightenment, at least a portion of exploratory objectives were now defined in terms of inquiry into the characteristics of *terrae incognitae*: the unknown lands. And this is what von Humboldt and Jefferson would have visited about.

In 1804, von Humboldt had just completed one of the world's first truly scientific explorations — a far-flung enterprise that took him from deep in the tropical forests of what is now Venezuela and Brazil to the upland basins and plateaus of Mexico. During these explorations, he gathered samples of plants and animals previously unknown to science, made observations about the soils and climate of these areas new to European scholars, and attempted to relate the natural conditions to human cultures by observing native customs and traditions in differing environmental settings. Within a week of von Humboldt's departure from Washington on his way back to his Prussian estate, an expedition conceived and sponsored by Jefferson — the Lewis and Clark Expedition — would depart on a trek across North America, armed with a set of instructions from Jefferson that were just as much based in Enlightenment science as had been the South American and Mesoamerican travels of the great German scholar.

Von Humboldt's travels and those of Lewis and Clark and other Jeffersonian explorers were a logical outgrowth of the traditional Enlightenment approach to inquiry about the natural world: first collect, catalogue, and identify within the context of some classification system (the Linnaean system of taxonomy for biology, for example); then attempt to analyze the "encyclopedia" of information gathered. It was in this intellectual framework that the science that underlay the explorations of Zebulon Montgomery Pike—a contemporary of Lewis and Clark—was framed. But it was framed in a uniquely American context in which some of the more traditional views of exploration involving commerce and empire also were part of the exploratory goals.

American Science and Geographic Intrigue in the Age of Jefferson

The contemporaneous explorations of Lewis and Clark, of Zebulon Pike, and of William Dunbar, George Hunter, Thomas Freeman, and Peter Custis in the lower valleys of the Red and Arkansas Rivers were all uniquely American explorations. Their goals were based both on Enlightenment science and the logical extension of American commerce and empire. There was, in American thought of the early nineteenth century, nothing contradictory in an explorer being some strange combination of merchant, scientist, and diplomat. After all, American science— as well-grounded in the European Enlightenment as it was— was still American.

The chief scientific organization of the time was "The American Philosophical Society Held at Philadelphia for Promoting Useful Knowledge"—a name that suggests that in the American Enlightenment high value was placed on utilitarian knowledge gathered for the promotion of American commercial or territorial (read "imperial") objectives. The goals of the Society were linked with those of the Republic: indeed, Thomas Jefferson served as its president during his two terms as president of the United States. Even though Zebulon Pike was not a direct product of Jefferson's administration, as were Lewis and Clark and the southwestern explorers Dunbar, Hunter, Freeman, and Custis, he was certainly no less committed to the concept of "useful" or utilitarian knowledge (science) as the bulwark of American scientific inquiry.

On the eve of his explorations up the Mississippi and into the American Southwest, Pike was under the command of General James Wilkinson, commander of American military forces in the West and governor of Louisiana Territory. Wilkinson, one of American history's most shadowy figures, had an intriguing past. He was a product of the University of Pennsylvania where his studies seemed destined to lead him to a medical career. He was, therefore, exposed to the same scientific thinking that drove Jefferson and von Humboldt and had significant understanding of what was then termed "natural history" (an amalgam of today's geography, geology, biology, and anthropology). He served with minimal distinction in the American Revolution, and after war's end, headed for Kentucky. Here, as a private citizen, he became involved in a Spanish conspiracy to separate the territories south of the Ohio River from the new republic and add them to what was then the Spanish-held Territory of Louisiana (defined as the western half of the Mississippi River drainage basin). By the time the conflict between the United States and the Indian nations of Ohio broke out, Wilkinson rejoined the U.S. Army and soon became the commander of the U.S. Army in the West—all the while maintaining his status as an agent of the Spanish colonial government in Mexico City.

When Jefferson dispatched Lewis and Clark, Wilkinson urged his Spanish employers to intercept the American explorers. But at the same time, the general seemed bent upon engaging in exploration of his own. Was he concerned that Lewis and Clark would grab all the glory, leaving none for an expedition—equally scientific, commercial, and imperial in scope as that of Lewis and Clark—sponsored by Wilkinson or, perhaps, by his employers in New Spain?

While we can know almost nothing about Wilkinson's true objectives in dispatching Pike, what we do know is that he had a long-term interest in the Louisiana–New Spain borderlands. Wilkinson wrote to Jefferson in June 1804 expressing his disappointment in missing von Humboldt and not "haveing his answers to the queries" that the general had wanted to put to the Baron about those borderlands. But there is additional evidence of Wilkinson's links to von Humboldt's view of New Spain and, therein, connections between the German scholar and the explorations of Zebulon Pike. Enter another of the more shadowy figures of American history—one who rivals and even surpasses General James Wilkinson in notoriety: Aaron Burr, who nearly became president of the United States, served as vice-president during Jefferson's first administration, killed Alexander Hamilton in a duel, was arrested for murder but not convicted, and later brought to trial on conspiracy charges dealing with a plot (in which Wilkinson was also implicated) to found a republic in the Southwest.

If anyone in the United States in 1804 would have been interested in getting a look at Alexander von Humboldt's maps, it would have been Aaron Burr and his probable co-conspirator, General James Wilkinson. According to a statement (possibly a legal deposition) by General Henry Lee, Burr had somehow obtained the original of the von Humboldt two-sheet map loaned to Gallatin by the German scholar. This map was then copied by an army sergeant in Wilkinson's command for Burr and Wilkinson. This sergeant was none other than Antoine Nau, a cartographer of some skill who later produced the maps that accompanied the published edition of Zebulon Pike's journals of his Southwestern expedition. Had Zebulon Pike seen the von Humboldt map before he departed? It would be amazing if he had not. He may have even had a copy of it in the field, and the significance of this will become apparent shortly.

Whatever Wilkinson's motives in sending Zebulon Pike out as an explorer, it was clear that he was dealing with a young army officer who had the same fascination with the West that Meriwether Lewis had articulated to Thomas Jefferson as early as 1792, when Lewis asked to be made part of a western expedition to be sponsored by the American Philosophical Society.

Pike grew up in an army family and received little formal education, although his continual efforts to improve himself were apparent by his reading lists while a young lieutenant on the Ohio frontier. It is clear from his letters and journals that, while sensitive about his lack of education, Pike was no less well educated than most Americans or even most officers in the U.S. Army — he was, for example, a much better speller than William Clark. And his reading seems to have included material on the trans-Mississippi West, as evidenced by his submission of a letter in the summer of 1803 to *The Medical Repository*, a respected periodical among the American intellectual community that often contained letters of interest on the Louisiana Territory.

Much of Pike's contribution, which was printed in 1804, was derived from Thomas Jefferson's report to Congress in July

1803. In this report, the president supported the actions of his administration in purchasing the Louisiana Territory from the French by describing the wonders of this new American territory. Like Jefferson, Pike described the geography and natural resources of the West, including Jefferson's famous "mountain of rock salt . . . 180 miles long and 45 miles wide," dimensions that Pike converted into standard Spanish leagues as "60 leagues by 15."

Pike also noted, as had Jefferson, that the Missouri River was the key to discovering a passage to the Pacific. In doing so, he reinforced the existing belief, derived largely from British exploratory literature, that somewhere in the interior of the continent was a height-of-land from which all major western rivers flowed. Pike also volunteered some new information: namely, that the mines of New Mexico were on the same line of latitude as St. Louis, and that the journey from St. Louis to New Mexico was "one-third . . . through the woods, and the rest through an immense prairie, where not a tree, shrub or knoll is seen to bound the prospect and the horizon only terminates the traveller's view for many a successive day." All in all, this was not a bad description of the southern Great Plains, albeit an abbreviated one.

Pike made no attempt to address a scientific question that was being debated at the time: was the newly acquired territory a vast trackless wasteland as the Spanish and some British scientific publications seemed to suggest? Or was it, as American and French literature posited, a rich gardenlike area, barren of trees—in Jefferson's phrase—"because the soil was too rich for the growth of forest trees?" But in Pike's description of an area where "not a tree, shrub, or knoll is seen," we see a foreshadowing of his later descriptions of the southern Great Plains which some would take as the origin of the myth of the Great American Desert.

In this letter to a leading American periodical—one read by the most prominent thinkers in the country—Pike demonstrated an interest in science and a grasp of the basics of western "natural history." It may have been this letter that drew Pike to Wilkinson's attention—or perhaps in the small army garrison in St. Louis it would have been natural that even officers as widely separated in rank as a lieutenant and a general could share their common interests in the natural history of the trans-Mississippi West. We do know that by July 1805 Wilkinson had selected Pike to lead an army exploration up the Mississippi River to attempt to ascertain the source of that river (a key point in the political geography of the continent, as various treaties used the Mississippi's source as a boundary marker).

It is apparent from the same letter in which Wilkinson informs Secretary of War Henry Dearborn that he was sending Pike "for the Head of the Mississippi" that the general was also thinking of an expedition to the West, particularly to the Comanches who, in Wilkinson's opinion, constituted "the most powerfull Nation of Savages on this Continent, and have it in their power to facilitate or impede our march to New Mexico, should such movement ever become Necessary." Concluding a treaty with the Comanches could also facilitate a march from New Mexico to St. Louis, should Wilkinson's Spanish employers find that "movement" necessary.

Pike's Mississippi Expedition

Pike's Mississippi River expedition succeeded primarily in that he was able to take a command up the river beyond the Falls of St. Anthony, winter over in one of the coldest parts of the continent, and return. His stated objectives on this journey were originally to proceed to the source of the Mississippi, although a letter from Wilkinson to Dearborn near the end of 1805 curiously suggested that if Pike in fact proceeded to the "the source of the River . . . he will have stretched his orders."

Yet Pike made an effort to discover one of the great riddles of the continent. He failed in the attempt to locate the Mississippi's source and it would be nearly two decades after his journey before what Henry Schoolcraft called "the last great riddle of North American geography" would be solved. Nevertheless, even though Pike disparaged his scientific achievements and claimed that he had done little beyond producing some fairly readable field maps, that in itself was a significant addition to scientific understanding. He acquired from British traders maps of the upper Mississippi country produced by David Thompson, perhaps the most skilled astronomer and geographer among North American explorers before John C. Fremont. These, along with his field notes, were given to Nicholas King (an English-born cartographer resident in Washington and highly knowledgeable about the American West) to produce maps for publication. The published maps, although not immediately recognized for their considerable value, formed the basis for later maps of the interior of the North American continent that were judged to be the most precise by the best of the Philadelphia scientists.

Of his own mapping efforts, Pike readily acknowledged inadequacies. He was not equipped, he noted, with the "instruments proper for celestial observations," and his readings of latitude and longitude would therefore, of necessity, be somewhat suspect. And since he did "not possess the qualifications of the naturalist," his assessment of the country was, he believed, limited to minimal commentary.

Pike lamented that his journey would "have little to strike the imagination," and by the time he returned to St. Louis in the spring of 1806, he was a discouraged scientific explorer. It must be remembered that this was his first exploratory venture, much of it accomplished while he and his men were hampered by deep snows and cold so severe that the ink in his pen froze. And, however minimal his scientific accomplishments might have been in his own mind, his descriptions of the course and navigability of the Mississippi, the character of the adjacent terrain and vegetation, and assessments of native peoples provided the first really clear look at the upper Mississippi Valley since the early French explorations of the late seventeenth century. Additionally, his diplomatic efforts with the Mississippi Valley native peoples had largely been successful (or so it seemed at the time) and he could correctly have assumed that he had contributed to the expansion of American commerce to the north, thereby placing at least some small impediments in the way of the British advance to the south.

If American Enlightenment explorers were mixtures of scientist, merchant, and diplomat, then Zebulon Pike on his maiden journey into *terrae incognitae* had satisfied most of the requisites of the Jeffersonian explorer. This was, in the final analysis, not bad for a rookie—and he was quickly to have the opportunity to make a more lasting name for himself as a contributor to science on a more far-ranging journey.

The Preparation of an Explorer

Zebulon Pike returned to the St. Louis garrison from his Mississippi River expedition on May 30, 1806. Before the end of June, he had orders from Wilkinson to embark on his southwest expedition with four exploratory objectives based in Indian diplomacy. He was to return some fifty Osage Indians who had been captured by the Potawatomies and ransomed by the United States to their home community. He was to engage in frontier diplomacy by effecting a peace treaty between the Osage and the Kansas nations. He was to attempt to contact and negotiate with the Comanche on the possibilities of a peace conference between the United States and the nation that Wilkinson had earlier referred to as "the most powerfull [Indian] nation." Finally, he was to "endeavour to make peace" between the Comanche and "the nations which inhabit the Country between us and them, particularly the Osage."

Wilkinson informed Pike that the return of the Osage to their home was "the primary objective of your expedition." This was disingenuous at best, given Wilkinson's concern about the Comanche. It was also misleading in the context of other objectives that Wilkinson laid down for Pike: to continue west to determine the sources of the Red and Arkansas Rivers. Here Wilkinson's instructions reveal both the tidy mind of someone trained in and dedicated to Enlightenment science and the devious thinking of a man who may have been attempting to serve two masters—the governments of the United States and New Spain—at the same time.

In language that began as if it were simply an afterthought, Wilkinson suggested to Pike that since his "Interview with the Cammanchees" would probably lead to the headwaters of the Red and Arkansas Rivers, he might just as well reconnoiter that territory and make a report. Of course, he should move with the greatest circumspection because "the affairs of Spain, & the United States appear to be on the point of amicable adjustment, and more over it is the desire of the President, to cultivate the Friendship & Harmonious Intercourse, of all the Nations of the Earth, & particularly our near neighbours the Spaniards."

Well. This is General James Wilkinson at either his best or worst—depending upon your point of view. In one fell swoop, he instructs Pike to move toward (and possibly beyond?) the very fringes of the legal definition of Louisiana Territory (the headwaters of the Mississippi's western tributaries) and at the same time warns the young explorer of the "desire of the President" for peace and harmony with all nations. Of all the people on the western frontier, no one knew better than General James Wilkinson how the Spanish officials would view an American exploring party moving anywhere near the sources of the Red or Arkansas Rivers—they would certainly not view it as "amicable." By invoking the wishes of Jefferson to preserve peace, tucked away in a message that instructs an American army officer to tread gingerly into territory occupied (legally or not—it makes no difference) by a foreign power, Wilkinson lent a degree of official approbation to Pike's expedition that it simply did not possess. And what is even more intriguing is that the remainder of Wilkinson's instructions had absolutely nothing to do with the Osages, the Comanche, or, for that matter, the Spanish.

Borrowing liberally from Jefferson's instructions to Meriwether Lewis (which Wilkinson could well have seen during the time that Lewis was in St. Louis prior to his departure in the spring of 1804), Wilkinson provides Pike with the kind of instructions which gave the southwestern expedition the scientific flavor that, when the diplomatic and commercial intrigue was added in, made Pike a quintessential explorer of the American Enlightenment. "In the course of your tour," Wilkinson instructed Pike:

> you are to remark particularly upon the Geographical structure, the Natural History; and population; of the country through which you may pass, taking particular care to collect & preserve, specimens of every thing curious in the mineral or botanical Worlds, which can be preserved & are portable: Let your courses be regulated by your compass, & your Distances by your Watch, to be noted in a field Book, & I would advise you when circumstances permit, to protract & lay down in a separate Book, the march of the Day at every evenings halt. The Instruments which I have furnished

you; will enable you to ascertain the variation of the magnetic needle and the Lattitude with exactitude, and at every remarkable point I wish you to employ your Telescope in observeing the Eclipses of Jupiters Satillites, having previously regulated your Watch by your Sextant, takeing care to note with great nicety the periods of immersion & emersion of the eclipsed Satillite. These observations may enable us after your return, by application to the appropriate Tables, to ascertain the Longitude. It is an object of much Interest with the Executive, to ascertain the Direction, extent, & navigation of the Arkansaw, & Red Rivers.

Wilkinson's instructions for Pike to explore the upper reaches of the Arkansas and Red Rivers are meant to appear to come from the president himself — "an object of much Interest with the Executive." These are slippery directions to give a young man who quite probably had no idea what he was in for. But they are also directions that indicate that Wilkinson's intentions — irrespective of his motivations regarding the borders of the United States and New Spain and the potential for conflict that travel into that borderland might bring — were not without scientific merit. For Wilkinson instructed Pike to do for the Southwest much of what Jefferson had instructed Meriwether Lewis to do for the Northwest: to come finally to grips with what was probably the most essential scientific question about the western interior of North America.

Was there a common source region for all major western streams? This was surely one of the questions that Wilkinson would have directed to von Humboldt to get "his answers to the queries," had the opportunity presented itself. But Wilkinson already possessed at least part of the answer that von Humboldt would have provided. On his map, the map that was borrowed or purloined from Gallatin, copied by Nau, and come into Wilkinson's possession, von Humboldt showed western streams such as the Red, Arkansas, and Rio Grande as having sources very close to those of the Missouri and Great River of the West. More important, this source region was close to Santa Fe, the heart of New Spain's Internal Provinces.

Lewis and Clark were searching for this common source area far to the north during their 1804–1806 expedition. General Wilkinson, unaware in the summer of 1806 of the success or failure of Jefferson's explorers, wanted to locate the source region himself—either in connection with the plotting that he and Burr had done to create their own fiefdom in the Southwest or in the interests of his Spanish employers. The instrument of Wilkinson's desire was to be Zebulon Montgomery Pike.

Let us then try to place Zebulon Pike into the correct scientific context on the eve of his Southwestern expedition and view the common state of knowledge of the interior of the American Southwest in 1806. It must first be noted that American knowledge of the area between St. Louis and Santa Fe, or between the Platte River and the Rio Grande, was extremely sketchy. No American explorer had yet managed to penetrate more than a few hundred miles up the Red River valley. The Spanish knew the area relatively well but, persisting in the geographical delusion of the proximity of the sources of the Rio Grande and Missouri and therefore viewing the Missouri River as a highway for the invasion of New Spain from the north and east, they kept their maps and journals and notes and military reports locked away in unreachable archives in Mexico City and Seville in Spain.

The best geographical understanding of the area was probably to be found on von Humboldt's map—and it was filled with conjecture and bad cartography based on limited Spanish explorations beyond the Rio Grande valley, particularly the explorations of a pair of Franciscan friars, Francisco Atanasio Dominguez and Silvestre Vélez de Escalante, and their military companion and cartographer, Bernardo de Miera y Pacheco. Given the secretive and non-scientific nature of Spanish exploration (Spain had not yet been much influenced by Enlightenment science) von Humboldt's map was little better than the maps produced by the French in early Louisiana Territory a century earlier. Geographical features and descriptions on the von Humboldt map appear to have been entered more to fill blank space than to illustrate known topography or rivers or native settlements or vegetative regions.

Where blank spaces exist on maps, the imagination is more than ready to fill them. In the geographical thought current in the early nineteenth century, the core geographical feature of the Southwest and Northwest was compressed into a single small area of land: the "pyramidal height-of-land," the common source area for western rivers that had been created out of rather flimsy evidence by American and British opportunists like Jonathan Carver and Robert Rogers and bought eagerly by ambitious imperialists like Thomas Jefferson—and James Wilkinson. This was the reason for the section in Wilkinson's instructions to Pike that the general deviously threw in as an afterthought and, even more deviously, made it appear to be consistent with Jefferson's wishes: "It is an object of much Interest with the Executive, to ascertain the Direction, extent, & navigation of the Arkansaw, & Red Rivers."

Well, of course. Whoever discovered the direction, extent, and navigation of these rivers would also discover the location of the sources of the Rio Grande, Missouri, Columbia and other western streams and open up half a continent to water travel by conquering armies or eager merchants. Armed with such intelligence, it is small wonder that Pike in the field often seemed confused and lost.

There were other components of existing science on the Southwest that had a bearing on Pike's expedition and its results. Not the least of these were the notions of the "utility" of the land—was it fertile soil suitable for the expansion of Jefferson's yeomanry or was it a desert expanse similar to the deserts known to the Spanish farther west between the Rio Grande and the Colorado? The Spanish had their opinions, based on the experiences of settlements in Texas and elsewhere: it was grassland suitable for raising livestock. But the Spanish information was not part of the general fund of knowledge, kept like the Spanish maps in secreted depositories.

French geographical information from their occupation of Louisiana Territory from the early 1700s to the end of the Seven Years' War in 1763 suggested that the great grasslands were somewhat more productive, but were still largely "meadows" where the "hump-backed kine," or buffalo, roved in such numbers that the area surely would support large herds of domesticated cattle and sheep and horses. The British, with their experience confined largely to the cooler, more humid north country, tended to see the area as desert-like because it did not produce trees. American opinion was molded most directly perhaps by Thomas Jefferson who recognized the treeless nature of the southern Plains but also viewed the area as a potential agricultural garden.

We do not know what Pike's opinion was of these conflicting geographies but we can guess. His letter to *The Medical Repository* bore more overtones of the Spanish desert than of the Jeffersonian garden. And so, young Zebulon Montgomery Pike in the summer of 1806 on the eve of his departure into the Southwest: possessed of little real scientific knowledge of the area he was about to traverse, supplied with faulty maps, provided with misleading (and perhaps illegal) instructions, loyal to a commander who did not deserve his loyalty — a poster child on how not to prepare an explorer embarking on what should have been a great expansion of Enlightenment science but ended up, on the whole, rather badly.

Pike's Southwest Expedition

Lieutenant Pike departed the U.S. army cantonment at Belle Fontaine, just up the Missouri from St. Louis, on July 15, 1806. He was accompanied by a command of twenty-two men, including Lieutenant James Wilkinson (the general's son), a surgeon (Dr. John Robinson, a Spanish sympathizer and probably a spy, who produced a notable map of the Southwest following the Pike expedition), a Spanish interpreter, and nineteen enlisted men. Also with the party were the fifty-one Osage Indians that Pike was returning to their home village.

After safely delivering the Osage to their "Grand Town" in western Missouri in late August, Pike and his party proceeded west through present-day Kansas (with a northern detour across the Smoky Hill tributary of the Kansas River to a point just north of the present Kansas–Nebraska border) during the remainder of the summer and fall of 1806. They reached the Great Bend of the Arkansas in mid-October, where Lieutenant Wilkinson detached from the main party and led a small group back down the Arkansas. Pike's intention from this point, based largely on his copy of the von Humboldt map, was to trace the Arkansas to its source and then cross over to the Red River's headwaters which in his view should be no great distance away.

By December, the expedition had reached the Royal Gorge of the Arkansas near present-day Cañon City, Colorado. Just above the Royal Gorge, Pike reached a branching of the Arkansas that he judged to represent its source of that river, since the forks lay approximately where the headwaters of the Arkansas appeared on the von Humboldt map. Here he made a fateful decision insuring that, for the remainder of his travels, he was—for all practical purposes—lost.

He followed what he believed to be a Spanish trail north from the main branch of the Arkansas past the later site of the mining town of Cripple Creek and ultimately ended up on the southernmost source waters of the South Platte. From this trail, Pike saw the peak that would later bear his name and be labeled on his maps as the "Highest Peak." Having reconnoitered what he thought was the absolute source of the Arkansas, his intent was then to turn south to the head of the Red River and Santa Fe—which his mental geography had close to the Red's headwaters. Such a plan made sense in terms of his geographical knowledge, based on von Humboldt's map—but it was a plan that had hard consequences for the success of his expedition and his final reputation. Turning south from the upper South Platte, he came again to the Arkansas drainage and turned west toward the main branch of the Arkansas, thinking that he was on the upper reaches of the Red River and close to Santa Fe.

It was now mid-December 1806 and Pike and his men were in trouble. They had no winter uniforms and they were in high country in a Rocky Mountain winter. Just as bad, Pike began to recognize the disjunction between the geography of the imagination and the geography of reality. In his journal he entered the momentous conclusion that "the geography of the country had turned out to be so different from our expectation; we were some what at a loss which course to pursue."

Although bewildered and on the upper waters of the Arkansas, Pike still believed he was on the Red River and, assuming that he was near its source and had achieved the instructions of Wilkinson to reconnoiter the headwaters of the

Arkansas and Red, he turned downstream—eventually coming to the Royal Gorge of the Arkansas he and his men had labored through weeks before. After struggling through the Royal Gorge in early January 1807, Pike finally recognized the magnitude of his mistake—he was not on the Red River but the Arkansas. His field notes inform us that Pike "now felt at considerable loss how to proceed." Indeed: his supplies had run short and he had no idea how or where to get more (not unlike Lewis and Clark during their struggle across the Bitterroot Range). He and his men had no horses for transportation or hunting to obtain animal hides or buffalo robes for warmth, and he was mightily confused about the geography of southern Colorado. Almost nothing that Pike did from this point would have eliminated the confusion in his physical and political geography.

He did not really know where the Red River was, nor did he really know whether or not he was still in American territory. He had two options: he could simply follow the Arkansas for a distance downstream and then strike out south for the Red River, supposed to lie in that direction; or he could cross the mountains on the western horizon, in the hopes of intercepting the Red River. Since the Red River heads far to the east in the Texas Panhandle, either choice would have increased his confusion. A trip down the Arkansas and then south would lead to the Canadian River, which he surely would have mistaken for the Red River. A trip across the Sangre de Cristo Range would place him in the Rio Grande valley, also the Red in his confused geography. There was no easy way out of this dilemma. Donald Jackson, the documentary editor of Pike's journals, has pointed out that nothing Pike ever did was easy. That certainly was the case as he sorted through the disjunctions between imaginary and real geography.

At the end of the first week of January 1807, Pike had made up his mind: they would cross over the mountains to the west and, hopefully, come to the source of the Red River. An exhausting and hazardous mountain crossing of more than two weeks finally brought Pike and his command to the San Luis Valley where, near the present-day Alamosa, Colorado, a log stockade was built on what Pike was sure was the Red. Given the supposed proximity to Santa Fe, Dr. Robinson left the party at the winter fort and struck out for the Spanish colonial capital. The remainder of the force fell into the daily routine of cutting wood, repairing equipment, and foraging for food. This routine was interrupted near the end of February when Spanish soldiers arrived to inform Pike that he was on the Rio Grande and, therefore, decidedly not in the American territory of Louisiana. Informed of this fact, Pike is supposed to have exclaimed "what . . . is not this the Red river?"

There has been conjecture that Pike knew exactly where he was, was under no illusions about not being in Spanish territory, and was simply dissembling. This is doubtful. The best geographical information available to Pike—the von Humboldt map—led inescapably to the conclusion that he was, in fact, on the upper Red River and in American territory. But a small and very weary American force was not going to argue with a larger, better-fed, and better-equipped force of Spanish soldiers, and for the next four months Pike and his men were the "guests" of the government of New Spain. They were taken first to Santa Fe and then south to Chihuahua, northeast through the Sierra Madre Oriental to San Antonio de Bexar, and finally, on June 30, 1807, back to Natchitoches, Louisiana—once again on American soil.

Bad luck, poor planning, questionable objectives, and a disastrous grasp of geography that was much inferior to his contemporary, William Clark, had all combined to make Zebulon Pike a failure. Although he beat Lewis and Clark to press by four years, he simply never was seen as a heroic figure as they were. His reports did not capture the imagination of the American public as did those of John C. Fremont, and although most Americans would recognize the name "Pike's Peak," few could tell you anything about its namesake. His bad luck continued when he was killed at the age of thirty-seven in the War of 1812 and history, in general, has not been kind to his reputation.

Assessing Pike's Scientific Accomplishments

While Pike's accomplishments as an Enlightenment explorer fall far short of those achieved by Lewis and Clark, his role in the development and assessment of the American West was still a significant one—but, as seems to be typical of Pike, that role was significant largely because of errors of understanding and imagination. In the published reports of Pike's journeys, there were two primary pieces of information and interpretation that continued to perpetuate myth and, by doing so, became significant in a historical context. The first of these was Pike's assessment of the land quality of the area between the Mississippi and the Rocky Mountains. Although Pike provided detailed information on the "natural history" of the southern Great Plains, unfortunately much of this information was either flat wrong or, at best, exaggerated.

In his letter to *The Medical Repository* in 1804, Pike had suggested the treelessness of the southern plains but had not used the word "desert." In his daily journals during the crossing of the plains in 1806 he consistently referred to the plains as "prairie" — a term equated in the American mind of the Jeffersonian Age as the equivalent of the English word "meadow." In fact, during his entire trek, Pike used the word "desert" only sparingly. Four years after his return, however, the published version of his journals carried the most negative descriptions of the southern plains, descriptions that some historians contend signaled the beginning of the "Great American Desert" myth that is supposed to have served as a mental barrier against rapid American migration into the lands beyond Texas. "These vast plains of the western hemisphere," Pike's published journals concluded, "may become in time equally celebrated as the sandy deserts of Africa; for I saw in my route, in various places, tracts of many leagues, where the wind had thrown up the sand, in all the fanciful forms of the Ocean's rolling wave, and on which not a speck of vegetable matter existed." The native inhabitants of this vast wasteland Pike compared to the "tribes of Tartary," and little was said about the herds of buffalo, deer, and antelope that flavor other early descriptions of the southern and central Great Plains region.

Pike's plains were very far indeed from the Jeffersonian Garden of the World — and Pike took a step further: "Our citizens being so prone to rambling and extending themselves, on the frontiers," he wrote, "will, through necessity, be constrained to limit their extent on the west, to the borders of the Missouri and Mississippi." If James Wilkinson had wanted to exclude an American population from the Southwest in order to preserve it for a Spanish population over which he might rule, he could not have made a better argument than did Zebulon Pike. We are left to wonder whether Pike's self-realized failings as an explorer colored his impressions of a landscape in bleak desert pastels, whether the "prairies" of the westbound journey were converted, by sheer disillusionment, to the "wastes of the Zahara."

Pike's second grand error was in his perpetuation of the concept of the core drainage area, the pyramidal height-of-land that gave rise to all major western streams. In his journals and in his maps (which, it must be noted in fairness to Pike, were more copies of von Humboldt's maps than they were carefully constructed cartographic evidence of a successful exploration), Pike persisted in the opinion that the sources of northern plains rivers such as the Missouri and Yellowstone headed in the same region as the southern plains rivers of the Arkansas and Rio Grande. On the second sheet of his major map, Pike showed the northernmost sources of the Platte and, across a range of mountains to the west, the "sources of the Arkansaw." Going by the scale of the map, about forty miles north of the sources of the Platte and Arkansas was the "Yellow Stone River. Branch of the Missouri."

During his trek north on the west side of Pikes Peak, the explorer claimed to have reached a point where he looked down on the source region of the Yellowstone, Platte, Arkansas, and Rio Grande. This is the area depicted in the northwestern corner of the "Chart of the internal parts of Louisiana" and to which Pike referred in his journal as "the grand reservoir of snows and fountains." The significance of this is not that Pike was wrong in compressing the nearly six hundred miles between the Yellowstone and Arkansas/Rio Grande headwaters. What makes the error significant is that Pike claimed to have viewed the region and this claim was picked up by William Clark, a much better cartographer and explorer who was, at the time Pike's map was published, preparing his own map summarizing the results of the Lewis and Clark Expedition.

On Clark's manuscript map of 1810 and his published map of 1814, immediately to the south of the southernmost portion of the Yellowstone drainage may be seen a replica of the northwest corner of Pike's "Chart" — with the sources of "Rio de la Platte," the "Arkansaw," the "Rio del Norte" or Rio Grande, the "Block House U.S. Factory in 1806" (Pike's winter cantonment), and just to the north of the "Block House" the label "Highest Peak." For the area that William Clark and Meriwether Lewis had seen and surveyed, Clark's map is highly accurate. For other areas, Clark relied upon information from members of Manuel Lisa's fur trading company, John Colter and George Drouillard, who had been in the Big Horn Basin and upper Yellowstone drainage in 1807–1808. He also relied on a fellow army officer and resident of St. Louis who must have been well known to him — Zebulon Montgomery Pike. By accepting Pike's erroneous and wishful cartography, Clark himself was guilty of perpetuating the myth of the common source area. Would he have done so had he not had Pike's map — from a source that he probably judged to be highly reliable?

There is no real way to measure the importance of Pike's two grand errors: the evaluation of the southern Plains as desert and the "grand reservoir of snows and fountains" from which issued all major western rivers. What we can say is that the errors have done Pike's reputation as an explorer little good and much damage. He has, consequently, long been dismissed as either a tool of Wilkinson's imperial (and illegal) ambitions or as an afterthought of Jeffersonian exploration who managed to get himself lost and confused, captured by the Spanish and hauled away in ignominy to Chihuahua, and then, finally and perhaps mercifully, killed by a stray British cannonball that missed Pike but struck a powder supply close enough to him that wounds from flying splinters cost him his life. But for all that, Pike was actually much more important as a shaper of the view of the American West in the late Jeffersonian and early Jacksonian periods than he has been given credit.

People may have forgotten Pike's maps quickly. But they didn't forget William Clark's map that was the master map of the American West until the 1840s — still containing the geographical misinformation from Pike. And potential migrants into west Texas and Kansas and New Mexico as late as the 1850s may have found Pike's descriptions of what an equally inept explorer, Stephen Long, would dub "The Great American Desert" just as important in avoiding the southern Plains as the forbidding presence of the Comanche. Zebulon Pike was not the first explorer who didn't know where he was, ran into trouble with authorities and was arrested, involved himself in conspiracies, and still left his tracks on the map. The name of Christopher Columbus comes immediately to mind.

John Logan Allen was born in Laramie, Wyoming, and earned a B.A. (1963) and M.A. (1964) from the University of Wyoming before completing his Ph.D. at Clark University in Worcester, Massachusetts in 1969. He taught geography at the University of Connecticut for many years and is currently the chair of the geography department at the University of Wyoming. He is member of the Lewis and Clark Trail Heritage Foundation and received their meritorious achievement award for his book, *Passage through the Garden* (1976). Allen served as a key consultant for the Colorado Springs Pioneers Museum in the development of the exhibit *Pike's World: Exploration and Empire in the Greater Southwest*. This essay was a scholarly result of the Museum's efforts.

Pike & Empire

James P. Ronda

Early in March 1807, in a small village outside Santa Fe, two men talked quietly about the future of New Spain and the ambitions of the young American republic. Lieutenant Zebulon Montgomery Pike had come to Santa Fe just days before under guard from his stockade on the Conejos River. The man Pike often called "my friend" was Bartholemew Fernandez, a Santa Fe resident and someone Pike once thought was an officer in the Spanish army. But in the snowy stillness of that March night, Fernandez sounded more like a civilian and a merchant than a soldier as he told Pike about the "great desire they felt for a change of affairs, and an open trade with the United States." Sensing an opportunity, Pike seized the moment, took a piece of chalk and began to draw a map on the floor. What he sketched out were the routes and connections between Louisiana and "North Mexico." Then, as if to say that the wish for a "change in affairs" might happen sometime soon, Pike gave "Mr. Bartholemew" a certificate addressed to American citizens identifying Fernandez as a friend and "man of influence." Fernandez was convinced that an American army would invade New Spain later that spring. Pike assured him that no invasion was in the works, but the certificate seemed to say "not this spring but sometime soon."

Where did this memorable conversation come from? Why was a junior officer in the American army deep in Spanish territory talking about the future shape of the continent? Answers to those questions take us back into the origins of "Manifest Destiny," the imperial rivalries that dominated North America in the early nineteenth century, and the tangled life of sometime-empire builder Zebulon Montgomery Pike. Pike traveled a long road to Santa Fe; the ideas he championed had been on the road even longer. To borrow a term from geology, Pike moved in a world of "suspect terrain" where boundaries, loyalties, and identities were constantly shifting and always uncertain.

Whether he knew it or not, young Lieutenant Pike was part of a long tradition of empire building. For Americans, that tradition had its beginnings in seventeenth-century England. English nationalism was an explosive mixture of religious passion and economic necessity, all fueled by an intense hatred of Catholic Spain. It was religion that most fully shaped the ideas that swirled around English expansionism. In sermon after sermon, both Puritan and Anglican clergy preached that the English nation had a special mission, a divine obligation to spread the Protestant faith throughout the world. "God is an Englishman," said one preacher, emphasizing that sense of the English as the new Israel, the chosen people of God. It was that powerful feeling of mission and "chosenness" that English colonists carried with them, whether they were bound for Massachusetts Bay or Virginia. One Puritan divine caught the temper of the time when he declared that God had sent the English on an "errand into the wilderness" to spread the true faith, making the world both godly and English.

As religious passions cooled in the eighteenth century, that English sense of sacred mission was steadily transformed. At a time of constant imperial conflict with France, the mission took on a more secular tone. Now it was Great Britain's national destiny to defeat France, wrest land from Indian hands, and become a real empire. Once it was the clergy who preached God's empire; now it was pamphleteers and politicians who promoted an imperial Britain.

No one better exemplified that secular British–American imperialism than Benjamin Franklin. A Franklin biographer wrote that "to Franklin the rise of the British Empire was the greatest phenomenon of the eighteenth century." While some political theorists took a darker view of empire and its consequences, Franklin and most others defined the word in positive terms. Empire promised power and prosperity. To build an empire was to take out an insurance policy for the future. In Franklin's view, America was at the very heart of the British Empire. Writing his "Observations Concerning the Increase of Mankind, Peopling of Countries, Etc." in 1751, Franklin predicted that America "in another Century will be more than the people of England, and the greatest Number of Englishmen will be on this Side [of] the Water." But this was not an argument for American independence. Instead, Franklin exclaimed "what an Accession of Power to the British Empire by Sea as well as Land!"

The American Revolution changed the location of power and destiny from Britain to the new nation. Once Britain had imagined itself exceptional among the nations of the world; now the American republic took on that role. God's will and the territorial expansion of the nation were fused in the fires of war and nation-building. South Carolinian William Henry Drayton captured that sense of American imperial mission and its religious overtones when he wrote in 1776 that "the Almighty has made choice of the present generation to erect the American Empire." Drayton looked to God for imperial validation; Boston revolutionary Samuel Adams substituted Nature for the deity. "We shall never be upon a solid Footing till Britain cedes to us what Nature designs we should have." Just what nature had in store for a land-hungry republic was a bit clearer in Jedediah Morse's influential 1789 *American Geography*. "We cannot but anticipate the period, as not far distant, when the AMERICAN EMPIRE will comprehend millions of souls, west of the Mississippi."

As for nature's American limits, Morse argued that "the Mississippi was never designed as the western boundary of the American empire." Revolutionaries and geographers soon found their words echoing in the popular press. On the eve of the Louisiana Purchase, the New York *Evening Post* boldly announced that "it belongs of *right* to the United States to regulate the future destiny of *North America*. The country is *ours*; ours is the right to its rivers and to all the sources of future opulence, power and happiness." God's empire promised salvation in heaven; the American empire promised heaven on earth. During the debate on the ratification of the Constitution, old revolutionary Patrick Henry paused to consider the nation's future. "Some way or other," he mused, "we must be a great and mighty empire."

These prophets of empire could define American expansion by their words but they lacked the power to transform ideas into political and diplomatic action. That power rested in Thomas Jefferson, third president of the United States. Like Franklin, Jefferson used the word "empire" in glowing terms.

Perhaps his most famous expression of imperial ambition came in the phrase "empire for liberty." Writing to James Madison in 1809, Jefferson predicted that "we should have such an empire for liberty as she has never surveyed since creation: and I am persuaded no constitution was ever before so well calculated as ours for extensive empire and self government." Behind those high-flown words was a harsh reality. As president, Jefferson had used all the powers of his office to gain Indian land by whatever means. If the empire of liberty had no place for native people, it also meant shoving aside Spanish, French, or British claims in the West. Jefferson made his imperial ambitions plain in an 1803 letter to Senator John C. Breckinridge. "When we are full on this side," he told Breckinridge, "we may lay off a range of States on the Western bank [of the Mississippi River] from the head to the mouth, and so, range after range, advancing compactly as we multiply." Here was the vision of an irresistible march across the continent, a march justified by the spread of liberty and made inevitable by the very design of nature. As Jefferson declared in his second inaugural address in 1805, "in my view, is it not better that the opposite bank of the Mississippi should be settled by our own brethren and children, than by strangers of another family?" And those strangers might be French, Spanish, British, or Native Americans.

Long before New York journalist John L. O'Sullivan coined the term "Manifest Destiny" in 1845, there was a fully formed expansionist ideology to energize and justify what George Washington had called "the rising American empire." That ideology, drawn from religious conviction, super-heated nationalism, and a fierce land hunger, was part of Zebulon Montgomery Pike's intellectual inheritance. Pike came to maturity in a world whose very language defined empire and territorial expansion as goals worthy of the best efforts anyone could muster. Pike embraced those ideas and blended them with his own restless ambition and exaggerated sense of self-importance. In the larger scheme of things, empire gave Pike a field on which to play out all his dreams of national honor and personal glory.

Zebulon Montgomery Pike was shaped by the climate of opinion that swirled around him. But it took one individual to draw him into the suspect terrain of imperial rivalry. Meriwether Lewis and William Clark had President Thomas Jefferson; Pike had General James Wilkinson. There was perhaps no more complex and dangerous figure on the early nineteenth-century western frontier than James Wilkinson. Commander of American forces in the West, sometime governor of the Louisiana Territory, Spanish secret agent, and co-conspirator with Aaron Burr, Wilkinson was what a recent historian has called "the perfect chameleon." But Wilkinson always remained true to his colors—the color of money and personal advancement. By the time Pike met Wilkinson, the general already had a long history in the shadowy world of deception and intrigue.

The summer of 1805 found Pike at Fort Massac in Illinois serving as district paymaster for the First Infantry Regiment. It was hardly a promising assignment for an officer hungry for advancement and eager for glory. Sometime during that summer, Wilkinson visited the post and selected Pike to lead a reconnaissance party up the Mississippi River. What drew Wilkinson to Pike remains unclear. The general did know Pike's father, Major Zebulon Pike, and the younger Pike's wife Clarissa was the daughter of a Kentucky friend. Wilkinson always had an entourage of young officers around him and perhaps he was looking to add another to that company. Without question or hesitation, Pike became Wilkinson's man. It was a decision that would haunt him for the rest of his life.

The exploration assigned to Pike seemed straightforward enough. Mapping the rivers of the Louisiana Purchase was high on Jefferson's list of western priorities. But Pike's journey up the Mississippi was not at the direction of the commander in chief but on orders from Wilkinson, and Wilkinson's reasons for sending Pike up north remain elusive. However, as Donald Jackson reminds us, Wilkinson was not a "complete charlatan," and Pike's first expedition may have been just what it seemed — a genuine military probe up an important river.

Whatever the reasons, Pike got his instructions from Wilkinson on July 30, 1805. He and his crew were to head up the Mississippi, plot the course of the river, and pay attention to what Jefferson called "the face of the country." Pike was also handed important Indian missions, including the purchase of land for two military posts and arrangements for Indian delegations to visit the Great Father. In addition, Pike was instructed to note the current state of the fur trade on the upper Mississippi. But there was nothing in those orders that directed him to launch a diplomatic offensive against British traders doing business in what is now Minnesota and the western Great Lakes. Because it is often said that Pike went north in search of the headwaters of the Mississippi, it should be noted that Wilkinson did not think this was an important expedition objective. He told Pike that finding the headwaters would be useful if it could be done in one season. Taken together, these instructions were not much different (if less detailed) than those Jefferson prepared for Lewis and Clark and the Thomas Freeman–Peter Custis expeditions. How Pike interpreted them would be another matter.

In so many ways, the Minnesota country at the beginning of the nineteenth century was a borderland frontier. Here the borders—both national and personal—were fluid and ill-defined. More important, Minnesota was a "middle ground," a place where peoples from diverse cultures met to trade and sometimes make war. The Minnesota country would be Pike's first borderland, the first place to give life to the ideas of empire he had inherited.

Pike had no experience in the complex world of Indian diplomacy. He had never been a participant at a major council, he knew little about the protocols and rituals that shaped such meetings, and he spoke no native language. Nonetheless, he was ordered to represent the United States at a gathering on contested ground and with Indians who were not much impressed by the power of the new nation. Heading upriver, Pike did not doubt that he could mold native realities to American patterns.

Perhaps the most important meeting Pike had with native people came near the end of September 1805 when he held council with representatives of the Santee and Mdewkanton Sioux. Pike and the Indian delegates met on an island at the confluence of the Minnesota and Mississippi Rivers within what is now the city limits of St. Paul. Pike blandly announced the Louisiana Purchase and then in a candid moment said he represented not the Great Father but General Wilkinson. Two issues then occupied Pike, both of them imperial in character.

Like Lewis and Clark, Pike had been instructed to scout out suitable locations for military establishments. Claiming that such posts would benefit native people, Pike asked the assembled representatives to sign a draft land purchase treaty. Thinking he had accomplished that, he then moved to an issue not covered by his instructions. Intertribal peace had long been a centerpiece for British Indian policy, and now it was on the American agenda as well. Taking matters into his own hands, Pike attempted to negotiate a peace between the eastern Sioux and their Chippewa neighbors. After listing all the advantages peace might bring, Pike concluded with a threat. "If the chiefs do not listen to the voice of their father and continue to commit murders on you and our traders," Pike warned, "they will call down the vengeance of the Americans."

At the end of the day, two Sioux chiefs signed a brief treaty document granting land for building the posts Pike sought. Pike later told Wilkinson that he had bought the land "for a Song." But he had neglected to fill in that portion of Article Two that specified the amount to be paid for the land. When Wilkinson wrote Secretary of War Henry Dearborn about the treaty, he tartly observed that Pike was "a much abler Soldier than Negotiator." But Pike thought he had done well, only later beginning to doubt that the peace he had negotiated was no more than a temporary truce.

Nothing more fully reveals Pike's expansive view of American empire than his ill-conceived foray into international diplomacy in the snows of northern Minnesota. During the first months of 1806, Pike and a small party sledded their way north in search of the headwaters of the Mississippi. What they found instead was a country fully in the hands of traders from Canada's North West Company. Established in 1787, the expansionist-minded Nor'westers had pushed west toward the Pacific and south into the Great Lakes. The Minnesota country was dotted with North West Company posts doing a brisk business with many Indians. This British presence was perfectly legal under the conditions of the 1794 Jay Treaty. That treaty allowed traders from both nations to "freely carry on trade and commerce with each other" and the several nations of Indians. But there were widely-recognized problems. Tensions between

British and American traders were compounded by charges that Nor'westers were smuggling trade goods and furs past the American customs house at Michilimackinac, and many in the federal government were persuaded that the Canadian company was a front for British imperial designs. Rumors of flags and medals being given to Indians by British traders only increased the troubles in Minnesota. Wilkinson had taken action against British interests on the Missouri River, but nothing had been done on the upper Mississippi. Pike was about to change that.

Few things more deeply offended Pike than the sight of the flags of other nations on lands claimed by the United States. For him, flags were the premier symbol of national sovereignty. They also had deep personal meanings linked to honor and identity. In early January 1806, Pike and his men visited British trader James Grant at his Cedar Lake post. Pike reported what happened next. "When we came in sight of his House, [I] discovered the Flag of Great Britain flying. I felt indignant, and cannot say what my feelings would have excited me to." Pike complained to Grant, prompting the trader to smoothly reply that the flag was not his but belonged to nearby Indians. "This was not much more agreeable to me," recalled Pike, and he decided to watch Grant and other traders carefully.

What he saw at other North West Company posts convinced Pike that British traders were indeed politicking among the Indians and posed a real threat to American sovereignty. In a certain way, Pike was right. Until the Treaty of Ghent in 1814, the British held on to their Great Lakes military posts in open defiance of agreements made at the end of the American Revolution, and they had not abandoned efforts at making alliances with Indians throughout the Old Northwest. At Leech Lake, Pike and trader Hugh McGillis had a spirited exchange about the presence of British flags. For Pike, those flags were more than a question of law and sovereignty—they were a personal insult to American honor. Sensing that the matter was a sensitive one, McGillis asked Pike if the British flag could be raised "by way of complement to ours, which had nearly arrived." Just as the Jay Treaty had allowed traders from both nations to work in the country, McGillis pragmatically thought two flags might be acceptable. Pike was silent on this, explaining later that "I had not yet explained to him my Ideas."

Those "Ideas" became dramatically clear in a letter Pike addressed to McGillis on February 7, 1806. Pike brusquely informed McGillis that he and other company traders were in American territory and had to obey import laws and customs regulations established by the federal government. While admitting that the Jay Treaty permitted the British to do business in the Minnesota country, Pike insisted that foreign traders had to pay appropriate customs duties, obtain trade licenses, and conform to all American laws. The explorer's winter tour had convinced him that that North West Company trade networks extended "to the center of our newly acquired territory of Louisiana." Pike knew that American traders often complained about unfair competition from their British rivals. In his mind, the North West Company not only challenged American power but cut into a vital part of the national economy. As Pike later explained to Wilkinson, "the Dignity and Honor of our Government requires that those Scoundrels be taught to geather their Skins in quiet . . . added to which those are the very instigators of the War between the Chiefs and Scioux in order that they may monopolize the trade of the Upper Mississippi."

Wilkinson once wrote that Pike "stretched his orders," but what the explorer did next went far beyond them. He brazenly deceived McGillis about the nature of his mission, telling the trader that "I have found, sir, your commerce and establishments, extending beyond our most exaggerated ideas, and in addition to the injury done our revenue, by the evasion of duties, other acts which are more particularly injurious to the *honor* and *dignity* of our government." Acting entirely on his own authority, Pike then issued a comprehensive set of demands. The North West Company was to stop distributing flags and medals to Indians, trade goods had to be registered and duties paid at Michilimackinac, and no company post could fly the British flag. None of this was ever part of Pike's official instructions; instead, the letter represented Pike's deeply felt personal and emotional sense of American empire. Pike had his first taste of imperial politics and diplomacy in northern Minnesota. It would not be his last.

When Wilkinson complained that Pike had "stretched his orders," the general was writing specifically about the explorer's ill-fated attempt to find the headwaters of the Mississippi. But for Wilkinson there was something appealing about an officer willing to go beyond the letter of the law. Perhaps it seemed to show initiative and the willingness to take risks. And in the spring of 1806, when Pike returned to St. Louis, Wilkinson was all about taking risks in a high-stakes game. The nature of his game has never been fully clear. Wilkinson continued to spy for Spain as Agent 13, collecting a handsome pension from his handlers. At the same time, he entertained a personal and financial interest in opening a direct trade towards Santa Fe despite New Spain being closed to American merchants. But most complex and murky was his relationship with ex-Vice President Aaron Burr. The Wilkinson–Burr conspiracy has long been the subject of scholarly debate. This much is plain: Burr and Wilkinson had invested their personal and political fortunes in the West, and over time they would fashion different plans, adopt different strategies, and then tell different stories to different audiences. Whatever their plans—whether invading Mexico to spark a war between the United States and Spain or the establishment of an independent republic in what was once New Spain—the conspirators needed to know more about Spain's southwestern empire.

The schemes hatched by Wilkinson and Burr played on the mutual fears and suspicions shared by Spain and the United States. Wilkinson was especially adept at pitting one nation against the other. While Spain had allied itself with the United States during the revolution, Spanish officials were increasingly convinced that the new republic had designs on Spanish territory. As early as 1783, one Spanish official warned that "a new and independent power has now arisen on our continent. Its people are active, industrious, and aggressive. It would be culpable negligence on our part not to thwart their schemes for conquest." Writing in 1796 from New Orleans, Governor Francisco Carondelet predicted that the Americans would soon invade Spanish territory. On the eve of the Louisiana Purchase, frontier army officer José Vidal described the Americans as "ambitious, restless, lawless, conniving, changeable, and turbulent." And news about the Lewis and Clark expedition supplied by Wilkinson as well as the successful interception of the Freeman–Custis expedition on the Red River only served to give substance to Spanish fears. If Spanish officials worried about an American invasion by either civilian adventurers or the American army, Jefferson and his cabinet were equally unsettled when they looked south. The Louisiana Purchase borders between the United States and Spanish territory were open to question and definition. Spain and the United States had vastly different views on the territorial reach of the purchase itself, and there were many unruly characters like Philip Nolan to trouble the contested border between Louisiana and Spanish Texas. No one was more skilled at increasing those tensions than James Wilkinson. In a series of letters written during 1805, Wilkinson filled Secretary of War Henry Dearborn with stories of Spanish treachery and the possibility of imminent attack. Early in the year Dearborn ordered a secret reconnaissance into Texas, thus providing at least some official authority for what would become Pike's second borderland exploration. In one especially explosive letter written in the fall of 1805, Wilkinson suggested measures to be taken "should it be necessary to take possession of New Mexico." Dearborn promptly responded, agreeing that such military operations were entirely possible.

It was in that atmosphere of intrigue, suspicion, and shadowy conspiracy that Wilkinson prepared for Pike's southwestern expedition. Wilkinson's instructions for Pike, dated June 24, 1806, gave the explorer three missions. His first objective was to return fifty-one Osage captives to their homes. Wilkinson always maintained that this was Pike's "primary object," but neither the general nor the lieutenant ever believed that tale. The second mission was more clearly imperial—a peace treaty between the Osage and Kansas Indians. But it was Pike's third goal that proved most difficult and ultimately most controversial. Wilkinson ordered the explorer to find and negotiate with the Comanches, a search that would surely take Pike into Spanish territory. Pike was told to "move with great circumspection," a polite way to say that he was on a spying mission. But the nature of that spying and who would benefit from it remain unexplained. Wilkinson probably knew that

Pike would be captured, although there is no evidence that he betrayed Pike as he had Lewis and Clark by informing Spanish officials of their presence in the West. How would the Spanish react to the presence of an American army officer and his party found on Spanish territory? Would that frontier incident spark a war between the two nations? What is clear is that Pike uncritically accepted his role as a spy. For him this was one more way to serve the greater cause of American empire. He had faced the British in Minnesota; now he was prepared to confront the Spanish on the southwestern frontier.

Imperial expansion in North America always involved diplomatic relations with native nations. Empire builders sought Indians as allies and trading partners—and in the case of the Anglo-Americans—as sources for land. Pike was not an especially skilled or experienced diplomat but he did have a sure grasp of American imperial aspirations and how native people fit in the republic's scheme of things. Peace, trade, and a whole-hearted acceptance of the Great Father in Washington were the essentials that Pike and his superiors demanded from the nation's "red children."

At the end of September 1806 the second Pike expedition was camped on a rise overlooking the Kitkehahki, or Republican, Pawnee village in what is now Webster County, Nebraska. On September 27, Pike's interpreter Antoine F. Baronet Vasquez (known in Zebulon Pike's 1810 book, *An Account of Expeditions to the Sources of the Mississippi* as Barony) came to camp with Pawnee chief White Wolf (known in Pike's *Account* as Characterish) and three other chiefs. Always alert to signs of rival empires, Pike could not miss seeing the large Spanish medal White Wolf was wearing around his neck; and if he didn't see it at that moment, Pike soon learned that the chief had a commission from Spanish officials dated in mid-June 1806. If the British were moving into the very center of Louisiana, then these objects were sure signs that Spain was also trespassing on the Purchase and luring Indians away from their new Great Father. Eager to impress the Pawnees, Pike offered food and gifts. The gifts were more than presents; they were symbols of imperial authority. Like other diplomats and explorers, Pike thought when Indians accepted such gifts they were also acknowledging American authority and sovereignty. Native leaders undoubtedly saw the gifts in another light. Pike gave White Wolf a gun, a gorget, and "other articles." The otherwise-unidentified "second chief" got a small American medal, while the remaining Pawnees received gorgets. Writing several days later to Wilkinson, Pike hoped that the gifts "would have a good effect, both as to attaching them to our government, and in our immediate intercourse."

While Pike was eager to get on with his Pawnee diplomacy, there was the matter of arranging peace between the Osage and Kansas Indians. Pike pursued that matter on September 28. No record survives of that negotiation, but Pike was convinced that the Indians had "smoked the pipe of peace." Like so many others, Pike easily confused peace with truce. On the Great Plains there was no permanent peace but only a long series of truces easily broken. Native leaders understood that; Pike did not.

The next day, September 29, was fully taken up with the great Pawnee council. Pike estimated that some four hundred warriors were present in the large village. As the Americans entered, something immediately caught Pike's eye. It was a Spanish flag hanging in the door of the council lodge. Pike had a long history with flags and he was about to add another chapter. No sooner had the gathering begun than Pike demanded the Spanish flag be hauled down, handed over to him, and an American flag put in its place. Pike admitted later that this was "carrying the pride of nations a little too far." The Pawnees had been impressed by the recent presence of a large Spanish force commanded by Lieutenant Facundo Melgares. Tipped off by Wilkinson, the Melgares expedition was in the field hoping to intercept Lewis and Clark just as Francisco Viana had recently halted the Freeman–Custis party. While Melgares did not visit the Republican Pawnees, a junior officer made known the Spanish presence and the desire to stop all American "interlopers." After replying to Pike's other requests, there was stony silence about handing over the Spanish flag. Pike decided to press the issue just as he had with the Nor'westers. He told the Indians that "it was impossible for the nation to have two fathers; that they must either be the children of the Spaniards or acknowledge their American father."

Two flags now carried the weight of rival empires. Like it or not, the Pawnees were caught between the Spanish and the

Americans. After a long and painful silence, a Pawnee elder got up and quietly took down the Spanish ensign. Pike then triumphantly raised the American standard over the village. The American officer may have thought he had won the day, but the Pawnees were both angry and fearful. As Pike later recalled, "every face in the council was clouded with sorrow, as if some great national Calamity was about to befall them." At that moment Pike must have known he had overreached. Realizing that he had embarrassed the Indians and put them at risk of Spanish reprisals, Pike offered a quick compromise. He returned the Spanish flag but insisted that it not be flown so long as the American expedition was present.

Pike was right about one thing. In the contest for empire in the West, flags were more than mere fabric. They represented imperial ambition and national honor. Pike once described flags as "the standard of an European power." For him, flags and medals were markers, emblems of empire. His Pawnee adventure suggests just how far Pike was willing to place those markers as well as the limits of American influence. The Pawnees got their compromise; in later years native people would not be so successful.

The rest of Pike's journey into the Southwest is an often-told story. It is a tale of geographic confusion, courage in the face of adversity, and eventual arrest at the hands of the Spanish. Pike once wrote to Wilkinson that a journey to Santa Fe under Spanish guard "would gratify our most sanguine expectations." Whatever those expectations, Pike and his men got that wish.

Historians and other scholars have paid much attention to the origins of Pike's second expedition and his various geographic bewilderments. But in the larger story of empire in the West those are sideshows. Perhaps Pike would have us look closer at the ideas and strategies embedded in his "Observations on New Spain." Written in 1808 and printed as an appendix to his *Account*, the "Observations" is a summary of what he learned about Spain's southwestern empire. More important, it presented Pike's geopolitical thinking about relations between Spain and the United States as well as the means to effect what his friend Bartholemew Fernandez called "a change of affairs." That meant political revolution and the extension of American power into what had been Spanish territory. Beyond anything else Pike ever wrote, "Observations on New Spain" reveals his vision of empire. To understand that document is to grasp something about the essential Pike.

Most of "Observations on New Spain" is a routine recounting of what Pike knew or thought he knew about large parts of Spanish North America. There are the predictable comments about terrain, climate, local customs, and military forces, and there are occasional flashes of unintended humor as when Pike compared Spanish women to "the ladies of Turkey." But near the end of the essay, Pike suddenly shifted focus and began a detailed geopolitical discussion of southwestern North America.

That analysis began with Pike's views on the consequences of Spanish rule. Betraying all the preconceptions and prejudices of a culture that was deeply anti-Spanish and profoundly anti-Catholic, Pike portrayed New Spain's government as filled with petty tyrants and greedy aristocrats who oppressed a generous, sober, and hospitable people. New Spain, so Pike believed, labored under the burdens of "restrictions, monopolies, prohibitions, seclusions, and supersitition." Pressing this theme, Pike argued that Spain kept its American possessions "so carefully secluded" from "all light" that her citizens "have vegetated like the acorn in the forest."

But Pike believed that change was in the air. Echoing what Bartholemew Fernandez told him, Pike insisted that opening the doors to free trade would make the country "rich and powerful." Yet it would take more than the power of the marketplace to produce political change. A Spanish official once wrote that so long as the United States and New Spain were neighbors they would be enemies. Pike turned that argument on its head. "The approximation of the United States, with the gigantic strides of French ambition, have begun to rouse their dormant qualities, and to call into action the powers of their minds, on the subject of their political situation." Believing that the people of New Spain would not turn to the British for help, Pike was convinced that only the United States could extend the empire of liberty to "North Mexico." Here Pike pulled no punches. "*They therefore have turned their eyes towards the United States*, as brethren of the same soil, in their vicinity, and who has within her powers ample resources of arms, ammunition, and even men to assist in securing their independence." For Pike the choice was clear. Either the United States would support a revolution or Spanish rule might continue. And if Napoleon's brother Joseph became King of Spain, a revived French empire would suddenly become the republic's dangerous southern neighbor.

Pike never pretended that American empire building in Spanish America would be done for the ideal of liberty alone. The economic rewards were sure to be substantial and enduring. American merchants from St. Louis would have ready partners in men like Bartholemew Fernandez and American ships would fill Mexican ports. "Even on the coast of the Pacific," Pike was sure, "no European nation could vie with us." Summing up all the prosperity empire seemed to promise, Pike confidently predicted "we would become their factors, agents, guardians, and, in short, tutelary genius." But Pike was not prepared to see Spanish-speaking Catholics as American citizens. A liberated New Spain would become a separate client state, a permanent but junior partner in "the rising American empire."

But none of this could happen without military intervention, and Pike openly promoted his plan for invading Spanish territory and prompting a revolution. It would take twenty thousand American troops "under good officers" fighting in concert with a force of "Mexican independents" to "create and effect the revolution." The entire cost of the adventure would be borne by the new government in Mexico City. Convinced that such an invasion would have widespread popular support, Pike insisted that the army act as "friends and protectors, not as plunderers." This was conquest without guilt, empire without shame.

Generations of preachers, politicians, and pamphleteers had offered their distinctive visions of empire that sounded almost millennial in passion and promise. The conquerors were really liberators, the conquered were grateful victims, and all would enjoy the benefits of heaven on earth, a glorious empire of liberty. Pike concluded his "Observations" with a prophetic vision that was at once remarkable yet representative of things to come.

> Should an Army of Americans ever march into the country, and be guided by these maxims, they will have only to march from province to province in triumph,

and be hailed by the united voices of grateful millions as their deliverers and saviors, whilst our national character would resound to the most distant nations of the earth.

Zebulon Montgomery Pike has suffered a strange and undeserved fate. Dismissed as either a young officer with little talent and consumed by ambition or the unwitting accomplice of an unscrupulous commander, Pike now seems a mere shadow. He appears an uncomplicated man of action with neither ideas nor intellect. In American memory Pike is recalled for a piece of the western landscape he neither climbed nor named. We trace his journeys but not the grand theories and bitter conflicts that shaped them. On the simplest level, Pike stands at the beginning of a long American fascination with the Southwest, one that finally exploded in the Mexican-American War and continues into our own time. The publication of his *Account* in 1810 revived interest in the Santa Fe trade and inspired an entire generation of soldier-explorers, including the redoubtable William H. Emory.

But it is in the elusive world of ideas that we can understand something deeper about Pike. Thomas Jefferson's empire of liberty faced four powerful opponents: France, Spain, Great Britain, and native nations. Unlike Lewis and Clark, Pike dealt directly with three of the four. What he said, what he wrote, and what he did drew on and was inspired by a venerable tradition of empire building, a tradition that Pike fully accepted and enthusiastically advanced. In Pike as geopolitical thinker, we can see all the twists and turns, fantasies and fabrications that made the West part of the United States. Pike really meant it when he talked about "the national objects" that guided his journeys. More than any other explorer of the age, Pike stands as the perfect emblem in the imperial war for the West.

James P. Ronda holds the H. G. Barnard Chair in Western American History at the University of Tulsa and is the past president of the Western History Association. He is a specialist in the history of the exploration of the American West and has authored many scholarly works including, *Finding the West: Explorations with Lewis and Clark* (2001); *Lewis and Clark Among the Indians* (2002); and *Beyond Lewis and Clark: The Army Explores the West* (2003). Ronda served as a key consultant for the Colorado Springs Pioneers Museum in the development of the exhibit *Pike's World: Exploration and Empire in the Greater Southwest*. This essay was a scholarly result of the Museum's efforts.

Notes

Any reassessment of Zebulon Montgomery Pike must begin with the definitive edition of his letters and journals prepared by Donald Jackson. Published by the University of Oklahoma Press in 1966, *The Journals of Zebulon Montgomery Pike, with Letters and Related Documents* is the cornerstone for all Pike research. Jackson's own thoughts on Pike can be found in his *Thomas Jefferson and the Stony Mountains: Exploring the West from Monticello* (Urbana: University of Illinois Press, 1981) and reprinted by the University of Oklahoma Press under the title *Thomas Jefferson and the Rocky Mountains*.

While the clash of empires has long been a staple in American historical writing, no scholar has put explorers at the center of that struggle as deftly as William H. Goetzmann. His superb *Exploration and Empire: The Explorer and the Artist in the Winning of the American West* (New York: Alfred A. Knopf, 1966) places Pike in broad context.

Two recent essays are useful in defining empire as central to the history of the West. They are: Jeremy Adelman and Stephen Aron, "From Borderlands to Borders: Empires and Nation-States, and the Peoples in Between in North America," *American Historical Review* 104 (June 1999), 814–841 and Stephen Aron, "Lessons in Conquest: Towards a Greater Western History," *Pacific Historical Review* 63 (May 1994), 125–147.

Peter S. Onuf's *Jefferson's Empire: The Language of American Nationhood* (Charlottesville: University of Virginia Press, 2000) makes a singular contribution to understanding Pike's imperial rhetoric, and no scholar has done more to bring the disciplines of history and geography to bear on American empires in conflict than D. W. Meinig. His *The Shaping of America: vol. 2: Continental America, 1800–1867* (New Haven: Yale University Press, 1993) is both ambitious and illuminating.

Pike played out his role as an agent of empire in two contested borderlands. The following works help locate Pike in what is now Minnesota: Gordon C. Davidson, *The North West Company* (Berkeley: University of California Press, 1918), Reginald C. Stuart, *U.S. Expansion and British North America, 1775–1871* (Charlotte: University of North Carolina Press, 1988), W. Stewart Wallace, ed., *Documents Relating to the North West Company* (Toronto: Champlain Society, 1934), and "The Diary of Thomas Connor [John Sayer]," in Charles M. Gates, ed., *Five Fur Traders of the Northwest* (St. Paul: Minnesota Historical Society, 1965). But it is the Spanish borderlands of the Southwest that are most associated with Pike as imperial explorer. No single book is more important for understanding that uncertain country than David J. Weber, *The Spanish Frontier in North America* (New Haven: Yale University Press, 1992).

A. P. Nasatir, ed., *Before Lewis and Clark: Documents Illustrating the History of the Missouri, 1785–1804*, 2 vols. (St. Louis: St. Louis Historical Documents Foundation, 1952) and Dan Flores, ed., *Jefferson and Southwestern Exploration: The Freeman and Custis Accounts of the Red River Expedition of 1806* (Norman: University of Oklahoma Press, 1984) are both valuable for tracing Spanish responses to what were perceived as incursions into their territory.

For all the important work done on Pike's era, there remain notable gaps. Eugene Hollon's *The Lost Pathfinder: Zebulon Montgomery Pike* (Norman: University of Oklahoma Press, 1949) is now largely out of date. Pike plainly deserves a modern biography firmly rooted in the documentary record as discovered by Donald Jackson. James Wilkinson, Pike's devious commander, also needs a modern biography, although the task there will be much more difficult. Wilkinson's papers are at the Chicago Historical Society, but as Donald Jackson once observed, the general "poisoned the well" by altering and rewriting many important documents. While the Wilkinson–Burr Conspiracy may never be fully sorted out, American ambitions in the Southwest remain a largely unexplored topic. One model for such an investigation might be John Miller Morris, *El Llano Estacado: Exploration and Imagination on the High Plains of Texas and New Mexico, 1536–1860* (Austin: Texas State Historical Association, 1997).

Pike's Southwestern Expedition: Outfitted or Illfated?

Don Headlee

On Tuesday, July 15, 1806, Zebulon Montgomery Pike, with a company made up of two lieutenants (including himself), one sergeant, two corporals, sixteen privates, one surgeon (civilian), one interpreter (civilian) and fifty-nine Indian men, women and children left from the landing at Cantonment Belle Fontaine, St. Louis, Missouri. Traveling on the muddy waters of the Missouri River they occupied two keelboats. All but two of the soldiers had accompanied Pike on his expedition on the Upper Mississippi in 1805. They were seasoned soldiers who had dutifully served Pike and had been selected by him and ordered to go on this second expedition. They had not volunteered, and as soldiers of the United States Army they had no other alternative but to obey a command or face a court-martial.

Pike's military career started early in his life. His father had started his own military career as a private volunteer during the Revolutionary War. During the elder Pike's command at Fort Massac, Illinois, young Zebulon Montgomery Pike was attached to his father's company, but he had served before this time carrying supplies to the military post of the Northwest. He spent several years distributing supplies to the forts up and down the Ohio and Mississippi Rivers. During 1796, while Pike was transporting supplies, James Wilkinson became the commanding general of the army. Wilkinson, who was acquainted with Pike and was well aware of his abilities as a soldier, had him commissioned as a second lieutenant in March 1799. Eight months later Pike was promoted to the rank of first lieutenant. Pike was not only looked upon in favor by Wilkinson, but it seemed obvious that he had plans for him.

The first task that Wilkinson assigned to Pike was to explore the upper Mississippi River and to find its source. As with other expeditions of this time period such as the Meriwether Lewis and William Clark expedition to the west, the need to ascertain the boundaries of the newly purchased land referred to as the Louisiana Purchase was paramount. With twenty men, a seventy-foot keelboat, equipment and goods costing approximately $2,000, Pike undertook this journey. It is not the purpose of this paper to discuss the importance of this journey and its accomplishments, but only to bring to attention that Zebulon Pike had previous experience in organizing an expedition before leaving on his second assignment set before him by General Wilkinson in July of 1806.

One major difference between the Lewis and Clark expedition and the Zebulon Pike expedition was the planning that took place before getting under way. We are aware of the months of activity and preparation that preceded the departure of the Lewis and Clark expedition from Camp Wood on the east bank of the Mississippi River, upstream from St. Louis (also called Camp Dubois). Pike's mission was through orders given to him by his commanding officer, General Wilkinson, not from President Thomas Jefferson. It is not the intent of this paper to determine the much-debated, and somewhat dubious, purposes of the Pike expedition into the southern part of the recently acquired Louisiana Territory. The intent here is to look at the preparation, or lack thereof, for Pike's expedition. To my knowledge, there are no records of the exact items and the number of these items that were taken on this journey. What has been used is an inventory made from Pike's journal and correspondence that relates to the expedition.

Pike received his orders to proceed without delay from Wilkinson in a letter dated June 24, 1806. His objectives were: (1) to deliver the Osage captives and a deputation of Pawnee, Otoe and Osage returning from Washington, D.C., to their homeland; (2) to try and accomplish a permanent peace between the Kansas and Osage Nations; (3) to create a "good understanding" with the Comanche, and if that endeavor was achieved, to make a peace between all Indian nations. Wilkinson also mentions that this would probably lead them into the vicinity of the headwaters of the Arkansas and Red Rivers approximate to the settlements of New Mexico. He cautioned Pike to take care and not alarm or offend the Spanish due to the delicate negotiations being made between Spain and the United States. He was instructed to take note of the geographical and natural history of the area and the population, and to collect and preserve specimens of everything curious in the mineral and botanical world. He was also instructed to use his compass and watch to note in a field book the course and distance of the day's march.

It was in this same letter that Wilkinson informed Pike he was to send his son, Lieutenant James Wilkinson, back down the Arkansas River properly equipped to take courses and distances. The party was to descend the Arkansas until they reached Fort Adams, a post on the Mississippi. Later it will be pointed out that Lieutenant Wilkinson brought to his father's attention the poorly equipped conditions under which he was to operate. Pike was told to descend the Red River, accompanied by a party of "respectable" Comanche, to the post at Natchitoches and wait for further orders. In the same letter, Wilkinson told Pike that he was to receive $600 worth of goods to take on his journey. He was admonished to render a strict accounting, vouched by documents attested to by one of his party. This $600 is a seemingly small amount compared to the $2,000 given Pike for his journey up the Mississippi in 1805.

From the examination of the goods and equipment mentioned in the journal and correspondence that related to Pike's expedition, the following categories will be used: clothing, scientific instruments, weapons, trade goods, and other equipment. Although precise information about many of the items to be mentioned is not available, we can still get a good perspective of them.

First, an examination of the clothing worn by members of the Pike expedition is of interest. It is easy to come quickly to the conclusion that the members in general of the party were ill-prepared to meet the weather conditions they were going to encounter. On December 3, 1805, Pike states,

> The hardships of the last voyage [1805] had now began, and had the climate only been as severe as the climate then was, some of the men must have perished, for they had no winter clothing, I wore myself cotton overalls, for I had not calculated on being out in that inclement season of the year.

The climate and general topography of this country was not entirely unknown. It had been traversed by explorers and traders long before Pike began his journey. As early as 1541, the Spanish explorer Coronado passed through this area seeking Quivira, the legendary city of gold. With the information that was available about the area, why did Pike leave so poorly clothed? As early as November 27 Pike mentions that the soldiers had light overalls on, no stockings, and in every way ill-provided to endure the inclemency of the region. On December 25 he states,

> . . . in the most inclement season not one person clothed for the winter, many without blankets, (having been obliged to cut them up for socks, &c.) and now laying down at night on the snow or wet ground; one side burning whilst the other pierced with cold wind: this was in part the situation of the party whilst some were endeavoring to make a miserable substitute of raw buffalo hide for shoes &c.

As early as November 8, Pike mentions that the party has halted to jerk meat and mend their moccasins. This indicates that their army footwear was now worn out and they needed to make part of their own clothing. Shoes must have still been in supply on October 20 because Pike mentions that the prize for the winner of a shooting match was a tent and a pair of shoes. It should be pointed out that at this shooting match their only remaining dog, standing at the foot of the tree in the grass, was struck by a ball and killed. Pike had reported on July 31 the loss of his dog, the misfortune being that this dog, given to him by Harry Fisher at Prairie des Chiens, was the only one to bring anything out of the water. At another shooting match on August 11, a prize of a jacket and a twist of tobacco was won by Pike. Pike was reputed to be an excellent marksman. He presented his prizes to the young fellow who waited on him, probably Private Thomas Dougherty. The next day Pike mentions the loss of some of his clothing, which was blown from the top of the cabin of the boat into the Osage and immediately sank.

In Pike's letter to General Wilkinson dated July 22, 1806, which would be early in the journey, he mentions that he gave each of the "young Savages" a "Soldiers Coate." Exactly what issue these coatees might have been is conjecture. Probably Pike's men were equipped with the new 1804 coatee. We know the giving of out-of-date military uniforms was often practiced as part of the gift-giving process. How many and what type of jacket Pike had in his possession is not known, but if they had been abundant, they would have been welcome in the days to come.

In the trip to Santa Fe, New Mexico, after their capture by the Spanish troops, he states that first consideration was ammunition, second was tools, and then came their clothing, which consisted of "leather, leggings, boots and mockinsons." He tells us that he left his uniform, clothing, trunks, etc., as did all the men except what they had on their backs. Importance was given to footwear that would protect their feet and legs from the cold. He describes himself and accompanying companions when arriving in Santa Fe, "I was dressed in a pair of blue trowsers, mockinsons, blanket coat and cap made of scarlet cloth, lined with fox skins and my poor fellows in leggings, breech cloths and leather coats and not a hat in the whole party." The local populace inquired as to their living standards, if they lived in houses or in camps like the Indians, even if they wore hats in their county. The party made a very uncouth impression on the inhabitants of Santa Fe.

Lieutenant Wilkinson's plight should not be forgotten. As he leaves to descend the Arkansas, in his letter to his father he writes, "I am now about undertaking a voyage more illy equipped than any other Officer, who ever was on Command, in point of Stores, Ammunition, Boats &n Men." He further states, "My men have no winter cloathing, and two of them no Blankets." In his April 6, 1807, report he refers to his men as being almost naked and that the tatters which covered them as comfortless. There can be little doubt as to the poorly equipped troops of the Pike expedition. But the reasons for such poor preparations by an experienced military person like Pike leaves a lot to speculation.

This was a military expedition assigned the task of gathering important data and information about an area of the newly acquired Louisiana Purchase, about which little or no information existed. General Wilkinson, in his letter to Secretary of War Henry Dearborn dated August 2, 1806, tells us that he had furnished Pike with $280 worth of instruments to enable him to take latitude of places. In Wilkinson's letter to Pike dated June 24, 1806, he states the following:

The Instruments which I have furnished you; will enable you to ascertain the variation of the magnetic needle and the Lattitude with exactitude, and at every remarkable point I wish you to employ your Telescope in observing Eclipses of Jupiters Satillites, having previously regulated and adjusted your Watch by your Sextant, taking care to note with great nicetty the periods of immersion & emersion of the eclipsed Satellite.

He mentions that longitude could be determined with the appropriate tables upon Pike's return. Wilkinson remarks on the importance of this knowledge in relation to the direction, extent and navigation of the Arkansas and Red Rivers. He also mentions that Lieutenant Wilkinson and Sergeant Joseph Ballinger were to be properly instructed and equipped to take courses and distances and remark on the soil and timber, etc., on their trip down the Arkansas. It has already been pointed out how poorly equipped Lieutenant Wilkinson was on his return trip.

Pike often makes reference to the adjustments made to his instruments. On August 23 he mentions he adjusted his instruments to take "equal altitudes and a meridional altitude of the sun" but missed the immersions of Jupiter's satellites due to clouds. Again, on August 24 he states that he spent nearly half a day adjusting the line of collimation in the telescopic sights of his theodolite. Whether due to Pike's adjustments or his lack of training in using these instruments, his range of error was usually thirty-five to forty-five miles on his latitudinal readings. At the home of a priest in San Juan on his journey from Chihuahua, the priest expressed his desire to see Pike's astronomical instruments. He only had with him his sextant and a large glass which magnified considerably. The rest of his instruments were with Sergeant William E. Meek and his party. The priest showed much surprise at the effect of the sextant and Pike remarked as to the lack of knowledge held by a person so versed in other sciences. He was informed by the priest that the Spanish government took great care in preventing the pursuit of any branch of science.

In Pike's letter to Sergeant Meek in Chihuahua dated April 26, 1807, he gives him permission to sell the telescope and theodolite along with all the tools in his possession. The sergeant was to keep an exact accounting of the money and to be responsible for it. He further instructed the sergeant to consult Dr. John H. Robinson or Juan Pedro Walker if the instruments were damaged so a lower price could be established. In the inventory of arms, equipment and other things that remained in the barracks belonging to the Americans and inventoried by Spanish Lieutenant Don Facundo Melgares, there was an achromatic telescope with a broken lens and the theodolite lacking several lenses and a with broken leg which did not sell.

One of the most interesting instruments carried by Pike was his Reaumur thermometer. The Reaumur thermometer was invented by Rene Antonie Ferchault de Reaumur and introduced in 1731. It saw widespread use in Europe, particularly in France and Germany. The Reaumur thermometer used zero degrees as the freezing point and 80 degrees as the boiling point. It was this thermometer that Pike used to take his temperature readings. We know that he carried a Reaumur on his journey up the Mississippi; he gives us a reading of 27 degrees below zero (29 degrees below zero Fahrenheit) on January 8, 1805, while in the present state of Minnesota. He gives a reading of 25 degrees Reaumur (88 degrees Fahrenheit) on August 11, 1806, when he noted that the party found the heat to be very oppressive, but this was August in Missouri. Perhaps the most historically significant reading came on November 27, 1806, when he took a reading of 9 degrees above zero Reaumur (52 degrees Fahrenheit) at the foot of the mountain he was climbing, then he reported a reading of 4 degrees below zero Reaumur (22 degrees Fahrenheit) at the top of the mountain. Here he states that the Grand Peak was still fifteen or sixteen miles from their location. In his journal we find the often-quoted statement, " . . . and would have taken a whole day's march to have arrived at its base, when I believe no human being could have ascended its pinical." In the Sangre de Cristo Mountains on January 17 he speaks of nine men having frozen feet. He gives us a reading of 18.5 degrees below zero Reaumur (10 degrees below zero Fahrenheit). As he travels north through Mexico on his journey to Natchitoches, he gives a reading of 30 degrees Reaumur (99.5 degrees Fahrenheit) in the vicinity of Santa Rosa, a town in the Coahuila Province. He speaks of the dust and drought which obliged them to march at night and to encamp without water. The thermometric observations made by Pike offer us another aspect of this historical journey.

A few other instruments always a part of any exploration party that were often mentioned in Pike's writings are the compass and spyglass. On January 23 he states, "... when I found it impossible to keep any course without the compass, continually in my hand, and then not being able to see more than 10 yards." On May 26, 1807, Pike writes in his journal, "and from a hill took a small survey, with my pencil and a pocket compass which I always carried with me." On June 2 he records, "In the day time were endeavoring to regulate our watches by my compass, and in an instant that my back was turned some person stole it; I could by no means recover it, and I had a strong suspicion that the theft was approved, as the instrument had occasioned great dissatisfaction." Of course the most famous use of his spyglass was on November 15 when he states, "At two o'clock in the afternoon I thought I could distinguish a mountain to our right, which appeared like a small blue cloud; viewed it with my spy glass, and was still more confirmed in my conjecture." This sighting was to lead him in quest of this "blue mountain" later to bear his name.

The importance of firearms on an expedition during this time period goes without debate. A careful search of the Pike journal about his trip through the Southwest will reveal terms like: gun, rifle, two-barreled shotgun and pistol. We are not given any manufacturer's names or caliber of the weapons mentioned, and the term "gun" is used in most general references. We do know that the standard infantry weapon at this time was the .69 caliber Springfield musket. This weapon was used by the military for many years to come. This is a smooth-bore flintlock that has a range for fairly accurate marksmanship up to fifty yards. We can assume with some degree of certainty that this was probably the weapon carried by the soldiers on Pike's expedition. It was a military expedition and with little doubt it was equipped with military weapons.

Of course, the most important use of their weapons was in procuring meat. Numerous journal entries end with an accounting of the game killed on that day. On September 14 Pike states, "I prevented the men shooting at the game, not merely because of the scarcity of ammunition, but, as I conceived, the laws of morality forbid it also." When Pike and Lieutenant Wilkinson divide the party and Wilkinson returns down the Arkansas to the post on the Mississippi, Wilkinson writes a letter to Pike dated October 26 in which he vents some of his frustrations, particularly regarding the equipment that he was allotted. On the back of the letter Pike makes remarks relating to the distribution of powder and lead and ball. He had given Wilkinson's party of five men nineteen pounds of powder and thirty-nine pounds of lead and ball along with four dozen cartridges. Pike kept for his party of sixteen thirty-five pounds of powder, forty pounds of lead and ten dozen cartridges. Assuming that most of Pike's men were equipped with the aforementioned .69 caliber musket, forty pounds of lead would produce approximately six hundred balls. This, with the ten dozen cartridges, would give around forty-five rounds to each of the sixteen men in the party. With the prospects of facing a long and unknown journey into an area about to undergo its coldest season, and with the necessity of hunting food and the need for possible defense against an enemy, the whole scene takes on a forbidding aura.

An interesting account on October 24 relates to the shooting of prairie dogs. Pike states, "We killed great numbers of them with our rifles and found them excellent meat, after they were exposed a night or two to the frost, by which means the rankness acquired by their subterraneous dwelling is corrected." It should be noted here that Pike's entry on the prairie dog was the best description of these creatures of that exploratory period.

It was not uncommon to have personal weapons on an army expedition. We know that the men with Lewis and Clark carried a variety of personal firearms, so we can assume that the same was true with the Pike expedition. The upkeep on their weapons was a problem faced by all expeditions. On January 5 Pike mentions that on examination of his gun he "discovered her bent" and shortly thereafter broke it off at the breech due to a fall on the side of a hill. He went back to camp and returned to hunt with a double-barreled gun. These double-barreled weapons are mentioned several times in Pike's journal. On October 2 he tells General Wilkinson in his letter that he had presented the Osage chief a "doubled barrel'd gun, gorget and other articles." In his letter of April 26, 1807, to Sergeant William Meek, Pike tells him to present Lieutenant Don

Facundo Melgares the better of the two-barreled shotguns and to exchange the other for a Spanish gun or one of the carbines which the American prisoners were able to procure, and to pay the difference in value. Earlier, on April 8, 1807, he had been shown the double-barreled gun of his host, the treasurer, Francisco Javier Trujillo. This weapon had been presented to him by William C. C. Claiborne, the governor of the Territory of Orleans.

Perhaps the most noted use of the guns was that Pike had his men conceal his writings in the barrels of their weapons. He writes on May 1, 1806,

> In the night I arose and after making my men charge all their pieces well, I took small books and rolled them in small rolls, and tore a fine shirt to pieces, and wrapt it round the paper and put them down the barrel of the guns, until we just had rooms for the tompions, which were then carefully put in.

Pike mentions his pistols several times in his journal. On November 22, 1806, when they encountered the war party of Grand Pawnee returning from an unsuccessful search for Comanche, he found himself surrounded by Pawnee endeavoring to steal his pistols. By December 14, in an inventory of their weapons given by Pike, he states, "Bursted one of our rifles, which was a great loss, as it made three guns which had bursted, and the five which had been broken on the march, one of my men was now armed with my sword and pistols." Among the items listed in Lieutenant Melgares' inventory of arms, equipment and other things remaining in the barracks and belonging to the Americans were: two broken carbines, several muskets (four of the muskets with bayonets), one musket with two barrels and an assortment of accouterments used with firearms.

The last group of items to be discussed and found mentioned in the journal and letters will include trade goods, an assortment of tools and other items needed for survival. Like the expedition of Lewis and Clark before them, Pike's expedition party left with a supply of trade goods to be used as gifts for the Indians they would meet on the journey. In his report to his father dated April 6, 1807, Lieutenant James Wilkinson mentions an intermediate-sized medal given to the Pawnee chief, Iskatoppe. The "peace medal" was a common gift to be given to the chiefs and the custom was to continue for many years to come. Another practice that was common for expeditions at the time was the presentation of an American flag to the Indians. Pike mentions a flag given on August 30 to the chief of the Little Village of the Osage along with other donations. On September 29 at the council with the Pawnees, Pike found a Spanish flag unfurled at the chief's door. He admonished them for flying the Spanish flag and it was replaced with the American flag. After perceiving the sorrowful countenance of the Pawnee, Pike returned the Spanish flag with the injunction that it was not to be hoisted during their stay. This was received with a shout of applause by the Pawnee.

Another interesting item given as a gift to the chiefs was the gorget. This item was a carryover of an antiquated piece of military equipment originally used to protect the throat. Pike presented gifts at the meeting with four principal chiefs of the Osage. He mentions giving "a doubled barrel'd gun, gorget and other articles (this man wore the grand Spanish medal) and the second the small medal you furnished me, with other articles; and each of the other a gorget in their turn."

All expeditions of the period took a supply of whiskey with them. It was the military custom of the time to ration a gill (one quarter pint) of whiskey to the men each evening. However, it was also a practice to give whiskey to the Indians as a part of gift giving. On July 29 Pike mentions that one or two gills of whiskey were given to three young Osage, which intoxicated them all. Other standard goods given as gifts were: carrots of tobacco, knives, fire steels and flints. All these items are mentioned in the November 22 entry relating to the meeting with the returning war party of Grand Pawnee. The demand for ammunition, corn, blankets and kettles by the Pawnee was refused. After the Pawnee showed contempt for the gifts given them—some throwing them away—Pike and his men began loading their horses. The Pawnee began taking items from the soldiers and Pike ordered his men to take their arms and separate themselves from the "savages," and he declared to them he would kill the first person who touched the baggage. They found that the Pawnee had managed to steal one sword, a tomahawk, a broad axe, five canteens and sundry other small articles.

In his additional instructions to Pike dated July 12, 1806, General Wilkinson states, "Dr. Robinson will accompany you as a volunteer. He will be furnished with medicines, and for the accommodations which you give him, he is bound to attend your sick." However, in Pike's journal we find no evidence of Dr. Robinson giving any medical attention to Pike's men. All references to Robinson by Pike mostly relate to him as a constant companion, whether hunting or exploring. In contrast, many references are made in the Lewis and Clark journals to the medicine practiced by both. We have an inventory of the medical supplies taken by Lewis and Clark, but only the vague mention of supplies for the Pike expedition. We can only assume that Dr. Robinson attended the medical needs of Pike's men.

In closing, the statement made by Pike in his letter to General Wilkinson on October 2, 1806, should give us an insight into the many reasons for this expedition. Pike writes, "Any number of men (who may reasonably be calculated on) would find no difficulty in marching the route we came with baggage wagons, field artillery and all the usual appendages of a small army; and if all the route to Santa Fe should be of the same description in case of war, I would pledge my life (and what is infinitely dearer, my honor) for a successful march of a reasonable body of troops, into the province of New Mexico." Forty years later this exact action took place as Colonel Stephen Watts Kearny and the Army of the West crossed the plains of Kansas and Colorado and entered into New Mexico for a bloodless conquest. They certainly were better equipped than those who went before them.

Don Headlee, a Corps of Engineers employee and park ranger at the John Martin Reservoir, has been involved with interpretive history for many years, mainly at Bent's Old Fort. Throughout the Lewis and Clark bicentennial commemoration he spoke to more than three thousand five hundred students and adults about that exploration and now presents programs about the Pike expedition.

Zebulon Pike in Colorado:
His Struggle to Survive

Bruce C. Paton

Zebulon Montgomery Pike's worst troubles began shortly after arriving near present-day Pueblo, Colorado, on November 11, 1806, and ended on February 26, 1807, when he was captured by the Spanish[1] — one hundred seven days during which he and his men faced death from starvation and exposure to an environment for which they were not prepared. Other potential enemies, the Pawnees and the Spaniards, did not materialize. There had been a brief scuffle with some Pawnees after the party had been reduced in numbers by the departure of Lieutenant James Wilkinson, but this had only hurt Pike's dignity and pride. The other enemies — lack of food and cold — would nearly kill them.

The American Alpine Club analyzes climbing accidents by looking at three circumstances surrounding the incident: the conditions before and at the time of the accident; actions taken leading up to and after the accident; and judgment, good and bad, before and after the accident.[2] These same three elements can be used to examine the one hundred seven days of Pike's near brush with death.

Conditions: Winter on the high plains and in the mountains of Colorado is an unpredictable and sometimes lethal season. Winter in 1806 started early. Even in late October, when Lieutenant Wilkinson left the expedition to return to St. Louis, the Arkansas River was turning to ice. Later, in the fullness of the Colorado winter, Pike's men post-holed through thigh-deep snow, faced days with temperatures as low as -9 degrees Fahrenheit and struggled against blizzards that stung their faces and froze their beards. [3]

Pike admitted that his men were totally unprepared for what they were asked to endure and, because the original intention was to turn back before winter set in, they came without warm clothing. During the climb of the Grand Peak in late November, Pike was dressed in cotton "overalls," as the standard military summer uniform was called, and had bare legs and no socks, "in every way ill provided to endure the inclemency of the region."[4] There was no mention in his writings of gloves or a fur hat. Not only were the clothes inadequate but they must have become wet, causing both discomfort and danger. (Heat loss is twenty-five times greater through wet clothing than through dry.)[5] The party was struggling through deep snow and Pike had the sense to realize that the summit was inaccessible and would be impossible for them to climb. Sensibly, he turned back.

As the expedition progressed, the lack of warm winter clothing became more important and even the blankets, essential for keeping the men warm at night, were cut up to make socks in a vain attempt to prevent frostbite.

After the failed attempt to climb the Grand Peak, the expedition moved northwest, following what Pike thought was a Spanish trail, circled a windswept, barren expanse prone to brutal winter ground blizzards, now called South Park, and—to their amazement—after making their way back through the Royal Gorge, found themselves at their starting point near Pueblo. By this time many of the men were already frostbitten and the strength of the group was diminishing daily. They were breaking up into separate parties of stragglers, each doing its best to survive. Pike himself was not discouraged and wrote that the cold was not as great as that experienced during the previous winter along the upper reaches of the Mississippi. His men may have had different opinions. But worse weather was to come, and before long, nine of the fifteen men had frostbitten feet.[6] Two men were totally incapacitated and were essentially abandoned with some ammunition and a token food supply.

Leaving the two incapacitated men behind in a flimsy fort, Pike headed south, then west across the Sangre de Cristo Mountains. He did not know precisely where he was in relation to the Rio Grande, Red, and Arkansas Rivers but hoped to get to the headwaters of the Rio Grande. Not only were the men suffering from lack of food, but the horses were unable to forage because of the depth of the snow and had become exhausted by plunging through deep snow. Eventually all of the horses died. As a result, the men were forced to carry heavy loads. What was in those loads is hard to imagine because they had no clothes, no tents, and virtually no food.

Traversing the Sangre de Cristos is tough even in summer and in winter would only be made nowadays by a well-equipped, experienced mountaineer. At one point Pike and Dr. John Robinson were nearly suicidal and contemplated abandoning the men, when they managed to shoot a bison and stagger into camp, laden with freshly-killed meat.[7]

One of the men, John Brown, complained that their sufferings were beyond human endurance, marching for three days through deep snow and carrying loads "only fit for horses." Pike did not see fit to respond immediately, but later turned on Brown and told him that if he ever spoke that way again he would shoot him.[8]

After traversing the Sangre de Cristo range and passing through or near the Great Sand Dunes, the expedition reached the great expanse of the San Luis Valley, where they built a small fort surrounded by a moat and with an entrance that could only be passed on hands and knees.[9] Some of the men were sent back over the mountains to rescue those who had been left behind. Two of the men could not return and sent Pike gangrenous toe bones as a reminder of their desperate plight.

Food was always in short supply. The game, seen earlier in such profusion on the plains that Pike thought it would supply food for the Indians for a hundred years, [10] had mostly migrated to warmer areas except for a few stragglers. Fortunately, either Pike or Dr. Robinson always seemed to shoot a bison or a deer when it was most needed, forestalling total starvation. But the lack of food did not seem to concern Pike. He wrote later in his diary, "I will not speak of diet as I conceive it to be beneath the serious consideration of a man on a voyage of such a nature."[11]

One other condition affected every action: the group was too small for the expedition. It was not large enough to defend itself against an attack by any force other than a few skirmishers — despite Pike's boast about being able to hold off an attack by one hundred Spanish dragoons. It was large enough to require a steady supply of meat, but not large enough to split up into a hunting party and a group that could build and defend a substantial winter shelter.

The "conditions" could hardly have been worse — a lack of winter clothing, barely enough food, no tents and no attempt to make winter quarters, inadequate maps, no friendly Indians (such as had helped Meriwether Lewis and William Clark), and a rugged terrain and altitude that the men had never experienced before.

Actions: In the face of such terrible conditions, Pike's actions increased, rather than decreased, the trials and dangers. His first bad decision was to keep going after November 11. He could have turned around or made a settled camp for the winter, but pride — and we can only guess at other possible motives or instructions — kept him going towards the mountains during the worst season of the year.

He did his best to feed the men but his best was borderline. The lack of game was beyond his control, but he could have stopped, rested and stocked up with meat.

His attempt to climb the gleaming mountain which he saw with a clarity that we seldom have today is fully understandable. In part, he wanted to climb so that he could spy out the land, but there must also have been an element of ego in wanting to be the first to summit such a mountain. His decision to turn back probably saved his life and that of his companions. If he had died on the slopes of the Grand Peak, the men left behind in the camp would probably have turned for home. They certainly would not have ascended the Arkansas River into South Park. They were already short of food and dressed in summer army uniforms made of cotton.

In many instances Pike's actions were impetuous, even foolhardy: the journey north into South Park along the faint traces of what he thought was a trail made by the Spanish dragoons; the failure to build a winter fort; the push through the Sangre de Cristo Mountains when he could have chosen a route farther south. Some of these actions were obviously due to his understandable lack of knowledge of the area. Had he known of the vastness of the mountains to the west he might not have ventured farther. He was an explorer, a risk-taker, and the thought of not going as far as he could, despite the obvious hazards of winter, was more than he could resist. He had behaved similarly while exploring the Mississippi, pushing beyond his orders, becoming separated from his men, and being driven by determination to find the elusive source of the river.[12, 13]

Most of these questionable actions were due to poor *judgment*. Pike had started life in remote military posts, inspired by the flamboyant behavior of General James Wilkinson, and was given responsibilities beyond his age and experience.[14] He had been successful in surviving hardships that would have deterred most men. These successful endeavors must have inflated his attitude towards what he could achieve. He was a very determined man, amazingly indifferent to discomfort, hunger and danger, and these characteristics affected his judgment. His decisions to proceed west rather than turning back as he had been ordered, to explore north and west from the Grand Peak and not to set up a sustainable, defensible winter fort and wait out the winter months, all fit with the character of a man who was certain he could overcome all difficulties, regardless of the season and weather.

Our interpretation of Pike's motives and judgment may be clouded by suspicions that he was a spy,[15] but that does not alter the weakness of many of his judgments that endangered his men.

Pike's decision to move south and then cross the Wet and Sangre de Cristo Mountains can be analyzed on a cost/benefit basis—a form of analysis that certainly never formally crossed Pike's mind but must have informally been part of his thinking.

The potential costs were the deaths of himself or his men from exposure or violence, increased disability among his men, death at the hands of the Spanish or unknown Indian tribes and—perhaps worst of all to Pike—personal failure and disgrace.

The potential benefits were success in exploring and mapping the western limits of the Louisiana Purchase, finding the limits of Spanish sovereignty, possible intentional capture by the Spanish (always a lottery because they might have killed him), and personal gain, fame and promotion.

The objective evidence on which he could make such a decision must have included the perilous condition of his men, the death of all his horses, the lack of food, the disappearance of most of the game to shoot, his total ignorance of the topography of the land before him, his equal ignorance of the whereabouts of the Spanish and what their reactions would be to his appearance in their territory, his lack of adequate clothing and shelter, and many other equally gloomy factors. A good general principle to follow in making decisions is that "when empirical evidence contradicts subjective judgment, empirical evidence should take priority."[16] Pike obviously put his personal objectives before the objective evidence.

Three medical conditions injured many members of the expedition and probably affected Pike's judgment, leading to injuries — starvation, hypothermia and frostbite.

Starvation:[17] The human body, even at rest, expends a basic amount of energy (the basal metabolic rate, BMR) to maintain life, protect against illnesses and heal wounds. The BMR for a 25-year-old man, five feet eight inches tall (Pike's height) and weighing one hundred eighty pounds is eighteen hundred calories per day. Raw bison meat has about one hundred calories in 3.5 ounces. Therefore, it would have been necessary for the men to eat 5.5 pounds of raw meat a day, without additional sources of calories, just to sustain their BMR. The greater the physical effort expended, the greater the need for calories. No wonder that the men of the Lewis and Clark expedition sometimes ate seven to nine pounds of meat a day.[18]

A diet of only one thousand to twelve hundred calories per day, as was the rule in most of the German concentration camps in World War II, kills in six to eight weeks. Pike's men never fell to that nadir of existence but frequently went two to three days without food while exerting themselves to exhaustion. If their ordeal had continued they would have become so weak that they would have been unable to march any longer.

There are many effects of starvation — weight loss, weakness, mental changes including apathy and sudden bursts of anger, and cravings for and dreams about food. Vitamin deficiencies, especially of vitamins B and C, cause serious diseases if the lack of nutrition is prolonged. Scurvy, due to the lack of vitamin C, was the bane of the sea-borne sailor's life.[19] The earliest explorers from Portugal, sailing down the coast of Africa found that the deadly symptoms of scurvy — swollen gums and rotting teeth, bleeding under the skin and severe weakness and excruciating pain — first appeared after about 100 days of sailing. Pike's men were very close to that dangerous border line when they were rescued by the Spanish. Bison meat and venison contain small amounts of vitamin C, which is destroyed by overcooking. They cannot have eaten any vegetables or fruits, the main sources of vitamin C, for many weeks. If they had not been taken to a warmer climate where they probably ate vegetables, they would have begun to develop scurvy. The symptoms of scurvy must have been familiar to Pike, and if his men had been dying from such an easily recognizable disease he would certainly have recorded their deterioration in his journals.

The diet of Pike's group was grossly deficient in many important factors for weeks at a time. The brain metabolizes only glucose that has to be obtained from carbohydrates, or substrates that result from the breakdown of other food components. The prolonged lack of carbohydrates could have seriously affected cognitive function, leading to faulty decisions.

Malnourished men, therefore, make poor decisions and are subject to violent temper tantrums. They become more and more apathetic until, at the end, death comes as a welcome release. John Brown's mutinous remarks may have been accentuated by near starvation, and Pike's reaction may have been more than just the natural response of a leader to an angry subordinate; it might have been the response of an angry, starving man.

After passing through the Sangre de Cristos, both Pike and Robinson were in despair. They went off by themselves, prepared to die. Fortunately, a bison came within shooting range, was killed and provided a good supply of meat for the men in the camp. A full stomach quickly restores morale.

The expedition could not have traveled at a worse time of year. The temperature was bitterly cold and the men were very poorly dressed. The chances of developing hypothermia were great.

Hypothermia is, technically, the reduction of core body temperature from 98 degrees Fahrenheit (37 degrees Celsius) to 95 degrees Fahrenheit (35 degrees Celsius), or lower.[20] Shivering begins before this temperature is reached, and as the body temperature falls below the critical level, all the basic physiologic reactions and functions slow down—cognitive skills and decision making become blurred, and confusion is an obvious indication of impending trouble. Shivering, the body's first attempt to maintain temperature by increasing metabolism, consumes—and therefore requires—a lot of energy. If the caloric intake is insufficient to maintain body temperature, the situation becomes even worse, with hypothermia developing with increasing rapidity. The combination of poor clothing, poor food intake, bitter temperatures, and severe wind chill was the ideal situation for developing hypothermia.

The mental changes that occur—confusion, inability to make correct decisions, apathy, and a strong feeling that lying down and taking a rest would solve the problem—added to the mental effects of starvation, must have affected Pike's ability to lead his men rationally. His decision to push ahead into the Sangre de Cristo Mountains in the middle of winter, not knowing what might lie on the other side, was not that of a sensible leader. Either he was affected by the combination of starvation and hypothermia, or he was driven to contact the Spanish by motives that we do not understand. To have endangered his men and himself by pushing into obviously high mountains, deeply covered with snow, when making a winter camp was an option, does not in retrospect seem to be a wise decision. This decision may well have been affected by physical factors that he did not understand and that were beyond his control.

Even before the weary, tattered group hauled their heavy loads into the mountains, frostbite had already taken a serious toll on the strength of the group. Two men had been left behind with frostbite so severe that they could not walk, and others had been frostbitten to a lesser degree.

Frostbite[21] is the local freezing of tissues that results in the development of blisters, painful swelling of the feet and, within about three weeks, black gangrene of the affected parts. Walking becomes impossible, and if a man removes his boots to warm his feet at a fire the swelling becomes even worse and he cannot get the boots back on again.

A few years later, in 1812, the Baron Jean Larrey, Surgeon-general to Napoleon, described in graphic detail the terrible conditions of the soldiers retreating from Moscow. Larrey ascribed much of the damage to the natural inclination of frozen men to warm themselves before a fire. We cannot be sure that this is what Pike's men did, but it would be very strange if they did not follow their natural instincts to build a fire and try to warm their feet. The results would have been painful and devastating, and that is why Larrey suggested that the cure for frostbite was to rub the parts with dry snow. (We now know that this is equally disastrous.)

No modern military unit would leave two men behind in the middle of a frozen wilderness with little hope of their survival. The only alternative would have been to build a substantial fort and sit out the winter. Even Pike realized the enormity of the demands that he was putting on his men, knowing they would be crippled for life and be paid a miserable pension.[22] Perhaps he thought that more men would be saved if the remainder pushed on than if they all stayed together. Fortunately, the Spanish eventually rescued those who had been abandoned, and, to some extent, relieved Pike's conscience.

Pike was a man with enormous energy and an incredible ability to withstand cold and privations that brought lesser men to their knees. His example must have helped the others to keep going. The will to live is an important part of survival under desperate circumstances but is difficult to define. It is more than mere determination, it is determination that knows no limits.

Luck often played a part in the survival of Pike's group—luck that a bison appeared like an offering from the gods at the last critical moment; luck that the Pawnees did not attack; luck that the elements, although bad, did not overwhelm them; luck that they were not struck by scurvy or other diseases; luck that the Spanish turned out to be remarkably friendly and did not kill them as unwanted intruders into their territory. Sometimes luck is more important than skill. But perhaps the most important factor was boldness. For, as the German philosopher Goethe wrote, "Boldness has genius and magic in it. Begin it now."

Bruce Paton, M.D., is a retired cardiac surgeon and wilderness medicine expert. An avid outdoorsman, Paton has contributed to numerous texts and articles related to backcountry medicine, including *Wilderness First Aid: Emergency Care for Remote Locations*. He is a former chairman of the Colorado Outward Bound School, as well as a past president of the Wilderness Medicine Society. His books include *Lewis and Clark: Doctors in the Wilderness*, and most recently, *Adventuring with Boldness: the Triumph of the Explorers*.

Notes

1. M. R. Montgomery, *Jefferson and the Gun-men. How the West was Almost Lost* (New York: Crown Publishers, 2000).

2. *Accidents in North America: Annual Report* (Golden, Colorado: American Alpine Club).

3. W. Eugene Hollon, *The Lost Pathfinder, Zebulon Montgomery Pike* (Norman: University of Oklahoma Press, 1949).

4. Montgomery, *Jefferson and the Gun-men*.

5. H. D. Backer, et al., *Wilderness First Aid* (Sudbury, Massachusetts: Jones and Bartlett, 1998).

6. Hollon, *The Lost Pathfinder*.

7. Montgomery, *Jefferson and the Gun-men*.

8. Hollon, *The Lost Pathfinder*.

9. Montgomery, *Jefferson and the Gun-men*.

10. Zebulon Montgomery Pike, *Journals and Letters with Related Documents*, edited by Donald Jackson (Norman: University of Oklahoma Press, 1966).

11. Montgomery, *Jefferson and the Gun-men*.

12. Ibid.

13. Hollon, *The Lost Pathfinder*.

14. Ibid.

15. Ibid.

16. D. Eddy, *Clinical Decision Making. From Theory to Practice* (Sudbury, Massachusetts: Jones and Bartlett, 1996).

17. B. C. Paton, *Adventuring with Boldness* (Golden, CO: Fulcrum Publishing, 2006).

18. B. C. Paton, *Lewis and Clark: Doctors in the Wilderness* (Golden, CO: Fulcrum Publishing, 2001).

19. K. J. Carpenter, *The History of Scurvy and Vitamin C* (Cambridge: Cambridge University Press, 1986).

20. H. D. Backer, et al., *Wilderness First Aid.* (Sudbury, Massachusetts: Jones and Bartlett, 1998).

21. Paton, *Lewis and Clark: Doctors in the Wilderness*.

22. Montgomery, *Jefferson and the Gun-men*.

Men, Missions & Consequences:
The Leadership Of Lieutenant Pike

John R. Sweet

Lieutenant Zebulon Montgomery Pike was a simple soldier, chosen to lead small units on complex missions, with limited assets, through uncharted wilderness, during a complex period of history. He was a reliable young officer—resourceful, energetic, ambitious and thoroughly committed to mission accomplishment. But in the summer of 1805, at the age of twenty-six, Lieutenant Pike's leadership abilities were largely untested, despite his nearly twelve years of military service. Apparently something about him had gained the notice of powerful senior leaders; something had caused him to stand out from the other junior officers in the small, poorly-funded U.S. Army. He had won no awards for gallantry in battle, had no reputation as a scholar or intellectual, did not come from a wealthy or well-connected family. Whatever it was about Lieutenant Pike that made him the best choice to head up a challenging operation, it was something intangible. He must have possessed those internal qualities that senior officers always desire in their subordinates. He had been born with, or had developed, or both, the much-sought-after ability to lead soldiers on long, difficult, hazardous missions. To General James Wilkinson, and likely to the other officers in the chain of command, Lieutenant Pike appeared have the character traits, the range of skills and the fortitude and determination that could influence men to follow him into harm's way. He was able to inspire men to accomplish their collective mission, whatever that may have been. Zebulon Pike's leadership was sorely tested, in exploration and in war, and it is worthy of a careful analysis.

The word "leadership" itself defies easy definition. Certainly it is to persuade, convince and inspire others to follow, thereby furthering the aims and objectives of the group.[1] It goes beyond simple planning, delegating and tasking. True leadership invokes and nurtures a powerful spirit of commitment and dedication, both in followers and in the leaders themselves, that cannot be easily described nor explained. Yet philosophers have attempted to do so for millennia. The Ancient Greeks sought to define and explain leadership by a systematic analysis of human nature, and were able to view it within the crucible of war and political strife.[2]

> Leadership to them was the art of inspiring the spirit and act of following, regardless of external circumstances. In more metaphysical terms, it was the art of turning the soul toward some purpose. . . . Leadership was the bridge between the personal, interpersonal, and the cosmological (visionary) levels.[3]

Xenophon and the Roman Cicero described it in action, while Plato and Aristotle derived it down to its very philosophical essence. Their terms and principles are with us still, slightly altered for a twenty-first century corporate/military audience,

> The issues of human sensitivity and meaning have never been separated from the art of leadership. Today we tell a leader to be himself; the ancients told him to "Know Thyself." Today we highlight the ideas of character and competence; the ancient Greeks taught the same but called it *areté* (excellence, moral virtue). Today we discuss vision; the ancients discussed the end (*telos*) and the idea (*eidos*). Today we demand respect and caring from leaders; the ancients conceptualized the moral equality of all humanity and the duty of the leader to be caretaker of the people.[4]

According to Xenophon in *Memorabilia,* Socrates argued that true leadership requires that followers act upon their own free will, without compulsion or coercion. Free men are persuaded through logic and reason to follow with mind, body and spirit, even in the direst of circumstances. But was a young junior army officer at the turn of the nineteenth century even vaguely aware of such classical notions? Had Lieutenant Zebulon Pike ever read Aristotle, much less internalized his ideas on leadership? Certainly during that neo-Classical time, the leadership philosophy of the ancients was present in contemporary wisdom. For instance, George Washington and many Continental Army officers possessed at least a basic knowledge of the classical works. These concepts, if not the Greek and Latin terms, had certainly trickled down to junior officers. Admittedly, there were numerous other influences upon early American ideas about leadership, not the least of which were several centuries of British military heritage.

Zebulon Pike had been born to a life of military service, and must have been inculcated with martial values and spirit from the very earliest age. His father, also named Zebulon Pike, served as a private in the infantry of the New Jersey state militia, later earning a commission in the Continental Army. He eventually was promoted to Captain, and his war record included Washington's 1776 New York campaign, Germantown, Monmouth "and also many skirmishes."[5] After the war, Captain Pike settled down to farm in western Pennsylvania. He reactivated his commission in the Pennsylvania militia during General Arthur St. Clair's ill-fated 1790 campaign in western Ohio against the Miami tribe under Little Turtle.

In 1792, Captain Pike accepted a commission in the small but growing regular U.S. Army and the next year he moved his wife and four children to Fort Washington, near the village of Cincinnati. General "Mad Anthony" Wayne's legion had been formed to bring about the final settlement of the Indian conflict in the Ohio River country. In 1794, a 15-year-old Zebulon Montgomery Pike entered the U.S. Army as a private, starting his famous career in a most humble fashion. It is unknown whether either of the Pikes participated in the decisive Battle of Fallen Timbers on August 20, but young Zebulon served during the wilderness guerilla campaign in the logistics train, transporting supplies to the various remote posts. Young Zebulon Pike did not enter the service as an officer, nor in an elite unit, nor in some glamorous duty assignment, well-positioned for advancement (although he did, apparently, serve for a time in his father's company). He served as an enlisted man and must have learned valuable leadership lessons by being a private, rather than starting in a leadership position. And Pike's later ideas about what motivates and inspires soldiers must surely have been based upon what had motivated and inspired him.[6]

Other scholars have stated my basic premise, that the fundamentals of leadership have a timeless quality. That despite changes in culture, customs and technology, the classical philosophers "sought to understand human nature and in doing so they arrived at ideas on leadership that transcend time and context."[7] If we analyze Pike's leadership qualities by applying the teachings of the ancients, and by subjecting them to twenty-first century U.S. Army standards, our study is neither an anachronism, nor is it guilty of pointless "presentism." Pike's command decisions *should* be seen within the context of the times in which he lived, and the army in which he served. But the leadership qualities that inspired those decisions can be analyzed according to basic standards which were identified in ancient times and are still applied in the U.S. Army today.

The basic U.S. Army authority on the topic of leadership is *FM 22-100, Army Leadership.* Although the text is clearly written for a modern audience, the ideas are derivative of the teachings of the classical philosophers, while citing examples from the history of the U.S. Army. They serve to illustrate the premise that leadership qualities are timeless and time-honored, that for the modern army leader General Washington can demonstrate the value called loyalty, just as Captain Sam Gibbons, 505th Parachute Infantry Regiment can illustrate initiative in the Normandy *bocage,* or Master Sergeant Gary Ivan Gordon and Sergeant First Class Randall Shugart demonstrated honor and sacrifice on the streets of Mogadishu. It is therefore appropriate that we subject Lieutenant Pike to analysis based upon *FM 22-100.*

Much the same as Aristotle, *FM 22-100* divides leadership into three categories, those of what a leader must "BE," "KNOW," and "DO." These roughly correspond to ancient ideas as follows. The "BE" category basically refers to character, including values and attributes. The seven U.S. Army values are known to every modern soldier, loyalty, duty, respect, selfless service, honor, integrity and personal courage. Personal attributes critical to leaders include mental, physical and emotional qualities. This corresponds to the *areté* of the ancients.[8]

The "KNOW" category refers, of course, to the knowledge or "skill set" that a leader must possess. It includes interpersonal, conceptual, technical and tactical skills—roughly the *paideia* of the ancients. The "DO" category is focused on a leader's actions. Rather than what he believes and/or knows, what does the army leader actually accomplish in terms of influencing others, planning and accomplishing missions, and improving the organization for future operations?[9] In the course of this paper we will analyze what the army leader Lieutenant Pike tried to "be," what he was able to be, what he "knew," and what he did.

Zebulon M. Pike served during a time of momentous military events, when vast armies clashed in epic battles deciding the fate of nations. But those battles were in Europe, far from the western frontier where Pike and his men toiled, and they scarcely seemed a part of the Napoleonic Age. But as removed as he was, Zebulon Pike must surely have read about the campaigns that ravaged Europe and redefined the military sciences. Army officers of the era certainly read accounts of the distant battles and, as far as possible, studied from afar the careers and strategies of Napoleon and his lieutenants. But Pike was not totally removed from these struggles for empire and influence. It was a militant and expansionist world that the young United States found itself in, and its military officers were the chief agents for defense and conquest, exploration, and expansion. For an ambitious soldier like young Lieutenant Pike, these special missions, with their opportunity for adventure and special recognition, were the next best assignment to a combat command.

Pike met Meriwether Lewis in Kaskaskia, Illinois, when the latter was recruiting personnel for his and William Clark's expedition to the Pacific. Surely Pike also hungered for such an assignment. When, on June 24, 1805, Pike received orders from General James Wilkinson to lead an expedition to explore the headwaters of the Mississippi, Pike must have been thrilled.[10] Here was the opportunity that an ambitious junior officer hopes for—a high-profile mission where he can prove himself capable of accomplishing his mission, fulfilling his duty and gaining distinction amongst his peers. This latter opportunity was critical in the small, peacetime U.S. Army where promotions came slowly.

Pike's mission up the Mississippi River, like his journey to the Rockies, was an army operation that had no special congressional or presidential endorsement. He received minimal funding and no special training or equipment. Pike was simply a lieutenant in the infantry, allocated twenty men, a seventy-foot keelboat and about $2,000 to outfit his expedition. Here Lieutenant Pike made an error he would repeat with tragic effect on his second expedition. He stated in his journal of August 9, 1805, that he was "provisioned for four months with orders to explore the source of the Mississippi making a general survey of the river and its boundaries, and its productions, both in the Animal, vegitable and mineral creation; also to include observations on the savage inhabitants of its banks."[11]

Pike set out with equipment and provisions enough to sustain his unit until late November, but by October the first snows had fallen and the expedition had only reached the vicinity of Little Falls in today's central Minnesota. To be sure, they had had a successful fall meeting with local British traders and informed them that they were operating in U.S. territory, had met with Sioux leaders near modern Minneapolis and purchased land for a post, and explored and mapped the main river drainage up to their current position. But it had been difficult as well. They had been pulling the flatboat upstream for weeks, and on October 16 they encountered the rapids near Little Falls. Snow had fallen the night before and Pike stated, "This was but poor encouragement for attacking the rapids, in which we were sure we must wade up to our necks . . . and after four hours work became perfectly useless in our limbs with cold."[12] This last effort had brought his best men to utter collapse. His boats were leaking and heavy with water. Exerting their utmost in freezing, fast current, poorly fed and worked to the point of exhaustion, Pike described the effects on his men,

> My Sergeant [Kenneman], one of the stoutest men I ever knew, broke a blood vessel, and vomited nearly two quarts of blood. One of my Corporals [Bradley] also evacuated nearly one pint of blood when he attempted to void his urine. These circumstances, with four of my men being rendered useless before who were left on shore, convinced me that, if I had no regard for my own health and constitution, I should have some for poor fellows who, to obey my orders were killing themselves.[13]

He opted to drop downriver a few miles to an earlier campsite and erect a pair of blockhouses and a stockade. There they would hunt and lay in a cache of meat, in preparation for his final movement north to the headwaters of the river. This was a decision that Pike would repeat during his Rocky Mountain expedition the following year. He would push ahead with his exploring mission until the men were incapable of proceeding further and his supplies were exhausted, and then erect winter quarters late in the season. True, Pike was probably not adequately equipped or funded for either of his expeditions, but he did little pre-planning to mitigate those shortages. In neither case did he have any apparent plan developed upon the event that he failed to achieve his objectives before the winter season set in. Nor is there any indication that he attempted to feverishly "scrounge up" from local sources the clothing and equipment he needed.

For this first mission up the Mississippi River such an oversight may be forgivable (although he had already spent a number of years traveling up and down the trails and river corridors of the Old Northwest and might have anticipated the rate of travel and the impacts of weather). But he would repeat this mistake—his failure to obtain sufficient clothing and equipment and to pre-plan a course of action if he was unable to complete his mission before winter—again on his trip west. This mistake forced the expedition to endure unnecessary suffering and materially impacted the success of his mission.

It is also important to note that Lieutenant Pike exceeded his orders by choosing to winter in the upper Mississippi and press on with his mission. In fact, General Wilkinson stated explicitly in his orders that, "You will proceed to ascend the main branch of the River, until you reach the source of it, or the season may forbid your further progress, without endangering your return before the waters have frozen up."[14] Lieutenant Pike would again liberally interpret his orders the next year. That mission would again be primarily diplomatic rather than scientific, when he was ordered to return Osage prisoners of war received by the U.S. government, facilitate peace negotiations between the Osages and the Kansas tribes, and meet with the Pawnee in order to coordinate a peace conference with the Comanche. This alone was quite a mission for a first lieutenant and his platoon to accomplish! But Pike seemed to have focused on Wilkinson's secondary mission,

> As your interview with the Cammanchees will probably lead you to the head Branches of the Arkansaw, and Red Rivers, you may find yourself approximately to the settlements of New Mexico. . . . It is an object of much

interest to the Executive, to ascertain the direction, extent
& navigation of the Arkansaw & Red Rivers; as therefore
may be compatible with these Instructions and practicable
to the means you may Command, I wish you to carry
your views to these subjects, and should circumstances
conspire to favour the enterprise, you may . . . descend
the Arkansaw.[15]

Obviously Lieutenant Pike was highly motivated to do his
duty and accomplish his mission, and to "exceed the standard,"
in modern military parlance. But both of his expeditions were
primarily diplomatic missions to western tribes, to obtain land for
an army post or to return prisoners to their villages, respectively,
and were only exploratory expeditions in a secondary sense.

In fact, during the expedition to the Rocky Mountains, Pike
developed his own "follow on" mission that was clearly in the
nature of an intelligence-gathering operation. An American
businessman had asked Lieutenant Pike to look into the status of
a trader (named Baptiste Lalande) that had traveled to Santa Fe in
1804, only to sell the businessman's goods at a nice profit and settle
in New Mexico on the proceeds.[16] Robinson and Pike concocted an
amateurish plan, whereby Robinson could infiltrate New Mexico,

When on the frontiers, the idea suggested itself to us of
making this claim [against Lalande] a pretext for Robinson
to visit Santa Fe. . . . Our views were to gain a knowledge
of the country, the prospect of trade, force, etc. whilst,
at the same time, our treaties with Spain guaranteed to
him . . . the right of seeking all just debts or demands.[17]

This particular operation was poorly thought out and
clumsily executed. What would the already-suspicious Spanish
authorities think of this American physician walking in out of the
northern wilderness? Nowhere in General Wilkinson's orders is
any operation of this nature even vaguely hinted at. Where did
Lieutenant Pike get the idea that this was within the scope of his
authority? Historians have speculated that there were additional,
secret orders given that sent the young lieutenant off on this
mission.[18] But no such orders have come to light, and Pike's journals

do not even hint at their existence, so we must assume that Pike developed these orders on his own initiative, based upon a liberal interpretation of his commander's intent.

He seemed to place greater emphasis on the secondary missions, i.e., carefully but quickly completing negotiations with the Indians before driving deeper into the wilderness. It was an age of exploration and empire, and Lieutenant Pike was well aware of the interest taken in the Lewis and Clark expedition. In Pike's defense, what lieutenant would not zealously pursue a secondary mission that was "of much interest to the Executive?" If his primary motive was to serve his nation by expanding its knowledge and solidifying its claim to new territory, then he was acting with honor, albeit rashly. If his primary motive was to gain fame and rank, then his service was far from "selfless." These are questions of character.

But as stated earlier, in both cases he was ill-equipped to execute prolonged exploratory missions. Although heavy wool winter uniforms were standard issue, on Pike's expedition across the Great Plains his men carried only their summer uniforms. Although it is true that Pike didn't understand the nature of the western mountains, his experience the previous winter should have impressed upon him the need to pack for worst-case scenarios and, if he was determined to accomplish his secondary missions to the headwaters of the Red and the Arkansas Rivers, to equip his men for a winter expedition.

Although he doggedly pursued his duty to his commanders, he failed in his duty to his men. Specifically, if he intended to stay out into the winter season, he did not ensure that they were adequately supplied or equipped. And if his intent had always been to erect a stockade and bivouac over the winter, then in both instances he waited until his supplies were gone and his men were exhausted and ill before doing so. This was a failure in leadership, in that he failed to plan for likely eventualities and did not learn from past experiences.

In at least two other areas Lieutenant Pike fell short of providing exemplary leadership. He sometimes applied harsh punishments, but he disciplined his soldiers in accordance with the army regulations of the day. However, on one occasion he overstepped even nineteenth-century army standards by threatening to summarily execute one of his men for complaining! And just as significantly, he repeatedly failed in one of his basic duties as a small-unit leader. He lost accountability of his personnel, leaving them lost and scattered over the landscape, at times injured and suffering.

In general, Lieutenant Pike's attitude towards discipline and corporal punishment was no harsher than other officers of his day, and certainly milder than some. In fact, although corporal punishments were acceptable and common in the U.S. Army of 1800, Pike apparently rarely applied them. In his journals of exploration there is only one instance mentioned in which he imposed flogging. On the voyage up the Mississippi River, Pike awoke on September 24, 1806, and "discovered my Flag to be gone off from my Boat—uncertain whether it had been stolen by the Indians, or fell overboard and floated away."[19] Pike was clearly upset, since his flag had such important symbolic significance to a nineteenth-century officer. It was a symbol of the United States, his command and his personal authority. Certainly he found its loss, by theft or otherwise, to be a personal and professional insult and a stain upon his honor. He sent out search parties and ordered "the instantaneous punishment of my guard (having given one an 100 lashes)."[20] A Sioux chief returned the flag the next day, saying it had floated downstream about three miles to his village.

One hundred lashes sounds like a draconian punishment, and indeed such a punishment would result in a prison sentence for an officer in the twentieth- or twenty-first-century U.S. Army. But how excessive did it seem at the time? The Lewis and Clark expedition sentenced men to be flogged on at least four separate occasions (though only three of the sentences were carried out). The crimes included stealing whiskey and getting drunk while on guard, sleeping while on guard, insubordination and compromising the security at Fort Mandan by climbing over the wall after dark (while observed by an Indian who copied the feat).[21] Does Pike's lost flag compare to these offenses? Perhaps it does, if the loss was due to a lack of vigilance. But if the flogging was simply a response to the lieutenant's injured pride and honor, then it was simply self-indulgent cruelty, a fact that was surely apparent to his men at the time. However, the journals give no indication of Pike's inner motives and it behooves us to give him the benefit of the doubt. However, what was most critical at the time was how the other men under his command accepted the punishment. If administered fairly and with adequate cause and explanation, it was likely acceptable to Pike's soldiers; if seen as arbitrary and unnecessary, the flogging no doubt eroded morale.

Pike's greatest transgression in administering discipline, at least to the twenty-first-century observer, had nothing to do with a punishment actually administered, but rather merely *threatened* to inflict. In January 1807 his men were suffering from hunger, exhaustion and the dismay of being lost in a vast wilderness with no hope of rescue. They were high in the Sangre de Cristo Range, trying to cross over into the (unbeknownst to them) Rio Grande drainage to the west. It had been a long and demoralizing week and the unit had already been dwindling away as men "fell out" from cold injuries,

> I determined to attempt the traverse of the mountain, in which we persevered, until the snow became so deep, it was impossible to proceed; when I again turned my face to the plain and for the first time in the voyage found myself discouraged; and for the first time I heard a man express himself in a seditious manner; he exclaimed, "that it was more than human nature could bear, to march three days without sustenance, through snow three feet deep, and carry burthens only fit for horses," &c. &c.

> As I knew very well the fidelity and attachment of the majority of the men, and even of this poor fellow, (only he could not endure fasting) and that it was in my power to chastise him, when I thought it proper, I passed it unnoticed for the moment, determined to notice it at a more auspicious time.[22]

But there was joy in camp that night. The party had turned back east and trudged down onto the plains of the Wet Mountain Valley. Lieutenant Pike and Dr. Robinson were ranging ahead of the main body hunting when they spotted a small buffalo herd. Pike ordered the men to set camp in a nearby patch of timber while he and the doctor went ahead to try their luck. Pike and Robinson managed to kill one and carried back a heavy load of meat, to the great joy of his starving soldiers. They all gorged themselves on the delicious fresh meat and warmed by the campfires; Pike felt the morale level of his troops rising as the day came to an end. It was this moment that he chose to address the "seditious" soldier from earlier in the day. As his journal entry is detailed regarding this event, and his intention so obviously an attempt at self-justification, it deserves to be quoted in its entirety,

> *Brown*, you this day presumed to make use of language which was seditious and mutinous; I then passed it over, pitying your situation and attributing it to your distress, rather than inclination to sow discontent amongst the party. Had I reserved provisions for ourselves, whilst you were starving; had we been marching along light and at ease whilst you were weighed down with burden; then you would have some pretext for your observations; but when we were equally hungry, weary, emaciated and charged with burden, which I believe my natural strength is less able to bear than any man's in the party; when we were always foremost in breaking the road, reconnoitering and the fatigues of the chase, it was the height of ingratitude in you to let an expression escape that which was indicative of discontent.[23]

Pike makes sure to emphasize that he shared every hardship with his soldiers, which, if true (and there is evidence that it was the case) indicates that he was not some selfish elitist. Curious, however, is his statement that "my natural strength is less able to bear [the burdens] than any man's in the party." Did Pike believe himself to be physically smaller or weaker than his soldiers, and therefore should be accorded special consideration? Even if such was the case, it is hardly dignified for him as an officer to mention it or expect special treatment. Curious indeed, is his belief that this soldier, for whatever reason, should feel gratitude towards his leader. Pike goes on to clearly state his expectations of Private John Brown, and of all soldiers under his command,

> Your ready compliance and firm perseverance I had reason to expect, as the leader of men and my companions, in

miseries and dangers. But your duty as a soldier called on your obedience to your officer, and a prohibition of such language, which for this time I will pardon, but assure you, should it ever be repeated, by instant *death*, I will revenge your ingratitude and punish your disobedience.

Perhaps what we see in this statement is an officer who has reached his own mental, emotional and physical limits. Although Pike's character attributes may have been sound, he had temporarily reached that point where he himself could no longer handle the stress of the mission and command. But if that was the case, then why did he wait until that evening when he was fed and well-rested to confront the soldier and make his threat? And the threat itself was a terribly foolish act. Although execution was an acceptable military punishment for some crimes, including dereliction of duty, it certainly was not administered for "griping." And execution was a rare punishment, handed down only after full, formal proceedings, not administered summarily in the field by frustrated and exhausted officers. This act must have been beyond the pale of acceptable behavior, even by early-nineteenth-century standards. However, when Pike's journals appeared in print in 1810 there was no outcry against his behavior. Perhaps in those days Americans, even soldiers, expected officers to remain aloof and wield authority with arbitrary sway.[24]

What *is* certain is that at the point where he threatened his soldier's life, he ceased to be a leader in the classical sense. American soldiers, like the Athenian hoplites, are duty-bound to serve the democracy, but they continue to be free men, not slaves. This was a critical distinction in antebellum America, just as it was in the classical world. Lieutenant Pike had failed to employ persuasion (*pietho*) to appeal to his men's sense of reason; instead he had threatened force (*bia*). When he chose to compel his men to his will, rather than persuade them to follow, he ceased to be a leader. He had, in terms familiar to Plato, become a tyrant.[25] At least he had in that instance.

And it is apparent that Pike *did* care what his men thought, and that he appreciated their service. In the same journal entry of January 24, 1807, he goes on to tell the entire party,

I take this opportunity likewise to assure you, soldiers generally of my thanks for obedience, perseverance and ready contempt of every danger which you have generally evinced; I assure you nothing shall be wanting on my part to procure you the rewards of our government and gratitude of our countrymen.[26]

Again, however, he promises to try to secure for his men tangible rewards, rather than appealing to some higher notion of national destiny. Was this because the promise of fame and rewards were what Lieutenant Pike believed would motivate his men, simply because that was what motivated Pike? Or did he know his men well, and could motivate them to drive on with the mission, even when poorly equipped, poorly supplied and in the face of nearly overwhelming obstacles? Regardless of the motives, it worked. Three days later he led them over the Sangre de Cristo Range at Medano Pass. There they descended into the Rio Grande drainage, descended into Spanish territory and descended into history.[27]

The other area in which Pike failed to provide exemplary leadership was in the realm of troop management, or failing to keep accountability of his personnel. A small-unit leader must know the whereabouts and status of his troops at all times — soldiers whose location is unknown become mission-ineffective. They cannot be supplied, given orders, or warned of impending danger. It is no mean feat to track the location and status of even twenty men in a field environment, and a junior officer is greatly aided in this by his senior non-commissioned officer (sergeant). On both of his expeditions, Lieutenant Pike displayed an unsettling tendency to allow his force to become separated and scattered across a wide expanse of wilderness, often for days at a time.

On the Mississippi expedition of 1805–1806, Pike often ranged ahead of the main body, which was slowly and laboriously pulling the flatboats upriver against the swift current. He scouted and reconnoitered, often meeting with Native Americans and traders along the way. He, very sensibly, acted as the "eyes and ears" of his unit as they pushed into little-known and unstable territory. Lieutenant Pike also hunted enthusiastically, both for the thrill of the chase and because game meat became absolutely essential for their survival after their supplies largely ran out in mid-October. Often out overnight, he usually took a companion or two along, and other men were also dispatched away from the main body for various details, so keeping accountability of personnel was understandably difficult. But Pike's behavior was almost cavalier, and eventually there would be tragic results.

Once he had made the decision to build a post for the winter, Pike began hunting in earnest. He had two designated hunters, Corporal Samuel Bradley and Private John Sparks, but Pike felt a need to contribute also. While the troops labored at building the log structures, the lieutenant ventured into the woods searching for meat for the larder. On October 22 he wounded a deer which got away, and when he returned later found that, "My men neglected their business, which convinced me that I must leave hunting alone and oversee the others."[28] But the next day he recorded, "Raised my other blockhouse, got all the property in the one completed. Killed a number of pheasants and ducks when visiting my canoe makers. Sleets of snow."[29]

As work on the buildings continued, a hunting camp was established a few miles downstream in better game country. Pike soon identified a favorite hunting buddy, Private Theodore Miller, "whose obliging disposition made him agreeable in the woods." Pike and Miller set out from the hunting camp on November 2. Pike felt that this hunt had to be successful. Previous to leaving the garrison Pike recorded in his journal, "I told my men that, having never killed an elk, I would kill one before I came back . . . it really was a very foolish resolution." Pike shot and wounded several elk, not recovering one until the next day. It wasn't until November 4 that Pike returned to his hunting camp, "to the great joy of my men, who had been to our little garrison to enquire for me, and obtaining no news had concluded we were killed by the Indians."[30] Pike had killed several deer and an elk, but had caused his men to waste time searching for him—time that could have been better spent hunting or improving their winter quarters.

On the other hand, Pike showed great concern when his men were out hunting and did not return as expected. On November 6, Pike was in a hunting camp with Miller, Sparks ,and Bradley when the three enlisted men went out to retrieve some downed game. Soon after they left a snow storm blew in and Pike grew anxious,

Waited all day with the greatest anxiety for my men. The river became nearly filled with snow, partly congealed into ice. My situation can more easily be imagined than described. Went down the river to the place where I understood the deer was killed, but discovered nothing of my men. This joined with the knowledge of the hostile Chipeways . . . Snow still continued falling very fast, and became nearly knee deep. Had great difficulty to procure wood sufficient to keep a fire all night. Ice in the river thickening.[31]

The next day Pike headed upstream to his stockade, leaving a message in the snow for his "lost men." "I determined to depart for the garrison," he wrote, "and when the river had froze come down on the ice with a party . . . to search for my poor boys." That afternoon Pike ran into a group of his soldiers marching down river from the stockade, searching for the overdue hunting party. Pike was exhausted and suffering by the time he made it to his blockhouses on November 9. But he immediately went about preparing boats and sleds in order to send a large rescue party downstream to search for his three men. However, on November 11 Bradley and Miller walked into the garrison, having left Private Sparks at the hunting camp to guard the sizable meat cache.

Over the next two weeks Pike struggled to get his meat supply (seventeen deer and two elk) from his downstream hunting camp to his blockhouses. He sent small groups of men back and forth, almost arbitrarily, in an increasingly complex logistical puzzle. On November 12 he "dispatched Miller and Huddleston to the lower hunting camp — Bradley and Brown hunting in those woods." On November 14 he took five men and went downriver to help bring in the meat, but the river was frozen so he stopped to camp part way. On November 16 "detached Corporal Meek and one private to the garrison to order the sleds down." His personnel accountability was in complete disarray; Pike had lost unit integrity and did not have a reasonable knowledge of the whereabouts of over half of his men.[32]

Each of these trips through the wintry Minnesota wilderness contained inherent risk. The wise command decision would have been to limit these trips to the fewest possible, and limited to large, well-supplied, adequately-equipped, and experienced groups. The risks were made readily apparent on November 17, when one of the privates staggered into Pike's camp,

> One of my men arrived, he having attempted to make camp the day before, got lost in the prairie—layed out all night and froze his toes. He informed that the corporal and the men I sent with him both got their toes frostbit—the former very badly.[33]

These were probably unnecessary cold-weather casualties that resulted in needless suffering and life-long injury. And any casualties significantly impact a unit's ability to accomplish its mission. Precious personnel assets ("my boys," as Pike referred to them) should be safeguarded from unnecessary risk and pointless hardships. On the other hand, Pike faced nearly all of the same hazards that he asked his men to endure. It can safely be said that he generally "led from the front."

Once the stockade was completed and a supply of meat laid in, Pike chose to lead a smaller party upstream to the headwaters of the Mississippi, thereby completing the secondary mission that he was determined to accomplish. This leg of the expedition was successful and largely casualty-free, due in no small part to the fine hospitality and assistance that Pike and his men encountered from several North West Company and independent traders that they encountered. The young lieutenant had completed nearly every aspect of his assignment, mainly due to his drive and determination, commitment to duty and his undeniable physical, mental and emotional toughness. Unfortunately, Pike was slow to learn from his mistakes. Perhaps so committed and determined of a character had a problem with self-assessment and did not easily admit his mistakes. Whatever the reason, he repeated his blunders the following winter and his men suffered as a result.

We return again to January 1807, when Pike's men had already been struggling along on short rations for several weeks. They were again subsisting on whatever game they could kill. Pike's unit was camped near Grape Creek in the Wet Mountain Valley when "we discovered that the feet of nine of our men were frozen." This time his entire unit was immobile, leaving only Pike, Dr.

Robinson and "two of the men least injured" to "hunt something to preserve existence." Pike and Robinson were fortunate and killed a buffalo on the second day. This saved the unit from utter starvation, but "on examining the feet of those who were frozen we found it impossible for two of them to proceed, and two others only without loads by the help of a stick."[34]

Now Pike had an agonizing leadership decision to make. In an area unsuited for a winter bivouac, he had to push on over the imposing mountains to a better location. But, through either poor decisions or bad luck or both, he had already pushed them so hard as to render two of his men unable to proceed. The two men were John Sparks (the hunter from the Mississippi River expedition), and Pike's personal "waiter" Thomas Dougherty. Pike describes what occurred the morning of January 22,

> I furnished the two poor lads who were to remain with ammunition and made use of every argument in my power to encourage them to have fortitude to resist their fate, and gave them assurance of my sending relief as soon as possible. We parted, but not without tears. We pursued our march, taking merely sufficient provisions for one meal in order to leave as much as possible for the two poor fellows who remained.[35]

Before the party had descended into the San Luis Valley, another man with frostbitten feet had been left behind in a lonely camp high in the mountains. By February 7 a stockade had been constructed in the valley and Pike began to divide his command even further. His interpreter and one soldier had been left with the horses near the site of today's Cañon City. Two frostbitten soldiers were in a camp up in the Wet Mountain Valley near modern Silvercliffe. Another injured soldier was watching a meat cache high in the Sangre de Cristos. In short, Lieutenant Pike had isolated, sometimes injured men scattered over more than one hundred miles of rugged, mountainous terrain in the dead of winter. And on that day he gave two seemingly conflicting orders. He dispatched a five-man detail to bring in his three injured stragglers and some baggage, and he sent Dr. Robinson south to Santa Fe on his strange intelligence-gathering mission. Even as he sought to consolidate his command, he further fragmented it.

Ten days later his rescue party returned,

> They informed me that two men would arrive the next day; one of them was Menaugh, who had been left alone on the 27th of January, but that the other two men, Dougherty and Sparks, were unable to come. They said that they had hailed them with tears of joy, and were in despair when they again left them with the chance of never seeing them more. They sent on to me some of the bones taken out of their feet, and conjured me by all that was sacred, not to leave them to perish far from the civilized world.[36]

Sending the bones of their frostbite-ruined feet seems to indicate an act of spite, a message sent to their commander in bitter anger. Or it could be interpreted differently — perhaps they remained steadfast and loyal to their platoon leader and it was simply a pitiable plea to be rescued. Certainly Pike would need his horses to accomplish this, and two days later he dispatched two more men on the long journey to retrieve them.[37] In the meantime, Pike was deeply affected by his men's gesture,

> Ah! Little did they know my heart if they could suspect me of conduct so ungenerous [as to abandon them]. No! Before they should be left I would for months have carried the end of a litter, in order to secure them, the happiness of once more seeing their native homes and being received in the bosom of a grateful country.

Pike goes on to complain of the low pay and the scant recognition that they would likely receive for their sacrifice. "These poor lads are to be invalids for life, made infirm at the commencement of manhood," the lieutenant wrote, ". . . for what is the pension? Not sufficient to buy a man his victuals! What man would even lose the smallest of his joints for such a trifling pittance?"[38]

Certainly Pike was concerned about his men's sacrifice and how it would impact their future. But better questions might have been, was the sacrifice of life and limb even necessary? Could these cold injuries have been prevented by better planning and appropriate equipment? Should the unit have gone into winter quarters much earlier, leaving scouting and exploring to smaller, well-supplied and healthy groups working at a reasonable pace? Although Pike regrets the crippling injuries that his men suffered, nowhere does he appear to take responsibility for them.

Zebulon Pike did not possess the scientific training to become a truly great explorer. Nor did he have leadership brilliance, nor the uncanny luck that tends to accompany military greatness. There is no reason to believe that, if ever placed in command of vast legions, he would have become one of America's finest generals. But he did seem to have the drive and determination, the courage and the sense of duty, that got missions accomplished.

As is well known, Pike was finally taken into custody by Spanish soldiers on February 27, 1807, and taken to Santa Fe. His scattered men were eventually all rounded up and later joined him under arrest. Regardless of what modern scholars may debate, the Spanish officials were certainly convinced that the lieutenant was a spy and he was kept under house arrest, first in Santa Fe then in Chihuahua City. The Spanish attempted to confiscate Lieutenant Pike's notes and sensitive papers, but he managed to hide the most critical ones in some of his men's rifle barrels. Pike and most of his men were released the following summer. Not only did these papers make it back to the United States, he surreptitiously continued his journaling during his entire time in Mexico. The result was a marvelously detailed description of Spain's frontier provinces, albeit more valuable from a military than a scientific perspective.

On this second expedition Pike seemed to snatch success from the jaws of defeat. Despite starvation, intense cold, capture and confinement, and the attempted confiscation of his notes, Lieutenant Pike managed to bring home the first useful geographical, scientific, military and cultural information about the United States' new southwestern territories and the Spanish provinces that lay across the distant border.[39]

Pike had been promoted to captain while he was detained in Mexico. His return was noted in the major U.S. newspapers of the day—a few denounced him as an accomplice in the Aaron Burr–General Wilkinson secession plot. Secretary of War Henry

Dearborn came to his defense, confirming that he was on a legitimate, government-sponsored exploring expedition. He was promoted to major in 1808, but he failed to get his men awarded double pay, as the Lewis and Clark expedition members had been. Since Pike and his men were on an army ordered and funded mission, they were simply doing their duty.

Pike was well known to the higher-ups in the government and he moved steadily through desirable commands and duty positions, involved in typical peacetime, in-garrison conflicts and controversies. He was as ambitious as ever, even more so now, and the promotions came quickly (major in 1808, lieutenant colonel in December of 1809). By the time war broke out in 1812, Pike had been promoted to full colonel and he was probably the most-esteemed field officer in the army.[40]

Colonel Pike was placed in command of the as-yet untrained Fifteenth Regiment. He assumed command in July 1812, and by late summer they were in upstate New York, training for the Canadian campaign. He wrote to his superior, General Wilkinson, "If we go into Canada, you will hear of my fame or of my death—for I am determined to seek the 'Bubble' even in the cannon's mouth."[41]

Pike apparently did an excellent job of training his amateur soldiers in the drill and tactics of modern, Napoleonic Age warfare. They went into garrison in Plattsburg, New York, and fought a successful skirmish during General Dearborn's aborted invasion of Quebec in November. The army then went into winter quarters and most of the officers left the area to live in town with their wives. Colonel Pike, however, remained with his regiment. In March he led his troops on a hard winter march to Sackets Harbor on Lake Ontario. There a fleet was being constructed and an army assembled for an assault on Upper Canada. In the meantime, Pike was promoted to brigadier general.[42]

"I embark tomorrow in the fleet at Sackets Harbor at the head of fifteen hundred choice troops on a secret expedition," Pike wrote to his father on April 22, "if success attends my steps, honor and glory await my name—if defeat, still it shall be said we died like brave men and conferred honor even in death on the American name."[43] For Pike, if the mission was not accomplished there was only one alternative. On the other hand, an attitude this fatalistic could not have been too reassuring to his men.

The campaign plan called for the control of Lake Ontario with the capture of strategic Kingston at the mouth of the lake, and the capture of York, the provincial capital (modern-day Toronto). York was selected as the first objective because it was more lightly defended, and Pike was chosen to lead the attack. General Dearborn maintained operational control but would remain on board the American flagship, the USS *Madison*, until the fighting was complete.

On the night of April 26, Pike wrote his last letter,

My Dear Clara—we are standing on and off the harbor of York which we shall attack at daylight in the morning. I shall dedicate these last moments to you, my love, and tomorrow throw all other ideas but my country to the wind . . . I have no new injunctions, no new charges to give you, nor new ideas to communicate, yet we love to communicate with those we love, more especially when we conceive it may be the last time in this world. Should I fail, defend my memory and only believe, had I lived, I would have aspired to deeds worthy of your husband. Remember me with a father's love, a father's care, to our daughter; and believe me, with the warmest sentiments of love and friendship. Yours.[44]

General Pike commanded the First Brigade, a mixed force consisting of one thousand seven hundred troops, mostly infantry, and a few pieces of field artillery. Providing fire support would be the American fleet under Commodore Isaac Chauncey, consisting of two transports and fourteen warships armed with one hundred twelve guns, including forty 32-pounders. York was defended by about six hundred troops, including about two hundred British regulars, the rest being Canadian militia. They were commanded by Major General Sir Roger Hale Sheaffe, commander of all Crown forces in Upper Canada. In addition, a group of about one hundred Indian auxiliaries was camped west of town, and would offer the first resistance. The harbor was defended by an earthen fort, equipped with about eight 18-pounders and a half-dozen 6-pound guns. A fortified battery had been erected just a few hundred yards west of the fort. Both positions overlooked the lake to the south, with the mouth of the harbor and the town to their rear. The Americans had numerical and fire superiority, but would have to assault a well-defended position from the water. On April 27, 1813, they launched the attack.[45]

The result was a complex but amazingly successful and well-timed amphibious operation that coordinated naval gunfire with a landing against a defended beach, an overland attack and then an assault against a fortified position. In many ways, the operation was a textbook example of Napoleonic-era military science in action.

First, the American fleet ably suppressed the guns of the enemy batteries. The landing force was inserted two miles west of the fort and the town, then they attacked to the east. Under fire from Indians and regulars, the first wave landed in rowboats and cleared the beach and tree line before pushing inland. Characteristically, Zebulon Pike chose to go ashore early, in the second wave with the 15th Infantry Regiment. In fact, he led the overland assault personally. His line consisted of elements of the 6th, 15th, 16th, and 21st Regiments, as well as a battery of the 3rd Artillery. They wheeled right and advanced eastward steadily and rapidly, despite the swampy, thickly wooded terrain and the stubborn delaying action by the enemy. Meanwhile, the naval gunfire kept raking across the enemy's left flank and other ships continued to bombard the fort. An accidental powder explosion rocked the western battery just before Pike's 16th Regiment swept over the ramparts. The position was theirs. The fort and the town lay ahead.

Pike had his force advance to within two hundred yards of the main fort, where he waited for his artillery to come forward. It was between 1,30 and 2,00 P.M. While he waited he sent a lieutenant forward with a reconnaissance party and interrogated a captured Canadian militiaman. At that point the earth shook from an explosion and a giant blast from the fort shot skyward. General Pike, still at the front, was amongst the fallen. He was hit in the back by a stone and the wound was clearly a fatal one, though he lingered for hours. As American surgeon William Beaumont noted in his diary, "Above 300 were wounded, and about 60 killed dead on the spot by stones of all dimensions falling like a shower of hail in the midst of our ranks."[46]

The fort's main powder magazine was below the southwest bastion near the waterfront. Constructed of solid stone and heavy timber, it held nearly five hundred barrels of powder and many other munitions. General Sheaffe ordered a sergeant to detonate the arsenal via a long, timed fuse. Whether this was done to inflict maximum casualties upon the Americans or simply to destroy the munitions is still subject to debate, but its effects were devastating.[47] The British-Canadian force suffered about twenty casualties as well.

To what degree does Pike bear the blame for these casualties? Was there a tactical blunder on his part? Since he had not yet entered the fort, he cannot be accused of lingering on the objective. Certainly he had pursued the attack with vigor. Unless he was privy to intelligence describing the location of the enemy powder magazine (and he probably was not), it is difficult to find him at fault for this disaster. It was merely one of the tragic fortunes of war, where no one was precisely to blame yet the suffering was widespread.

Nineteenth-century accounts claim that Pike lay there in the dust, mortally wounded, but said to his men gathered around, "Push on my brave fellows and avenge your general."[48] As unlikely as it sounds, it would have been in keeping with Pike's nature. He was absolutely committed to accomplishing his mission, whatever the cost. Pike was carried back to one of the ships where he was laid on a cot. At his request, the captured British colors were brought to him and placed under his head for a pillow. He expired within a few hours, along with many of his men.

Undoubtedly Zebulon Pike was a leader—free men followed him. They followed him through hunger and cold and exhaustion. They followed him into captivity. And eventually some followed him to their deaths. But they also followed him to success and victory and onto the pages of history. We can never know how many of those soldiers ever knew or cared that they would, in a small way, contribute to or share in Pike's fame. More significantly, did Pike's successful missions contribute to the survival and growth of the young United States? That is also subject to debate, but Pike certainly believed so, and those missions were conceived and conducted with that assumption.

Pike was a simple soldier, but less simple as a human being. He was certainly a leader with character. Did he live up to "The Seven Army Values?" He was loyal to his superiors, often to a fault. He lobbied for his men, trying to secure for them rewards and payment for their efforts. On the other hand, he sometimes led them beyond their abilities and, perhaps, subjected them to needless hardship and suffering. His sense of duty was strong, and he never failed in his duty to his nation or the army. His duty to his men may be another story, however. Pike seemed to show respect, to superiors and subordinates, although he criticized some of his superiors in private correspondence.

Was Pike's service "selfless?" His unbridled ambition and hunger for fame and "honor" seem to deny this. Pike served his nation and the army with every fiber of his being, but he expected to be promoted and well-rewarded for his service and accomplishments. Zebulon Pike was not selfless. As for honor, in writing he used the term "honor" in the sense that it conveys fame and notoriety—rather than "principled uprightness of character." But Pike was a man of integrity, not given to lying or cheating. Perhaps he demonstrated honor in every sense. Of the final "Army Value," personal courage, there can be no doubt. In the historical record there is practically no example of his ever hesitating in the face of danger. Zebulon Pike was forthright, and if he feared anything it was ignominy and failure. But was he bold and courageous to the point of recklessness?

Pike certainly knew the craft and science of soldiering, perhaps as well as any of his contemporaries in the U.S. Army. He had spent years as an enlisted soldier and as an anonymous lieutenant before ever leading his first expedition. When, only seven years later, he was called upon to lead a major assault, he was able to plan and coordinate a complex combined-arms operation that was one of the army's great accomplishments of the war.

On his explorations, Lieutenant Pike was somewhat impetuous and did not learn from his mistakes. Solutions that could have been derived from hard-learned lessons (i.e. securing adequate supplies and clothing, no matter what) were not implemented. But in war, General Pike seemed to have incorporated all that he had learned, leading from the front in an attack that was textbook perfect, until the earth exploded in front of him. As is common in war, he had no second chance in which to implement that hard-learned lesson.

Pike's character, combined with his knowledge, experience and talent, combined to give him excellence and moral virtue—

areté to the ancients. He was not a perfect leader, he was not a perfect man. But he was repeatedly chosen to lead complex and important operations, because he had the drive and determination, the commitment and sense of duty, to get missions accomplished. Zebulon Pike is not a figure of mythic greatness—he was too human and too flawed for that. But he deserves a place in history, and the importance of that place should be determined by the importance of the missions that he accomplished.

John Sweet is a teacher, scholar, and Colorado National Guard officer living in Palmer Lake, Colorado. He has spent nearly thirty years studying and writing about the western fur trade and exploration, the frontier military, and Native American history. His work has appeared in scholarly journals and popular magazines. Mr. Sweet has taught at nearby colleges and currently teaches at the Classical Academy in Colorado Springs. In November 2001 he entered the military and now serves as a field artillery officer. Mark L. Gardner read Mr. Sweet's paper at the Symposium as he had been called to active duty.

Notes

1. *FM 22-100, Army Leadership* (Washington, D.C.: Department of the Army, Aug. 1999), Page 1-Paragraph 4, offers the following definition, "Leadership is influencing people—by providing purpose, direction and motivation—while operating to accomplish the mission and improving the organization."

2. A contemporary, highly readable description of classical ideas on leadership can be found in Christopher D. Kolenda's "What is Leadership, Some Classical Ideas", from *Leadership, The Warrior's Art* (Carlisle, PA: Army War College Foundation Press, 2001), 3-25.

3. Ibid., 5.

4. Ibid.

5. W. Eugene Hollon, *The Lost Pathfinder, Zebulon Montgomery Pike* (Norman: University of Oklahoma, 1949), 7-8. For basic biographical information on Pike I have relied on Hollon's classic work, supplemented by Harvey L. Carter's *Zebulon Montgomery Pike, Pathfinder and Patriot* (Colorado Springs: Dentan Printing Co., 1956).

6. Hollon, *Lost Pathfinder*, 19-20; Carter, 4-5.

7. Kolenda, "What is Leadership," 4.

8. *FM 22-100*, 2-2 to 2-22.

9. *FM 22-100*, 2-24 to 2-28.

10. Hollon, *Lost Pathfinder*, 52.

11. Donald Jackson, ed., *The Journals of Zebulon Montgomery Pike* Vol. I (Norman: University of Oklahoma Press, 1966), 6. I have utilized Jackson's collection of Pike-related primary documents almost exclusively, as it is thoroughly annotated and remains the premier collection to date.

12. Jackson, *Journals*, 48.

13. Ibid.

14. Wilkinson to Pike, July 30, 1805, from Jackson, *Journals*, 3.

15. Wilkinsin to Pike, June 24, 1806, from Jackson, *Journals*, 285-287.

16. Jackson, *Journals*, 378; Hollon, *Lost Pathfinder*, 178.

17. Jackson, *Journals*, 378-379.

18. Hollon hints that there may have been more to the orders and the mission than meets the historian's eye, suggesting that Pike wanted to be discovered and taken into Santa Fe by Spanish authorities, for "there he could obtain information that General Wilkinson greatly desired." Hollon, *Lost Pathfinder*, 136-138; Dr. Harvey Carter speculates that Pike, still thinking himself in U.S. territory, although frozen and starving, wanted to solicit Spanish help for his shattered command. Carter, *Pathfinder and Patriot*, 17.

19. Jackson, *Journals*, Vol 1, 39.

20. Ibid.

21. Stephen Ambrose, *Undaunted Courage* (New York: Simon & Schuster, 1996), 147-150; 181-182; 192. Ambrose makes use of Donald Jackson's *Jefferson and the Stony Mountains, Exploring the West from Monticello* (Urbana: University of Illinois Press, 1978.) It should be kept in mind that Lewis and Clark conducted hasty, but formal, court martial proceedings prior to administering punishment. It is unclear from the journals whether Pike did so or not.

22. Jackson, *Journals*, 371-372. Entry for Sat., Jan. 24, 1807.

23. Ibid., 372.

24. Hollon, *Lost Pathfinder*, 176.

25. Kolenda, "What is Leadership," 7-8.

26. Jackson, *Journals*, Vol. I, 373.

27. Ibid., 373.

28. Ibid., 50-51.

29. Ibid., 51.

30. Ibid., 53-56.

31. Ibid., 56-57.

32. All of the above quotes are from Jackson, *Journals*, 58-59.
33. Ibid., 59-60.
34. Ibid., 369-370.
35. Ibid., 370.
36. Ibid., 381.
37. Ibid., 381-382.
38. Ibid., 381.
39. Hollon, *Lost Pathfinder*, 139-157; Carter, *Pathfinder and Patriot*, 20-24. All except one of Pike's soldiers made it home to the United States. Private Theodore Miller was stabbed to death by Sergeant William Meek while in Spanish custody at Carrizal, Mexico. Meek was apparently held by the Spanish until 1820, when he returned to the U.S. Transcripts of his Spanish court martial proceedings are in Jackson, *Journals*, Vol. II, 209-223.
40. Hollon, *Lost Pathfinder*, 200.
41. Ibid., 202.
42. Ibid., 210. For general history on the Lake Ontario campaign of 1813, I have used John R. Elting's *Amateurs to Arms!, A Military History of the War of 1812* (Chapel Hill, NC: Algonquin Books of Chapel Hill, 1991). But also highly useful is *The Encyclopedia of the War of 1812* (Santa Barbara, Calif.: ABC-CLIO, 1997) edited by David S. and Jeanne Heidler. The article on "The Battle of York" (pp. 568-569) by Richard V. Barbuto was very informative.
43. Hollon, *Lost Pathfinder*, 212.
44. Ibid., 217.
45. Apparently no definitive, balanced account of the Battle of York has been written, but Charles W. Humphries' "The Capture of York" from *Ontario History* 51 (Winter 1959), 1-24, is one of the most complete. Written from a Canadian perspective, it is nonetheless more balanced than Barlow Cumberland's *The Battle of York* (Toronto: W. Briggs, 1913.) An interesting discussion of sources and historiography is found in Milo Quaife's *The Yankees Capture York* (Detroit: Wayne University Press, 1955.)
46. Myer, Jesse, ed., *The Life and Letters of Dr. William Beaumont* (St. Louis: C.V. Mosby Co., 1912), 44-45.
47. Ibid., Dr. Beaumont, who was present at the battle and treated the wounded wrote in his journal, ". . .they devised the inhuman project of blowing up their magazine (containing 300 bbls. powder) the explosion of which, shocking to mention, has almost totally destroyed our Army." Interestingly, Beaumont never mentions Pike in his journal.
48. Hollon, *Lost Pathfinder*, 213-214.

Aaron Burr, James Wilkinson, Zebulon Pike & the Great Louisiana Conspiracy: A Veteran Prosecutor & Amateur Historian Looks at the Evidence[1]

John M. Hutchins

Introduction: The Great Louisiana "Whodunit"

The Meriwether Lewis and William Clark expedition into the virgin lands of the Northwest is considered a great story to the many historians ensnared in its toils. It also is thought the epitome of high adventure by modern white-water rafters, wannabe mountain men, and hopeful fly fishermen. But the 1804–1806 voyage of Lewis and Clark lacks a couple of essential ingredients to make it really popular literature. It has some grizzly bear hunting, some near-starvation, and a bit of Indian fighting. But it lacks a central core of espionage, secret codes, skullduggery, and betrayal. Thus, although the circumstances surrounding the 1809 death of Meriwether Lewis has provided a few conspiracy-theorist historians with a convoluted tale of murder, the trek to the Pacific, chronicled by so many participants, appears to be one of the most open narratives in American history.

Ironically, it is that poor second cousin to the Lewis and Clark voyage, the Southwestern travels of Lieutenant Zebulon Montgomery Pike, that provides true grist for the conspiracy theory mill. Pike's expedition, unlike that of Captains Lewis and Clark, may not invite being studied to death, but well it should. The Arkansas and Red River expedition of 1806–1807 provides, if not so much drama, an element of mystery which will not, and probably can not, go away.

This difference is accounted for by the simple facts that Lewis and Clark were sent on their way by President Thomas Jefferson, were openly funded by Congress, and were largely successful in their endeavors. Pike, on the other hand, was ordered into a contested region by one man, of questionable character, largely accountable to no one, and Pike was only marginally successful.

The latter situation has caused many to ask, with reason, what were the real goals of Pike's expedition and, perhaps more importantly, what did Pike know and when did he know it?

But even questions are difficult to formulate when it comes to Pike's mission. Like a mystery board game, we may speculate on the cards dealt out and announce, for example, that we suspect Aaron Burr, on Blennerhassett Island, with a slightly-used dueling pistol. Or, we can accuse General James Wilkinson, in the Sabine Neutral Ground, with the missing letter to General Nemesio Salcedo. But, unlike the typical such game, we don't even know for sure what the crime was. Was the American Union to be dismembered? Was New Spain to be invaded? Was there treason? Was there espionage? Was there, in fact, murder most foul?

Therefore, if one is a young historian looking to make a name for oneself with a lifelong challenge, if one is a frustrated middle-ager looking for an affair with an unclimbable mountain, if one is slipping slowly into madness and wishes to accelerate the descent, then the Burr Conspiracy is for that person. There is an almost-unlimited amount of evidence, whether direct, circumstantial, material, relevant, obscure, or collateral. And, by the way, the best evidence probably is long gone. Or, tantalizingly, the best evidence may yet be awaiting discovery, perhaps in the form of a misfiled letter deep in the mildewy vaults of Castro's Cuba. In any event, this rocky field of scholarship lies out there for historians to plow at their risk.

Yet this modern treasure hunt is complicated further by the essential principle that there is a difference between sufficient evidence in a legal sense and sufficient proof in an academic sense. In a way, the burden of proof beyond a reasonable doubt in the criminal arena is less demanding than the burden required to satisfy historical certainty. This dichotomy is amply demonstrated by the seemingly inexhaustible number of tireless Burke-and-Hare historians who wish to dig up the dead, literally and figuratively, and undo controversial convictions or cultural judgments suffered by a wide-ranging list of victims and villains.

Thus, any search will not be easy. The logical place to start, perhaps, is to round up the usual suspects. But, when these cards are dealt, there may be a joker or two.

Game Piece Number 1: President Jefferson

As far-fetched as it is to our modern ideals and imbedded trust in our institutions, the first suspect is none other than the third president of the United States, Thomas Jefferson. This brilliant man was full of contradictions and, while the champion of the small farmer, was himself no mere country bumpkin. He could play the violin, but he also was capable of playing hardball politics and deadly diplomatic games. Indeed, during our nation's early problems with the cutthroats of Tripoli, when the Articles of Confederation provided the rules in play, Jefferson advocated smashing the pirates with broadsides, while John Adams preferred buying them off.[2] Also, Jefferson was quite capable of demonstrating a belief that the end justified the means, both in elections and in running the government.

As for defending his recent purchase of Louisiana, during the spring of 1806 when relations with Spain looked gloomy, President Jefferson drew up a contingency plan whereby Britain would be approached to help to defend the new land of the Louisiana Purchase against Spanish and French threats. In exchange, the United States would join the war against Napoleon, since France would be supporting the Spanish position.[3]

But these contingency plans by the head of state are a legitimate function of government planning. Jefferson did not actually ask Congress to declare war, and he obviously did not wish for the Union to come apart. Jefferson was no plaster saint. At least one historian claimed the president wanted Meriwether Lewis dead. Still, even though Jefferson's attacks on Burr were evidence of blindly obsessive and vindictive behavior and his continuing public support for his equivalent to a chairman of the joint chiefs of staff was reckless negligence, this president fails as a knowing conspirator when it comes to a plan like the supposed "Great Louisiana Conspiracy."

Game Piece Number 2: Colonel Burr

Our second suspect is, naturally, the man with whom the Louisiana Conspiracy forever is associated: Aaron Burr. Nonetheless, if Zebulon Pike is known primarily for being the namesake of a mountain he could not climb, then Aaron Burr is remembered, not for his being put on trial for his life, but for killing Alexander Hamilton in a duel in 1804.

When Burr was arrested, he was charged with both treason and with a misdemeanor. The treason alleged Burr hoped to detach the western part of the United States and form an independent empire. According to William Eaton, a soldier of fortune and one of the chief witnesses against him, Burr had "a project of revolutionizing the western country, separating it from the Union, establishing a monarchy there, of which he was to be the sovereign, New Orleans to be his capital; organizing a force on the Mississippi, and extending conquest to Mexico."[4]

Indeed, Burr can be condemned with his own words, which, like so much of the evidence in this case, were discovered a hundred years too late. In August 1804, Burr contacted the British ambassador Anthony Merry and, according to Merry, offered "to lend his assistance to his Majesty's government in any manner in which they may think fit to employ him, particularly in endeavoring to effect a separation of the western part of the United States from that which lies between the Atlantic and the mountains, in its whole extent."[5]

But the question remains whether Burr was merely talking wildly in his inchoate scheming, or was he serious? As William Clark wrote when he heard in January 1807 of the report by Eaton of the "most desperate and violent" plot, it made Burr seem to be "little short of a second Bonaparte." On the other hand, Clark also noted that the story "was of such a violent nature that it is scarcely credible that a man in his proper senses could be possessed of such mistaken . . . idea of the disposition of the American people."[6]

As for the misdemeanor charge, this count accused Burr of "preparing the means of a military expedition against Mexico, a territory of the King of Spain, with whom the United States were at peace."[7] Thus, this charged Burr with a violation of a neutrality statute passed during the presidency of George Washington.

Although a violation of this act was a misdemeanor, there were many at the time who viewed such interference in international relations as putting the American Union itself in jeopardy through treason. As the federalist attorney general of Massachusetts, James Sullivan, said in Boston in early 1807, in referring to the accusations against Burr, a plot to engage the "country in foreign wars, in order to benefit a few great men who would become the leaders," would result in war and "the parched earth of my country drenched with the blood of my fellow men." Those who fomented such activity, Sullivan indicated, were neither "friends to the peace of [our] country," nor "lovers of [our] country."[8]

Thus, according to this thinking, those, like Burr, who would disturb the peace of the nation and hazard a war with a foreign power, were, at least in the traditional and British sense, committing a form of treason. While a national leader like Jefferson legitimately could contemplate such a policy, a private citizen could not.

Burr was not tried for both treason and the misdemeanor in the same proceeding. The treason trial proceeded first and the venue was in republican Virginia, which probably turned out to be a tactical error. Americans knew of celebrated English treason trials, and Virginians in particular would be familiar with the treason trial of Sir Walter Raleigh. Not only had Raleigh been held accountable for mere words (many of them not his own) but his trial "throughout was conducted in a manner which would now seem utterly unjust."[9]

In any event, when Chief Justice John Marshall got hold of the case, he greatly restricted the traditional view of what constituted treasonous behavior. For him—and he was aided by both the constitutional definition and by the limiting words of the indictment—treason could be no less than actively levying war against the United States at the particular location singled out in the indictment. If Burr had not actually done that, he was no traitor. Inchoate planning, even if it involved directing others at a distance, was not enough. Because Burr was not placed at the location of the active levying of war, the jury was obligated to acquit, which it reluctantly did.

As for the misdemeanor, organizing an expedition against Spain, the prosecution was hampered by a lack of available witnesses. The jury had to acquit on this charge, as well.[10] In any event, since there had recently almost been a war with Spain, finding a jury to convict anyone of filibustering (unauthorized warfare) would have been problematic. There was, after all, only a very fine emotional line between organizing volunteers to serve the United States in fighting Spanish forces and outfitting filibusters to invade Spanish colonial possessions. In a related case that same year, a jury acquitted two associates of Burr named Colonel Lewis Kerr and James Workman, who also were charged with enlisting men to invade Spanish Mexico.[11]

But this was not the end of the legal problems for Burr. Prosecutors wanted to bring charges against Burr in the western federal districts of Ohio, Kentucky, or Mississippi, so there was still another hearing before Marshall. What is important about this commitment proceeding is the fact that Marshall allowed lots of testimony and evidence, questionable or not, into the hearing.[12] However, further prosecutions of Burr did not occur, despite the wrath of Thomas Jefferson.

Game Piece Number 3: General Wilkinson

Our third suspect must be General James Wilkinson, the man everyone loves to hate. As head of the small U.S. Army, Wilkinson was the premier accuser of Burr. He also was considered, at the least, as Burr's personal Judas.

Wilkinson had been a young soldier in the American War of Independence. His claims to fame during that conflict included being slippery enough to elude capture in 1776 when General Charles Lee was taken by British dragoons, and being involved in the Conway Cabal against Washington. Also, early in the war, Wilkinson had met Aaron Burr and they remained close. Later, Vice President Burr would be instrumental in getting Wilkinson appointed to the governorship of Louisiana Territory.[13]

At about the time Pike and his men left on their southwestern expedition, rumors were rampant about what was going on, and Wilkinson was considered every bit as much a player as Burr. An Ohio paper, dated July 19, 1806, opined:

> We ... look on Wilkinson but as another Julius Caesar. ... Wilkinson and Burr we have very good reason to believe understand each other and are the two men most to be dreaded in the union. The former is an accomplished sycophant, with considerable military and political talents, and an early address to all men of whatever persuasion, religious or political—in the company of ladies and gentlemen he is a finished courtier, and when with blackguards, he knows not his match as a complete blackguard. ... Wilkinson never stop[s] at any means by which a favorite purpose can be effected.[14]

Many modern historians have continued to have this belief in a Burr–Wilkinson plot and some have seen the Arkansas expedition as a part of the overall scheme. Wilkinson himself supposedly indicated that Pike's mission was of a "secret nature."[15] In 1959, an American Heritage team comprised of Alvin Josephy, Peter Lyon, and Francis Russell wrote,

> Probably without Pike's knowledge, General Wilkinson ... had become involved in a variety of schemes for personal enrichment and glory. He was dabbling privately in the Missouri River fur trade, planning to send secret agents to the Northwest to trade with the Indians and gather geographic knowledge for his own use, and had joined a conspiracy with Aaron Burr to erect an independent empire in the Southwest. To secure information about that part of the continent, he ordered Zebulon Pike [on his] expedition. Pike's written orders were to explore the headwaters of the Red and Arkansas Rivers. ... In secret instructions Wilkinson apparently also directed Pike to get himself arrested by the Spanish and taken to Santa Fe so that he could spy on that city.[16]

Obviously, all of the expeditions sent out by General Wilkinson, including the one to the Southwest, appeared to benefit the United States and provided Wilkinson with *prima facie* situations of plausible deniability. Not only did these voyages have instructions to explore or reconnoiter on behalf of the republic, but, as General Wilkinson pointed out in an 1805 letter to the secretary of war, "They serve to instruct our young officers and also our soldiery, on subjects which may hereafter become interesting to the United States."[17]

However, like many modern politicians, Wilkinson had no qualms about furthering his personal ambitions and increasing his private fortune while in public service. For example, it certainly was no accident that Wilkinson's instructions to Pike also included directions to look for interesting minerals. Wilkinson knew of the views of Baron Alexander von Humboldt, who travelled through New Spain in 1802–1803. Humboldt had noted that prior geographers had spoken of New Mexico "as a country rich in mines, and of vast extent."[18] Humboldt disagreed with the "rumor up and down Europe of the immensity of the Mexican wealth," and with the "very exaggerated ideas relative to the abundance of gold and silver employed in New Spain in plate, furniture, kitchen utensils, and harness."[19] However, even he noted that one would be astonished at seeing in Santa Fe, "people of the lowest order barefooted with enormous silver spurs on, or at finding silver cups and plates a little more common there than in France and England."[20]

Not only would the vague promise of such mineral wealth interest the venality of Wilkinson, it also would serve the goals of the Burr conspiracy. According to General William Eaton, Burr would gain "volunteers to his standard from all quarters of the union," since there was "the vast extent of territory of the United States, west of the Allegheny mountains, which offered to adventurers with a view on the mines of Mexico."[21]

But these best-laid plans of Burr and Wilkinson, whatever they were, went astray, and there was a falling out of these two scoundrels. William Eaton believed that it was his accusations regarding the conspiracy that caused Wilkinson to suddenly switch sides. "It was not until my public exposure had alarmed General Wilkinson in his camp," wrote Eaton, "that he, though more than two years acquainted with the treasonable plot, thought of *betraying* his *fellow traitor*, and *becoming a patriot* by *turning states evidence*."[22] Eaton, according to a friend, Charles Prentiss, "firmly believed that Wilkinson was equally guilty with Burr."[23]

While observers at the time, and some historians since, have discredited witnesses like Eaton, there is much to support the allegations regarding Wilkinson's criminality in delaying sounding the alarm. The same Richmond grand jury which indicted Burr narrowly failed having the votes to indict Wilkinson for misprision of treason.[24] And, during Burr's trial in Richmond, Justice Marshall was well aware that Wilkinson's failure to expose the plot to light in a timely manner could subject the general to accusations of misprision of treason.[25]

Because of Wilkinson being the center of cross-examination by the defense, Pike's name actually came up during the proceedings against Burr. Timothy Kibby, whom Wilkinson had solicited to join an expedition against Mexico, executed an affidavit stating that Wilkinson had told him that Pike and his men carried documents that would make them "as safe at Santa Fe as at Philadelphia."[26] When Wilkinson testified at the commitment hearing after Burr's two acquittals, the general was cross-examined by Burr's lawyers about the instructions he gave Lieutenant Pike and about the conversation with Kibby. According to Harman Blennerhassett, who was accused of hosting recruitment for Burr's frontier army, "Nothing could be got out of him as to the former, and as to any dealing with Kibby . . . he would no more confess it," than he would admit to being in the Conway Cabal against Washington. Wilkinson "produced two copies of alleged instructions to Pike. These papers, being of his own manufacture, left his adversaries, of course to content themselves with whatever effect the suspicions arising from their questions might produce."[27]

While it would be many years before access to Spanish archives would damn Wilkinson conclusively as a payee of a foreign—and not particularly friendly—government, there certainly were rumors and accusations of this status at the time. Colonel Thomas Butler, who was court-martialled by Wilkinson in 1803, claimed to his friends that the real reason which caused Wilkinson to turn against him with such vitriol was because Butler had vigorously expressed himself as believing the rumors that the commanding general was a spy in the pay of the Spanish.[28] The U.S. district attorney of Kentucky, a federalist subordinate who was smarter than his republican president, wrote Jefferson in early 1806 about his concerns of a Spanish plot. Of General Wilkinson, this lawyer warned, "I am convinced [that he] has been for years, and now is, a pensioner of Spain."[29] Daniel Clark, who had long been familiar with Wilkinson's business affairs, knew (and told Congress) that the general had "for years been the pensioner of a foreign power," and that the payments were made "for the dismemberment and ruin of his country."[30] Burr himself claimed in 1807 that his chief accuser was "a man notoriously the pensioner of a foreign government."[31]

If the evidence of Wilkinson's secret Spanish salary, as well as knowledge of his activities on behalf of Spain (including notifying the Spaniards of Lewis and Clark and suggesting that they be stopped) had been known positively, it is likely that even Justice Marshall would have had no inclination to water down charges of treason against such a person in a position of trust. Presumably, many of Wilkinson's actions regarding troop movements along the Spanish border in Louisiana could be viewed as overt acts in levying war against his country. At the least, Wilkinson would have been guilty of the very things that Sir Walter Raleigh unjustly stood accused of by the prosecuting Lord Edward Coke: "Thou hast a Spanish heart, and thyself art a spider of hell."[32]

While many historians today think Burr was guilty of some sort of murky treason, with Wilkinson the facts seem clearer and the vote is virtually unanimous. Almost without exception, historians concede that Wilkinson was a guilty man who escaped merited punishment. There simply does not seem to be much doubt about his criminal and reprehensible conduct, especially after his correspondence with his Spanish masters came to light.

If nothing else, Wilkinson, instead of surviving two courts-martial held after the Burr trial, should have been convicted in such a military tribunal. Article 57 of the Articles of War prohibited corresponding "with the enemy, or giving intelligence, directly or indirectly," and "death or other punishment" was authorized. Even if Spain was not a declared enemy, Article 101 contained no language subject to lawyer-like argument. It stated merely, "Spies shall suffer death." Finally, there was that catch-all for the commissioned officer, Article 83, conduct which was "unbecoming an officer and gentlemen."[33] Certainly, in better military circles, Wilkinson deserved dismissal, if not worse, under that provision alone.

Game Piece Number 4: William Duane

But if Wilkinson would be the favorite suspect of every guest at a mystery weekend at a bed and breakfast, there is another playing piece that would be unknown to most of the participants. This is the piece representing William Duane.

William Duane was born in upstate New York in 1760, his father thereafter being killed by Indians about the time of the Pontiac Conspiracy. His mother, a Catholic, took him to Ireland to be educated. At nineteen, Duane was cut off from his family for insisting on marrying a Protestant, and the young man became a printer to support himself. He stood aloof from the war in his homeland and emigrated to India in 1784, where he started a newspaper and became very successful.[34]

However, Duane was on the road to becoming radicalized. While in India, in supporting the demands of troops against the local government, he was arrested and deported to England, losing his fortune in the process. After more successful newspaper publishing in Britain, he returned to the new United States in 1795. He joined the *Aurora*, a newspaper notorious for its anti-administration stance and an organ largely responsible for the election of Jefferson in 1800. He was rewarded with several military appointments under the republican administrations of Jefferson and James Madison.[35]

However, before John Adams was tossed out of office, Duane had the dubious honor of being arrested under the Alien and Sedition Acts. He also was subjected to various other legal prosecutions for his anti-federalist journalistic endeavors.[36]

As a journalist and as a person, Duane would turn on anyone who betrayed whatever or whomever Duane believed in and he pulled no punches in attacking. For example, when James Callender, who had been paid by Jefferson to write scurrilous things about President Adams for the 1800 election, flipped sides and began writing similar material about the man from Monticello, Duane showed no mercy. Duane wrote in the *Aurora* that Callender had given his wife venereal disease and then let her die alone while he had "his usual pint of brandy at breakfast."[37]

Although he might have had reckless opinions, Duane believed in the primacy of historical truth, writing, at the time of Pike's expedition, that "an oath is a solemnity that should be warily entered into and when it is used to establish the belief of facts which never took place, it is perjury and an abominable crime."[38] Obviously, the federalists did not think well of Duane or of his integrity. After the bitter election of 1800, John Adams included him among the "group of foreign liars" who helped Jefferson and his republicans win.[39]

Thus, in character and personality, Duane was almost the opposite of the suave and urbane General Wilkinson. Duane would speak his mind regardless of the consequences. Subtle and underhanded double-dealing was not his forte. During the preparations for the Burr treason trial, Duane went to Harman Blennerhassett, a fellow Irish-American, and used dire threats to try to get Blennerhassett to turn state's evidence.[40]

Like Jefferson, William Duane does not seem like a viable suspect, or even player, in this convoluted mystery. However, before deciding, one had better wait until the last scene of this somewhat meandering production.

Game Piece Number 5: Doctor Robinson

While he was not so blessed when he went on his earlier expedition to the upper reaches of the Mississippi, Pike had a trained physician along with him on his march to the Rocky Mountains, John Hamilton Robinson. Although army surgeons were not considered line officers, medical doctors were professional men and "gentlemen who, by their education and studies, are supposed to possess many qualifications for investigating nature, beside their importance in case of diseases or bodily injuries."[41]

Robinson is another enigma related to Pike's venture. Wilkinson had specifically appointed Robinson right before the trip began, instructing Pike, "Doctor Robinson will accompany you as a volunteer. He will be furnished medicines, and for accommodation which you give him he is bound to attend your sick."[42] Robinson also claimed that he was the attorney-in-fact for one William Morrison of Kaskaskia, Illinois, who was owed money by Baptista Lalande, who had become a resident of Santa Fe.[43]

Robinson was a Virginian and three years younger than Pike. After his medical training, Robinson moved in 1804 to St. Louis and married the sister-in-law of Dr. Antoine Saugrain, a gentleman who had been the recipient of a large Spanish land grant in 1800. Saugrain also had been a doctor in the service of the Spanish military hospital at St. Louis prior to the Louisiana Purchase and apparently was close to Lieutenant-Governor Don Carlos DeLassus, the official who reluctantly handed St. Louis over to the Americans in early 1804.[44] It has been presumed that Saugrain introduced Robinson to Wilkinson when the expedition to the Southwest was being organized.[45]

Robinson, during the entire voyage, was a companion to Pike and an able member of the expedition. However, in the dead of winter, he separated from Pike and headed to Santa Fe, supposedly to collect the debt due Morrison. Pike, in his journal, admitted that these "pecuniary demands" were "in some degree spurious." Once Robinson was picked up by the Spanish, he claimed he was a French doctor who had separated from a party of hunters.[46] Robinson also later confidentially told the Spanish that he desired "to become a vassal of His Catholic Majesty" and to explore to the northern regions for Spain, in opposition to American and British claims.[47]

The Robinson scenario could have seemed familiar to some. A year before Robinson set off with Pike, General Wilkinson had asked Secretary of War Henry Dearborn that Wilkinson be given discretion to determine who could enter Louisiana for trading with the Indians. Otherwise, Wilkinson opined, the government could not control "the sinister projects of sordid loose individuals" or "the political enterprises of foreign powers." Specifically, Wilkinson warned that, a Spaniard interested to convey direct information from the seat of our Government over land to Mexico — he has but to employ an agent clothed with American citizenship, to send him either to purchase a few goods, claim a license, ship up the Missouri into the Osage, the Kansas or Platte Rivers, and from thence take an Indian guide and traverse the country to Santa Fe.[48]

Was it therefore a coincidence that Robinson, recruited by Wilkinson, tramped off by himself towards Santa Fe? One historian, Thomas Abernethy, has asserted that, while Pike himself was in ignorance about the true nature of his expedition, Robinson was not. Professor Abernethy concluded that "it was certainly he to whom Wilkinson confided his secret instructions."[49]

As noted, General Wilkinson supposedly said to Timothy Kibby that Pike and his party had documents with them that would provide them absolute safety. Just what these documents were — whether Pike's published orders or something else — has never been answered satisfactorily. Curiously, six years later, when Robinson returned to Chihuahua as an envoy of Secretary of State James Monroe to speak with Governor Salcedo, Salcedo asked if Robinson had the customary letter to deliver from his president. Robinson somewhat arrogantly answered that he had no letter, "for he himself was the letter."[50]

Robinson's later years were just as murky. During the War of 1812, he would become involved with filibustering in Texas, supporting the efforts of José Alvarez de Toledo against the Spanish. But, before Robinson could join Toledo, the Tejano patriots, assisted by American volunteers, were slaughtered at the Battle of the Medina on August 18, 1813, or cut down as they fled to the refuge of Louisiana. Although most of the dead were never identified, it was reported at the time that a son of General Wilkinson was one of the volunteers on Toledo's staff and was one of those killed.[51] James B. Wilkinson, who had been with Pike and was promoted to captain in 1808, is listed in U.S. Army records as having died on September 7, 1813.[52] Presumably, this was the Wilkinson with Toledo who was mortally wounded as a filibuster.[53] This final, curious relationship between Wilkinson

HUTCHINS • 153

and Robinson in another Mexican scheme, fatal to General Wilkinson's explorer son, seems to prove that Robinson was, at least, a filibuster at heart.

Game Piece Number 6: Lieutenant Pike

Zebulon M. Pike seemingly needs no defenders when it comes to the Burr Conspiracy. Milo Quaife, a noted historian of American exploration, wrote,

> Pike himself . . . plainly and emphatically denied that he had received any instructions from Wilkinson, either verbal or written, associating his enterprise in any way with the activities of Burr. Having in view of Pike's character and integrity, this seems to me conclusive.[54]

Indeed, anyone questioning this fervent doctrine runs the risk of being pelted with verbal abuse, if not San Luis Valley tomatoes. One Colorado defender has relegated Pike's critics to the ranks of eastern dudes. The criticism of Pike, wrote Professor Archer Hulbert,

> is due to the fact that—as usual—our journals and documents on western travel have been edited by Atlantic Americans—or at least by those so ignorant of western lore and plainsmanship that judgment gives way to an inaccuracy that mitigates against a clear understanding and smacks of everything but scholarship.[55]

But, perhaps, there are none so blind as those who will not see. Circumstantially, a player of the Burr mystery game would have no difficulty filling out the checklist of suspicions when it came to Zebulon Montgomery Pike. As a practical matter, if General Wilkinson had been caught red-handed in his spying and double-dealing, there is no way that his lieutenant would not have been targeted as a potential co-conspirator. Pike, who had not even known that he was about to be promoted to captain when he set off to the Southwest, later expressed a bitterness that would have supplied a motive for betraying his trust. "Colonel Butler's vacancy should have given me a captaincy nearly a year sooner than I obtained it," he wrote to his father. "Many others have similar causes of complaint," he continued, "and should my country attempt to do us such injustice, may my right arm [wither] from my body if I would ever again extend it to save her from ruin and slavery."[56] These are words reminiscent of those uttered by the character Philip Nolan in the short story by Edward Everett Hale, *The Man Without a Country*. Thus, even if he were a naive innocent, Pike almost certainly would have been disbelieved and held accountable for his presumed active participation in Wilkinson's plotting.

First of all, while historians marvel at Pike's continued loyalty to General Wilkinson, they overlook the fact that Pike was the general's protégé. Pike, like many a young officer in modern times, "hitched his wagon to a star." General Wilkinson, in turn, had selected Pike personally to carry out the general's orders in the Southwest. Especially with a man of Wilkinson's lack of scruples, this choice alone has some significance.[57] As Judge John Lucas wrote from St. Louis in 1805 regarding an officer who had run afoul of Wilkinson, "An officer who is faithful to his duties and respects the laws of his country . . . is not a man that will suit Mr. Wilkinson."[58] Similarly, an Ohio newspaper, just before Pike left on his Southwest expedition, concluded, "Wilkinson has the American army, few as they are, devoted to him. . . . He has by one means or other, ground down to ciphers every officer in the army, who would not pay court to him . . . and there is scarcely now one soldier but is devoted to him."[59]

Second, it is not hard to imagine that Pike's southwestern venture strategically was aimed at Burr's ambitions every bit as much as it supported ostensible goals of the United States. Whether Pike's mission was projected to ignite a war, to open communications with dissident New Mexicans, or to distract the Spanish by misdirection, it would not be illogical to assume it was part of a greater conspiracy. According to the testimony of General Eaton, a man who proved in Tripoli what a small force of adventurers under a committed officer could do, Burr was quite adamant in his belief "that the influence of General Wilkinson, with his army, the promise of double pay and rations, the ambition of his officers, and the prospect of plunder and military achievements, would bring the army generally into the measure."[60] Indeed, in the Richmond courtroom, Eaton bristled at Burr's personal cross-examination of him and, undoubtedly glaring at Burr, fairly shouted, "You spoke of *your* riflemen, *your* infantry, *your* cavalry. It was with the same view, you mentioned to me that that man [pointing to General Wilkinson, just behind him] was to have been the first to aid you."[61]

Aaron Burr, according to General Eaton, had "agents [who] were in the western country" ready to strike.[62] Was Zebulon M. Pike one of those minions? Eaton also testified "that the army and the commander in chief were ready to act at [Burr's] signal."[63] Was Pike included in that number? Those are the million-dollar questions.

But mere association is not enough to convict someone of being in a conspiracy. The evidence against Pike would have to be more than coincidental or circumstantial. The evidence would have to prove that Pike knowingly joined the conspiracy, accepted its goals, or participated in its concealment. Did Pike do anything which could be seen as overt acts in aiding the carrying out or concealment of any criminal designs on the part of Wilkinson? He certainly did, when one examines the personnel who accompanied the voyage.

Other Game Tokens: A Tale of Two Sergeants

Lieutenant Pike had twenty fellow members of the U.S. Army who accompanied him on his expedition west. Many of them had been with Pike on his earlier journey up the Mississippi. One of these men was Henry Kennerman, who had been considered, by Pike, during the expedition of 1805–1806, "one of the stoutest men" he had ever known. But Corporal William Meek had reported misconduct on Kennerman's part, and Pike had broken Kennerman down to private. When Pike's second expedition passed through Missouri on its way west, Private Kennerman disappeared and the lieutenant reported him as a deserter. Unlike Elvis, Kennerman has not been seen since.

But if good men were hard to find in 1806, sergeants were not. One of Pike's new men on the second expedition was Joseph Ballinger, who previously had served Wilkinson in his contacts with Spanish authorities, which included the delivery of two mule-loads of Spanish silver.[64] Ballinger, in fact, had done business dealings for Wilkinson way back in 1789, at the same time that a young adventurer named Philip Nolan had been involved in similar projects involving Wilkinson.[65] Presumably on the instructions of Wilkinson, Pike had recruited civilian Ballinger for a five-year enlistment just before the Southwestern Expedition started and promoted him to sergeant the same day.[66]

Ballinger did not reach the Mexican mountains with Pike. Instead, he accompanied the general's son, Lieutenant James B. Wilkinson, when the lieutenant's small party split off from Pike and headed down the Arkansas. Before they left, Ballinger wrote a rather familiar letter to General Wilkinson and put it in Pike's care. The letter included comments about the general holding Ballinger's pay for him and about Ballinger wanting "to make some money" for the general by trading in horses.[67] As with many presumably offhand comments dealing with these events, the reference to horse trading is curious. The real Philip Nolan, that young and intimate associate of Wilkinson, also presumably known by Ballinger, had been a supposed horse trader in Spanish Texas, where he was killed by Spanish troops in 1801. From the perspective of the Spanish, Nolan's horse trading was a mere pretext, filibustering was his goal, and even the pens he erected, supposedly as corrals, were really small forts.[68]

Further, Pike cannot be said to have been a mere spectator when it came to Ballinger's involvement in the expedition and with Ballinger's later unavailability during the Burr controversy. For, after Pike returned to civilization, he submitted paperwork that claimed that Ballinger had enlisted in 1802 and this entitled Ballinger to a discharge after only about a year of service.[69] Thus, even if Pike could not be accused of having connived in getting Ballinger on the expedition in order to do something illegal, he obviously falsified a document which put Ballinger beyond government process and made him unavailable as a potential witness. Indeed, when Congress started looking into Wilkinson's relationship with Burr in 1808, there was a report that Ballinger, a supposed friend of Burr, had been recruiting Indian allies for Burr during his travels with Pike.[70] However, by this time, civilian Ballinger reportedly was beyond congressional subpoena, having returned to "the Spanish provinces."[71]

If this were the only example of such seemingly obstructive activity on the part of Pike , it would be a weak argument that he was protecting Wilkinson. But it is not the only example. There is the story of a third, and deadlier, sergeant.

On February 26, 1807, when Pike was taken south from his Conejos River stockade, he had with him only six of his remaining fourteen enlisted men. The others, in various stages of misery, had to be collected by the Spanish before they followed in Pike's wake, first to Santa Fe and then to Chihuahua. One of these stragglers was William Meek, now a sergeant. Pike left Meek written instructions that Pike was entrusting his trunk, with his papers, to Meek's safekeeping. If the trunk was opened by the Spanish, Pike instructed Meek to give the Spanish officer in charge "my Letter," whatever letter that was.[72]

During the trip of Pike's men southward as they followed their leader, at the village of Carrizal an extraordinary event occurred that apparently was rediscovered by Colorado Springs historian, Harvey Carter, at the time of the sesquicentennial of Pike's 1806 expedition in 1956. On May 7, 1807, "Sergeant Meek quarreled with Theodore Miller, both men having been drinking brandy, and Meek killed Miller with a saber."[73]

The Spaniards, fortunately in true Spanish style, held an inquisition in Carrizal and took testimony. It was related that Meek and Miller had a "verbal difference" in Santa Fe, and Miller thereafter feared for his life.[74] As for the fatal altercation in Carrizal, it started when Sergeant Meek accused Miller of having stolen some vermillion (vermillion, among other uses, was a very valuable trade good, being used by Indians for paint; however, vermillion, known as cinnabar or mercuric sulfide, also was used for making ink, an obvious requirement to write letters or to take notes). Miller then countered that it was Meek who had stolen the vermillion belonging to Lieutenant Pike. The two soldiers then started fistfighting but were separated by Corporal Jeremiah Jackson.[75] According to Private Patrick Smith, "Meek had calmed down," but he then obtained a saber and charged on Miller, crying, "This is the way American sergeants punish their soldiers!" Miller had no time to say anything other than to gasp three times, "I am dead."[76] As for Meek, he was heard to say, "Well, good."[77]

To the investigating Spanish, Meek first claimed that Miller had become drunk, had disobeyed an order to go to his quarters, and then had assaulted Meek. When confronted with the conflicting testimony of his fellow American soldiers, Meek changed his story. Meek now told the Spanish that, if soldiers offended any officer or sergeant, such miscreants "are deprived of their lives, death being administered by the one offended, and that, using this right which the military law gives him, he proceeded in the punishment of Miller applying to him the penalty of the ordinance." Finally, when this theory of summary judgment was challenged by the circumstances of the first fight, Meek claimed that he got his saber, "not with the intention of killing him but rather of punishing him with it, and to frighten him, not knowing if Miller had with him his knife."[78]

Curiously, even after he dispatched Miller, Meek claimed that "he loved him like a brother." While the two had argued in Santa Fe, according to the sergeant they had reconciled after Miller had apologized, saying that he had been under the influence of brandy.[79] As for the intake of brandy by both Meek and Miller at Carrizal, both Spanish and American witnesses agreed that the two had not consumed enough to make them unconscious of their actions.[80]

There was a followup proceeding in Chihuahua, and more testimony was taken. Sergeant Meek somewhat modified his testimony, still contending that he legally was justified by military law in taking Miller's life.[81] He retracted his first confession, claiming that it was translated inaccurately.[82] In addition, Meek's subordinates now tended to corroborate some of Meek's version of Miller's insubordination and they also now assailed Miller's character and sobriety.[83] Yet this was the same reliable Miller whom Pike said had an "obliging disposition" which "made him agreeable in the woods."[84]

This sad and seemingly inexplicable affair actually amounts to more than just a footnote to the Pike expedition. It did, at the least, affect the contemporary perception of the legitimacy of Pike's mission. An anonymous letter, appearing December 1809 in the *Gazette* newspaper of New Orleans, made a serious accusation about the death of Private Miller. The writer of the letter wrote,

> I have seen a communication in the *Courier*, announcing the return of Captain D. Hughes, with the prisoners left by Major Pike in the Spanish provinces in the year 1807, with the exception of a Sergeant Meek, who was detained for having killed one of the party, who declared the purpose of Major Pike's journey was different from the one announced.[85]

The letter-writer than went on to say,

> Is General Wilkinson and his myrmidons reduced to the alternative of putting to death the witness of their treachery? "Dead men tell no tales" and perhaps the general might have escaped the justice of his country a little longer had he adopted the measures of Sergeant Meek for suppressing evidence.[86]

The *Gazette* was not the only newspaper to discuss the affray. A year before, the New Orleans *Courier* had mentioned it, as noted by the *Gazette*, although it concluded that Meek had "nobly taken the life of one of the party, who attempted by an insinuation to inculpate the motives of the expedition."[87]

Historian Eugene Hollon, who brought the newspaper innuendo of the *Gazette* to light, dismissed the tale as being of "doubtful" veracity.[88] But Hollon wrote his biography of Pike before the story of the killing of Miller by Meek had been resurrected and discussed by Harvey Carter. Subsequent historians have followed Hollon's lead, not examining the accusation or the murder with a critical eye.

Were there no additional evidence other than anonymous newspaper reports, Hollon might have been justified in his dismissive attitude. However, there is long-standing corroborative evidence regarding this newspaper allegation. That evidence was provided by Zebulon M. Pike himself.

On July 5, 1807, Pike wrote a lengthy letter to General Wilkinson from Natchitoches. In this missive, Pike told Wilkinson of his efforts to conceal some of his documents from the Spanish, a subterfuge participated in by his men. Pike said of his men,

> . . . in whose breasts lay the whole secret of my papers, and whom I frequently, when in the Spanish territories, was obliged to punish several for outrages committed when in a state of intoxication, yet never did one offer, or show a disposition to discover it. It is certain they knew *instant death* would follow; but still their fidelity to their trust is remarkable.[89]

Despite this fidelity, Pike also assured the general that he had given his men orders regarding releasing information and would "dispose" of his men "in such a manner as not to put it in their power to give things much publicity."[90]

In the same letter, Pike mentioned Sergeant Meek several times in an oblique manner, noting that "the sergeant killed one of his men, in consequence of some improper conduct, and the general [Salcedo] accuses him of great intractability, as he is pleased to term it."[91] Pike also opined that Salcedo erroneously believed that he could "procure some information" from Meek since the sergeant was detached from his commander.

Then, immediately following the discussion of Sergeant Meek, Pike launched into a discussion that reads like an appeal for emoluments, backed up with an implicit threat. It also includes a request for the general's input as to what should be the publicly stated goals of the recently completed expedition. Pike wrote,

> From the foregoing statement your excellency will observe that I yet possess immense matter, the result of one year's travel, in a country desert and populated, which have *both* been long the subject of curiosity to the philosopher, the anxious desires of the miser, and the waking thoughts and sleeping dreams of the man of *ambition* and the *aspiring* soul, and in our present critical situation, I do conceive, immensely important, and which opens a scene for the *generosity* and *aggrandisement* of our country, with a wide and splendid field for harvests of honor for individuals. But my papers are in

a mutilated state. . . . These circumstances would make it necessary . . . to assort the matter. . . . Also, with respect to the Spanish country, I must know the extent of the objects in view, in order to embrace those points in my reports.[92]

Finally, this extraordinary letter in its final paragraphs dealt with the Burr conspiracy. Pike mentioned the newspapers he had seen while in Spanish custody, in addition to making an assertion that he was not fully informed in what was going on. Pike wrote,

We had heard in the Spanish dominions of the convulsions of the western country, originating in Mr. Burr's plans, and that you were implicated; sometimes that you was arrested, sometimes superceded &c. Those reports (although I never gave credit to them) gave me great unhappiness, as I conceived that the shafts of calumny were aiming at your fame and honor, in a foreign country, where they had hitherto stood high, and were revered and respected by every class. At St. Antonio colonel Cordero informed me of the truth of the statement, which took a load from my breast and made me comparatively happy, and I hope ere long will the villainy be unmasked and malignity and slander hide their heads. . . . A letter addressed to me Cincinnatti, Ohio, may possibly reach me on my route, when I hope to receive the approbation of my conduct. Many letters written to me, addressed to this place, have been secreted or destroyed: possibly the general can give me a hint on the subject.[93]

Pike's letter has been critically eyed before, by historian Jerome Smiley, who noted at length that the correspondence indicated Pike suppressed the true secret of the expedition, promised to tailor his report to fit the then-current situation, and hoped that Wilkinson would not turn against his lieutenant as he had against Burr.[94] But even Smiley did not know the details about the murderous encounter between the sergeant and the private.

Thus, the affair with Sergeant Meek and Private Miller, in context with Pike's letter, provides much in the way of proof that Pike knowingly was involved, to some extent, with what he thought were his general's secret plans. As noted, Pike curiously stated to Wilkinson that his men were subject to "instant death" if they attempted to give away the secrets of the expedition. As Pike well knew, Private Miller certainly was given such a punishment when he committed an act of "improper conduct." Further, this punishment was meted out by Pike's probably most trusted noncommissioned officer. Finally, it is curious that the murder occurred after Miller was accused by his sergeant of having stolen some of the lieutenant's vermillion.

Pike at least admitted to something amounting to concealment after the fact when he indicated that his men would be dispersed and not be able to give publicity regarding the secrets of the expedition. Apparently, with the dearth of other narratives by expedition members, this occurred; certainly it is known that Ballinger was properly disposed of so as not to provide publicity to inquiring minds in Congress. Related to this pattern of cover up, Pike also used language to his superior that could be construed as a type of extortion regarding his being in possession of information that would excite the "ambitious" man and the "aspiring" soul.

The Meek–Miller affair was unmentioned by Pike in his journals. In fact, Pike seemed to show more concern about the survivors of the Philip Nolan expedition than he did for imprisoned Sergeant Meek.[95] It appears that the murder was not investigated by anyone (other than the Spanish) for many years. Nonetheless, contemporary newspapers got wind of it—with the sources being almost certainly some of Pike's returning men—and the information indicated that Miller was killed by Meek to prevent Miller from telling the Spanish what he thought was really going on. Whatever that secret was, neither was it ever shared with Pike's countrymen on his return.

Winners and Losers: Evidence Beyond a Reasonable Doubt

Pike, when he headed west, did not have to be a member of Wilkinson's inner circle in order to be in legal hot water. Even if Pike was not a principal to any traitorous designs involving Burr or Wilkinson, he still could have been legally culpable if he knew vaguely what was going on, which is not improbable. "Misprisions . . . are . . . all such high offences as are under the degree of capital, but nearly bordering thereon."[96] Misprision of treason traditionally "consist[ed] in the bare knowledge and concealment of treason, without any degree of assent thereto."[97] As previously noted, when Wilkinson testified against Burr in Richmond, he and Chief Justice Marshall knew that Wilkinson, when asked about when he first knew of Burr's scheme, ran the risks of admitting guilt regarding misprision of treason. Marshall, while not allowing Wilkinson to refuse to answer based on the Fifth Amendment, did allow Wilkinson to acknowledge just the date he reported his knowledge to the president.

However, misprision of treason was not the only charge which potentially faced Pike. Since Burr was not convicted of treason, it is important to note that there was also misprision of any felony, which "is the concealment of a felony which a man knows, but never assented to."[98] In addition, there was another offence which could be alleged against Pike regarding his relationship with his commanding general. Since General Wilkinson was never convicted of anything (but only because the evidence remained hidden during his lifetime), it is also important to note that Pike's apparent efforts to prevent his men from giving "publicity" during the pendency of the Burr trial likely were criminal. For "to endeavour to dissuade a witness from giving evidence . . . [is among] high misprisions . . . and punishable by fine and imprisonment."[99]

Finally, Pike, like Wilkinson, did not potentially just face the wrath of civilian courts. Pike also was subject to the same military law as Wilkinson. With the evidence which could be arrayed against him, circumstantial and otherwise, it would be extremely optimistic to presume that Pike would not have been convicted at least of Article 83, conduct unbecoming an officer and a gentleman. An unsympathetic court of officers could conclude a violation of that article from the mere admission that Pike lied to Governor Allencaster about Doctor Robinson, especially if Pike could not establish that he was doing so for the good of the nation. As for Pike granting Sergeant Ballinger's fraudulent discharge, honest men have been ensnared for less.

All of this is not to say definitely that Pike was guilty of treason or other heinous crimes beyond misprision, including serious military offenses, only that the evidence was there to support such reasonable judgments. Actual guilt here would hinge on Pike's personal culpability, dependent on his knowledge and intent. But it is clear that, if General Wilkinson's active spying on behalf of Spain had been discovered a century earlier than it was, then there also was more than sufficient evidence to convict Pike along with his superior. It would strain credulity to expect a reasonable jury or court-martial to believe in Pike's innocence.

But, with the facts as they played out, Pike should not have been brought to the bar even if he had been guilty of serious misconduct. Since neither Burr nor Wilkinson were held accountable for their criminal actions, it would have been a miscarriage of justice for Pike, the underling, to have been convicted of anything. He would have been as the hapless Lieutenant Philip Nolan in Hale's *The Man Without a Country*, a virtual scapegoat.

Winners and Losers: A Few Final Words

Realistically, it appears that Pike was playing a game of wits with Wilkinson once Pike, probably initially ignorant of the real purpose of his expedition, discovered that he still knew much more than the general wanted told. This hardly was commendable conduct on the part of Pike. Yet there still is hope for those who believe in the relative purity of Zebulon Montgomery Pike among such a cast of scoundrels. While speculative, it need not be based on an unrealistic and uncritical view that Pike was a naive youngster.

In *Citizen Kane*, the young reporter's editor believes that an examination of a dying man's last words will provide all-important answers about the man and what made him tick. At the end of his frustrated search, the reporter himself thinks that, even if the last thing said was comprehensible, it would only amount to a piece of the puzzle in a complicated life. Perhaps the last words of Zebulon Montgomery Pike, in the manner of those of Charles Foster Kane, can shed some light on the Burr Conspiracy and whether a twenty-something lieutenant ever had any evil designs against his country that amounted to treason. What were those words?

Pike's exact last words, as he lay dying in Canada, are virtually forgotten to history. It is well known that he asked that a friend be notified to look out after someone, undoubtedly his wife Clarissa. But the quaint modesty of the times meant that the contemporary newspaper reports contained a blank for Clarissa's name and identified the friend to whom he entrusted her safekeeping only with the capital letter "D."

"D" was Duane. Apparently, only one work which was written during the lifetimes of Pike's contemporaries contains the unexpunged version of these virtual last words.[100] That Pike was sending his message to the often-notorious William Duane is clear when read in conjunction with the stilted but vague words which appeared in the *Aurora* regarding Pike's death.[101]

Duane and Pike had become friends in the years after the Burr troubles. Duane was fascinated with military science, as was Pike. Duane apparently served closely with Pike when Duane was an assistant adjutant general and Pike was his superior officer.[102]

What is the significance of these last words? Only this: William Duane was not the type of man who would befriend or forgive someone whom he believed had attempted to betray or destroy the republic of Thomas Jefferson. William Duane was many things, but he was neither lukewarm nor a hypocrite. By being one of Pike's most-trusted friends, this hotheaded and worldly man exhibited his trust in Pike. Consequently, it seems clear that Duane was confident that Pike never intended to do his country harm, whether in 1806 or at any other time. On the bloody battlefield of York, Duane, though not present, vouched for Pike's fidelity.

Thus, as an ambitious officer, Pike did try to impress and even to manipulate the master manipulator who was commanding general of the U.S. Army, but it would appear that Pike never was in on the real dark secrets of Wilkinson. Pike spied and lied, but he was out of the loop and he thought it was for his country, even if it was virtual filibustering. Only afterwards did he figure out that the stories about Wilkinson probably were true, but even then he helped in the coverup. Z. M. Pike was an Oliver North. He was no Benedict Arnold.

Therefore, when about to meet his Maker, this mortally wounded patriot did not call out for the still-powerful General Wilkinson. Pike called out for Duane, the rabble-rousing radical who cared deeply about people and causes. Like the name of *Rosebud*, the name of Duane presumably evoked in the dying Pike a sense of the days of youthful crusading and of those snowy times in the Colorado Rockies, when glorious excitement was the honorable goal.

John M. Hutchins, J.D., is a long-time (local, state, federal, and military) prosecuting attorney now in Denver, who has previously served as an elected City Councilman and City Charter Commission Member in Northglenn, Colorado. He served as a captain in the U.S. Army and is a retired major, U.S. Army Reserve. Mr. Hutchins has been a guide at the University of Colorado Museum, a Civil War reenactor, and is a member of the Denver Posse of Westerners. Mr. Hutchins has received historical writing awards from the U.S. Army Historical Center and from the Westerners International. He also is the author of "Captain Pike's Feint Up the Middle and the Spanish-American Cold War of 1805-1808," *The Denver Westerners Roundup*, Vol. LXIII, No. 1 (Jan.-Feb. 2007).

Notes

1. The author relies on *The Chicago Manual of Style* (Chicago: University of Chicago Press, 2003) [15th Edition] in this paper. Therefore, such items as spelling, capitalization, and punctuation in contemporary quotations mostly have been modernized or otherwise made to conform to the recommended style. The views, opinions, and speculations herein expressed are those of the author.
2. Gardner W. Allen, *Our Navy and the Barbary Corsairs* (Boston and New York: Houghton Mifflin Company, 1905), 35-36.
3. Dan L. Flores, ed., *Jefferson & Southwestern Exploration: The Freeman & Custis Accounts of the Red River Expedition of 1806* (Norman: University of Oklahoma Press, 1984), 89.
4. Ebenezer Merriam, ed., *The Life of the Late Gen. William Eaton . . . Principally Collected From His Correspondence and Other Manuscripts* (Brookfield, Mass.: E. Merriam & Co., 1813), 397.
5. Nathan Schachner, *Aaron Burr* (New York: A. S. Barnes & Company, Inc., 1961), 285-286.
6. James J. Holmberg, ed., *Dear Brother: Letters of William Clark to Jonathan Clark* (New Haven: Yale University Press, 2002), 119.
7. The most complete transcript of the proceedings is found in David Robertson, *Reports of the Trials of Colonel Aaron Burr, (Late Vice President of the United States,) for Treason and for a Misdemeanor, In Preparing the Means of a Military Expedition Against Mexico, a Territory of the King of Spain, With Whom the United States Were at Peace*, 2 vols. (Philadelphia: Hopkins & Earle, 1808).
8. T. Lloyd and Geo. Caines, *Trial of Thomas O. Selfridge, Attorney*

at Law, Before the Hon. Isaac Parker, Esquire; for Killing Charles Austin, on the Public Exchange, in Boston, August 4, 1806 (Boston: Russell and Cutler, Belcher and Armstrong, and Oliver and Munroe, 1807), 136.

9. Louise Creighton, *Life of Sir Walter Ralegh* (London: Rivingtons, 1877), 165.

10. Matthew L. Davis, *Memoirs of Aaron Burr*, 2 vols. (New York: Harper & Brothers, 1837), 2:385.

11. See *United States v. Workman, et al.*, 28 Fed. Cases 771 (D. Terr. Orleans 1807).

12. Schachner, *Aaron Burr*, 441-443.

13. Ibid., 291, 294.

14. *New Hampshire Sentinel*, "Domestic," August 23, 1806, 2-3.

15. James Ripley Jacobs, *Tarnished Warrior: Major-General James Wilkinson* (New York: The Macmillan Company, 1938), 224-225.

16. Alvin M. Josephy, Jr., Peter Lyon, Francis Russell, *The American Heritage Book of the Pioneer Spirit* (New York: American Heritage Publishing Co., Inc., 1959), 156-157.

17. Donald Jackson, ed., *The Journals of Zebulon Montgomery Pike, With Letters and Related Documents*, 2 vols. (Norman: University of Oklahoma Press, 1966), 1:232.

18. Alexander de Humboldt, *Political Essay on the Kingdom of New Spain*, 2 vols. (London: Longman, Hurst, Rees, Orme, and Brown, 1811), 2:307.

19. Humboldt, *Kingdom of New Spain*, 1:175.

20. Ibid., 1:176.

21. Robertson, *Reports of the Trials of Colonel Aaron Burr*, 1:477.

22. Merriam, *Life of the Late Gen. William Eaton*, 405.

23. Ibid., 403.

24. Joseph Wheelan, *Jefferson's Vendetta: The Pursuit of Aaron Burr and the Judiciary* (New York: Carroll & Graf Publishers, 2006), 169.

25. Baker, Leonard, *John Marshall: A Life in Law* (New York: Macmillan Publishing Co., Inc., 1974), 488-490.

26. Jackson, *Journals of Zebulon Montgomery Pike*, 2:248.

27. Raymond E. Fitch, ed., *Breaking with Burr: Harman Blennerhassett's Journal, 1807* (Athens: Ohio University Press, 1988), 116.

28. Royal Ornan Shreve, *The Finished Scoundrel: General James Wilkinson, Sometime Commander-in-Chief of the Army of the United States, Who Made Intrigue a Trade and Treason a Profession* (Indianapolis: The Bobbs-Merrill Company, 1933), 229.

29. Henry Adams, *History of the United States of America During the Second Administration of Thomas Jefferson*, 2 vols. (New York: Charles Scribner's Sons, 1898), 1:270.

30. Daniel Clark, *Proofs of the Corruption of Gen. James Wilkinson, and of his Connexion with Aaron Burr, with A Full Refutation of his Slanderous Allegations in Relation to the Character of the Principal Witness Against Him* (Philadelphia: Wm. Hall, Jun. & Geo. W. Pierre, 1809), 4 [facsimile].

31. Baker, *John Marshall: A Life in Law*, 461.

32. Creighton, *Life of Sir Walter Ralegh*, 170-171.

33. Isaac Maltby, *A Treatise on Courts Martial and Military Law* (Boston: Thomas B. Wait and Company, 1813), 11 [facsimile]

34. *The National Cyclopaedia of American Biography*, Vol. VIII (New York: James T. White & Company, 1898), 180; Allen C. Clark, *William Duane* (Washington, D.C.: Press of W. F. Roberts Company, 1905), 8-10.

35. *National Cyclopaedia of American Biography*, Vol. VIII, 180.

36. See Eric Burn, *Infamous Scribblers: The Founding Fathers and the Rowdy Beginnings of American Journalism* (New York: Public Affairs, 2006), 366-368.

37. Willard Sterne Randall, *Thomas Jefferson: A Life* (New York: Henry Holt and Company, 1993), 556.

38. William Duane, *Experience the Test of Government: In Eighteen Essays* (Philadelphia: William Duane, 1807), 59.

39. Saul K. Padover, *Jefferson: A Great American's Life and Ideas* (New York: Mentor New American Library, 1970), 115.

40. Fitch, *Breaking with Burr*, xxx-xxxi.

41. Henry Whiting, "Life of Zebulon Montgomery Pike," Jared Sparks, ed., *The Library of American Biography, Second Series*, Vol. V (Boston: Charles C. Little and James Brown, 1845), 226.

42. Harold A. Bierck, Jr., "Dr. John Hamilton Robinson," *The Louisiana Historical Quarterly*, Vol. 25, No. 3 (June 1942), 645.

43. Ibid., 646.

44. Louis Houck, *A History of Missouri, From the Earliest Explorations and Settlements Until the Admission of the State into the Union*, 3 vols. (Chicago: R. R. Donnelly & Sons Company, 1908), 3:80, 2:28 note, 2:63, 2:365.

45. Bierck, "Dr. John Hamilton Robinson," 644-645.

46. Ibid., 647.

47. Ibid., 647-648.

48. Clarence Edwin Carter, ed., *The Territorial Papers of the United States, Vol. XIII: The Territory of Louisiana–Missouri, 1803–1806* (Washington, D.C.: Government Printing Office, 1948), 197.

49. Thomas Perkins Abernethy, *The South in the New Nation: Vol. IV of A History of the South* (Baton Rouge: Louisiana State University Press, 1976), 279.

50. Bierck, "Dr. John Hamilton Robinson," 653.

51. See Bierck, "Dr. John Hamilton Robinson," 656-659; Hubert H. Bancroft, ed., *History of the North Mexican States and Texas, 1801-1889* (San Francisco: The History Company, 1889), II:27-31; Odie B. Faulk, *The Last Years of Spanish Texas, 1778-1821* (The Hague: Mouton & Co., 1964), 135-136 note 5; *Weekly Register*, "From the Red River Herald–Extra," October 9, 1813, 104.

52. Francis B. Heitman, *Historical Register and Dictionary of the United States Army, From its Organization, September 29, 1789, to March 2, 1903*, Vol. I (Urbana: University of Illinois Press, 1965), 1037.

53. Ted Schwarz and Robert H. Thonoff, *Forgotten Battlefield of the First Texas Revolution: The Battle of Medina, August 18, 1813* (Austin, Texas: Eakin Press, 1985), 126.

54. Milo Milton Quaife, ed., *The Southwestern Expedition of Zebulon M. Pike* (Chicago: The Lakeside Press, 1925), xv.

55. Stephen Harding Hart and Archer Butler Hulbert, eds., *Zebulon Pike's Arkansaw Journal: In Search of the Southern Louisiana Purchase Boundary Line* (Denver: The Stewart Commission of Colorado College and the Denver Public Library, 1932), lxiii.

56. W. Eugene Hollon, *The Lost Pathfinder, Zebulon Montgomery Pike* (Norman: University of Oklahoma Press, 1949), 172.

57. Pike's first voyage up the Mississippi might have been a mere test of his loyalties and capabilities. Wilkinson also sent an 1805 expedition up the Osage River under Lieutenant George Peter, and Pike apparently believed that he was in competition with Peter for selection to command the trek up the Arkansas. See Jackson, *Journals of Zebulon Montgomery Pike*, 1:xxvi note 2. For the Southwestern Expedition, Pike thought that he was selected over Peter, whom Wilkinson apparently favored initially. See Jackson, *Journals of Zebulon Montgomery Pike*, 1:xxiv. Indeed, Wilkinson, in a letter to Secretary of War Henry Dearborn in late October 1805, noted that Lieutenant Peter had completed his mission to the Osage, and, at the same time, complained that Pike had virtually disappeared up the Mississippi. See Carter, *Territorial Papers of the United States, Vol. XIII*, 248.

58. Carter, *Territorial Papers of the United States, Vol. XIII*, 289.

59. *New Hampshire Sentinel*, "Domestic," August 23, 1806, 2-3.

60. Robertson, *Reports of the Trials of Colonel Aaron Burr*, 1:476.

61. Ibid., 1:483.

62. Ibid., 1:484.

63. Ibid., 1:484.

64. See Jackson, *Journals of Zebulon Montgomery Pike*, 2:155 note; Shreve, *The Finished Scoundrel*, 82-83.

65. See Clark, *Proofs of the Corruption of Gen. James Wilkinson*, endnotes 28, 29, 32.

66. See Jackson, *Journals of Zebulon Montgomery Pike*, 2:155 note, 2:299.

67. Jackson, *Journals of Zebulon Montgomery Pike*, 2:154-155.

68. See Hubert Howe Bancroft, *History of Mexico, 1804-1824*, (New York: McGraw-Hill Book Company, 1967), 33.

69. Jackson, *Journals of Zebulon Montgomery Pike*, 2:155 note.

70. Ibid., 2:297.

71. Ibid., 2:303.

72. Ibid., 2:206-207.

73. Harvey L. Carter, "A Soldier With Pike Tried for Murder," *The Colorado Magazine*, Vol. XXXIII, No. 3 (July 1956), 218.

74. Ibid., 225.

75. Ibid., 223-224.

76. Ibid., 225.

77. Jackson, *Journals of Zebulon Montgomery Pike*, 2:215.

78. Carter, "A Soldier With Pike Tried for Murder," 226-228.

79. Ibid., 229.

80. Ibid., 231 note.

81. Ibid., 232 note.

82. Jackson, *Journals of Zebulon Montgomery Pike*, 2:219-220.

83. Carter, "A Soldier With Pike Tried for Murder," 232 note.

84. Zebulon Pike, *An Account of Expeditions to the Sources of the Mississippi, and Through the Western Parts of Louisiana* (Philadelphia: C. & A. Conrad, 1810), 38.

85. Hollon, *The Lost Pathfinder*, 166.

86. Ibid., 167.

87. Carter, "A Soldier With Pike Tried for Murder," 218.

88. Hollon, *The Lost Pathfinder*, 167. The *Gazette* was no friend of the Wilkinson clique. Wilkinson had arrested its editor during his arbitrary conduct in New Orleans upon the exposure of Burr's expedition. Wheelan, *Jefferson's Vendetta*, 169.

89. Jackson, *Journals of Zebulon Montgomery Pike*, 2:242.

90. Ibid., 2:242.

91. Ibid., 2:241.

92. Ibid., 2:241. The last thing Wilkinson probably wanted was his lieutenant truthfully to tell all he knew about his expeditions. Pike volunteered to testify for his general at the second of Wilkinson's courts-martial, but he was not called. Thomas Robson Hay, *The Admirable Trumpeter: A Biography of General James Wilkinson* (Garden City, N.Y.: Doubleday, Doran & Company, Inc., 1941), 227. Supposedly, Pike had been placed under arrest by General Wade Hampton, an enemy of

Wilkinson, to prevent Pike from testifying. Hollon, *The Lost Pathfinder*, p. 192. However, affidavits were admissible at courts-martial, and Wilkinson had Pike answer specific interrogatories (posited by Wilkinson) in a document prepared *two years* before the second court-martial. In this statement, which apparently was not introduced, Pike vouched for his general's integrity and described any Burr–Wilkinson relationship as innocent. See John Upton Terrell, *Zebulon Pike: The Life and Times of an Adventurer* (New York: Weybright and Talley, 1968), 231-232.

93. Jackson, *Journals of Zebulon Montgomery Pike*, 2:243-244.

94. Jerome C. Smiley, *Semi-Centennial History of the State of Colorado*, Vol. 1 (Chicago: The Lewis Publishing Company, 1913), 81-87.

95. Pike wrote a letter pleading for the release of Nolan's men, and in a later letter less emotionally said that the detention of "my sergeant and party" was a private injury to Pike and an insult to the U.S. government. See Pike, *An Account of Expeditions to the Sources of the Mississippi, and Through the Western Parts of Louisiana*, Appendix to Part III, 82-85. Meek was not released from Spanish confinement until 1820. Donald Jackson, "Zebulon Pike's Damned Rascals," *Occasional Papers, No. 1*, (Colorado Springs: Pikes Peak Posse of the Westerners, 1979), 6.

96. William Blackstone, *Commentaries on the Laws of England, Book the Fourth*, (Oxford, 1769), 119 [facsimile].

97. Ibid., 120.

98. Ibid., 121.

99. Ibid., 126.

100. See Nafis and Cornish, *Life of General Jacob Brown, to Which are Added the Memoirs of Generals Ripley and Pike*, (New York: Sheldon, Lamport and Blakeman, 1855), 254-255.

101. *Weekly Register*, "From the Aurora," June 5, 1813, 225.

102. See Heitman, *Historical Register and Dictionary of the United States Army*, I:385, 792.

Enemies & Friends:
Zebulon Montgomery Pike & Facundo Melgares in the Struggle for Control of the Louisiana Purchase

Leo E. Oliva

Lieutenant[1] Zebulon Montgomery Pike's Southwest Expedition (1806–1807) through a portion of the Louisiana Purchase encountered many obstacles, including bitter winter conditions in the Rocky Mountains and arrest and detention by Spanish troops in northern New Spain. Although all missions assigned to this small exploring party were not achieved, in the long run the lands traversed by the expedition plus the valuable information compiled by Pike and published in his journals and reports contributed significantly to the later boundary settlement between the United States and Spain in 1819, the opening of the Santa Fe trade between the Missouri Valley and New Mexico in 1821, and the acquisition of the American Southwest in 1848. For two centuries Pike's significant contributions to an expanding nation have been overshadowed by the Corps of Discovery led by Meriwether Lewis and William Clark.

As part of this bicentennial commemoration, it is time to give Pike and his small band of soldiers, once described by him as a "Dam'd set of Rascels," the credit they deserve in the struggle for control of the Louisiana Purchase and to look more closely at the relationship between Pike and Lieutenant Facundo Melgares, who led an expedition of six hundred Spanish troops from New Mexico to the Great Plains just prior to Pike's venture and with whom Pike spent considerable time and learned much during his detention in New Spain. Pike became aware of the Spanish mission to the Great Plains when he arrived at the Pawnee village on the Republican River in present Nebraska, where Melgares had visited a few weeks before. Pike's party followed the return route of Melgares south to the Arkansas River and along that stream into present Colorado to the point where the Spaniards left that river to head back to Santa Fe. Interestingly, almost everything known about Melgares's 1806 trip is obtained from Pike's journal, for the records of that Spanish expedition have not been found (it is possible they were destroyed by a fire at the archives in Chihuahua City).

The history of these two expeditions and their respective leaders became more intertwined after the capture of Lieutenant Pike's exploring party near the Rio Grande in present southern Colorado and detention in Santa Fe and Chihuahua, during a portion of which time Lieutenant Melgares was Pike's guard, overseer, and guide. The two enemies — for such they were, as military officers of nations competing for control of the Louisiana Purchase through which they both traveled at a time when both nations feared war between them might break out any time — became friends. Pike learned much about the Great Plains and the provinces of northern New Spain from Melgares, and that information, along with Pike's own astute observations of the people and culture of the region published in his journal of the expedition in 1810, sparked increased interest in the United States to attempt to open trade with New Mexico. Those trading efforts were thwarted so long as Spain retained control of the colony of New Spain (later Mexico) but bore fruitful economic results for both the United States and northern Mexico following Mexican independence from Spanish rule in 1821. It is evident that everyone who ventured forth from the United States to establish contact with northern Mexico after 1811 benefited from Pike's expedition and journal (including information provided by Melgares), either directly or indirectly. It was Facundo Melgares, governor of New Mexico from 1818 to 1822, who welcomed the first successful U.S. trade expedition to Santa Fe in 1821.

Both Pike and Melgares were sent by their respective governments into the disputed region of the Louisiana Purchase (the boundaries of which had not been defined) with a major purpose to secure friendship, trade relations, and alliances with several Indian tribes of the region, including the Osage, Kansa, Pawnee, and Comanche. Pike was especially directed to open talks with the leaders of the Comanche tribe because they were most closely tied to New Spain. The policy of seeking Indian spheres of influence had been used by all nations involved in the contest for North America. Indian allies were considered to be the key element to establish effective control and eventual domination of a vast region, including the Great Plains and a portion of the Rocky Mountains.

France was initially most successful in developing alliances with the Indians of the region (except for the Comanches who remained in the Spanish sphere of influence), but that European power was eliminated as a contender for control of North America at the close of the French and Indian War in 1763.[2] Then Britain and Spain competed for favors with the tribes and control of the region, and the new United States entered the contest after winning independence from Britain in 1783. England continued to trade with the Plains Indians, but the main contest, after the sale of Louisiana Territory by France to the United States in 1803, was between the United States and Spain. Immediately, the United States increased efforts to establish and consolidate control over trade with various tribes (many of whom were traditional enemies), thereby hoping to establish domination of the lands they occupied. At the same time, Spain pursued trade and alliances with Plains tribes and attempted to use them against the United States.[3]

A critical issue in this pursuit of control was the establishment of the boundaries of the Louisiana Purchase. Spain claimed almost everything west of the Mississippi River and prohibited U.S. citizens from entering the territory. The United States viewed the Louisiana Purchase as a hunting license to seek more lands and hoped to push that boundary as far west as possible. The boundary issue was not settled until the Adams–Onís Treaty (or Transcontinental Treaty) of 1819.[4] For all these reasons, the expeditions led by Melgares and Pike comprised an important round of an expanded contest between those two nations for a huge portion of North America. It was a contest to be won quickly by the United States, thanks especially to Pike but also to Napoleon Bonaparte who sold Louisiana to the United States and, perhaps more importantly, occupied Spain from 1808 to 1814, during and after which Spanish domination in the New World quickly deteriorated.[5]

Although they never encountered each other on the Plains, the paths of Melgares and Pike met up at the village of the Pawnees on the Republican River in present southern Nebraska. A look at the two expeditions provides insight into what was at stake in the disputed region of Louisiana Territory. It provides understanding about why the Spanish were so apprehensive about Pike and other U.S. explorers, and it also reveals what the U.S. hoped to achieve in the American West. Although Spanish explorers periodically ventured into the region beginning in 1541, and established claims to much of the western portion of North America, Spain did not attempt to establish settlements north of New Mexico and Texas. The French, with their aggressive policies of expanding trade and influence with tribal Americans, were the first and most successful in winning alliances and trade arrangements with many tribes, including the Osage, Kansa, Pawnee, and others. They were not successful, however, in winning over the Comanches, with whom, after 1786, Spain held dominion.[6]

Spain continued to consider New Mexico and lands to the north and east as a buffer zone where foreign threats could be countered before they reached more economically important places, such as Chihuahua.[7] Following the removal of France from the competition for the Great Plains at the close of the French and Indian War, Spain acquired French Louisiana and began an effort to become the favored trading partner of those tribes with whom the French had held sway. The major competition faced by Spain was that of the new United States, which soon developed great interest in the region west of the Mississippi Valley and in opening the Mississippi River to navigation for its citizens. Time and energy were on the side of the young and vigorous United States and against the declining colonial, mercantilist empire of Spain.[8]

Some Spanish officials were concerned about the potential threat of the United States. In November 1794 François Hector, Baron de Carondelet, governor of Spanish Louisiana, warned his superiors in Madrid that efforts should be made to counteract the trans-Mississippi interests of the United States, warning that, if they were not stopped, "in time they will demand the possession of the rich mines of the interior provinces of the very kingdom of Mexico." He declared the U.S. was "advancing with an incredible rapidity." Carondelet recognized the importance of keeping the Indian tribes friendly to Spain and in opposition to the U.S. He proposed "one hundred thousand pesos increase annually for the Indian department, for the purchase of arms, ammunition, and presents, which are necessary to employ the nations with efficacy." He also outlined a detailed plan for the defense of Louisiana from the U.S.[9]

The United States continued to put pressure on Spain to open the Mississippi River to navigation. In 1795, Spain, feeling more vulnerable because of changes in the balance of power in Europe and facing possible war with Britain, agreed to the Treaty of Lorenzo el Real (also called the Treaty of Friendship, Boundaries, and Navigation but best known as Pinckney's Treaty), and granted concessions to the United States by opening the lower Mississippi to commerce.[10] The following year Governor Carondelet informed the Marquis de Branciforte at New Orleans that this did not stop U.S. citizens from entering lands west of the Mississippi River.

> Your Excellency will see himself obliged to take beforehand the most active measures to oppose the introduction of those restless people, who are a sort of determined bandits, armed with carbines, who frequently cross the Mississippi in numbers, with the intention of reconnoitering, of hunting, and if they like the country, of establishing themselves in the *Provincias Internas*, whose Indians they will arm to both further their fur trade and to make the Spaniards uneasy.[11]

A few years later, because of the French Revolution and Napoleon's desire to regain control of Louisiana, Spain realized it could not defend Louisiana if Britain decided to take it, so an offer from Napoleon to return Louisiana to France was worked out in 1800, an agreement kept secret for nearly two years. France agreed that Louisiana could never be sold to a third party, only back to Spain.[12]

When Napoleon sold Louisiana to the United States in 1803, Spain refused to recognize the deal because it violated the terms by which the territory had been returned to France. Spanish officials also prepared to meet U.S. expansion into the disputed lands. President Thomas Jefferson set the Meriwether Lewis and William Clark expedition into motion prior to the Louisiana Purchase, and Jefferson was determined to explore the West in the face of objections from Spain. Lieutenant Pike's expedition would also be part of that effort, even though he was sent out by General James Wilkinson. Jefferson approved Pike's mission and praised its accomplishments.[13] Spanish officials became fearful of intrusions, some even expecting an actual invasion from the United States.[14] Several efforts were made by both sides to improve their respective claims to portions of the region. Melgares and Pike were both part of that endeavor.

General James Wilkinson, head of the U.S. Army and also a paid agent for the Spanish government, sent a secret warning to Spanish officials in the late winter of 1804 about the Lewis and Clark expedition and suggested ways that Spain could protect her claims from U.S. intrusions. He wrote,

> an express ought immediately to be sent to the governor of Santa Fé, and another to the captain-general of Chihuaga [Chihuahua] in order that they may detach a sufficient body of chasseurs to intercept Captain Lewis and his party who are on the Missouri River, and force them to retire or take them prisoners.

Wilkinson emphasized the importance of Spain "winning the affection" of various Indian tribes and "increasing their jealousy against the United States." By providing arms and ammunition to the Indians, Spain could employ them "not only in checking the extension of American settlements, but also, if necessary, in destroying every settlement located west of the Mississippi."[15] Wilkinson also warned against U.S. incursions in Texas and New Mexico, suggesting that Spain insist that the Mississippi River be the boundary between Spain and the U.S.[16] Wilkinson declared,

> It is very probable that the United States will demand possession of one part of the right bank of the Mississippi, in order to check the smuggling that will necessarily prevail if the above-mentioned side belonged to any other nation, and also to favor the collection of its revenues. The true policy of Spain requires obstinate resistance to such a demand by asking [for] the right bank of the Mississippi in its entirety.[17]

He even recommended that Spanish troops be sent to destroy Daniel Boone's settlement on the Missouri River. In fact, all settlers from the U.S. located west of the Mississippi should be destroyed because, "if those settlers be allowed to advance, they will very quickly explore the right path which will lead them to the capital of Santa Fé."[18] It is not clear if Wilkinson was just betraying Lewis and Clark, Jefferson, and the U.S., or, as Warren Cook observed, "the possibility must not be overlooked that, rather than aiding Madrid, he may have been setting the stage for incidents that would provide an excuse to declare war and invade Spanish borderlands."[19]

Thus Spanish troops were sent out to attempt to intercept Lewis and Clark, and some of these were on the Great Plains a few weeks ahead of Zebulon M. Pike's expedition in 1806. Lewis and Clark escaped all contact with Spanish troops, but Pike followed in their footsteps from the Pawnee village in present Nebraska to the point where the Spanish troops left the Arkansas River in present Colorado, and, later, he was taken into custody and detained by Spanish troops and government officials. General Wilkinson undoubtedly contributed to the search for and capture of U.S. explorers, in this case the very man he sent to find the sources of the Arkansas and Red Rivers and to attempt to open friendly relations with several tribes of Indians.

Sebastián Calvo, Marquis de Casa Calvo, former military governor of Louisiana and then-member of the Louisiana boundary commission, initially directed Spanish Governor Carlos Dehault Delassus at St. Louis, in January 1804, to permit Lewis and Clark to proceed without opposition: "you will not put any obstacle to impede Capt. Merry Weather Lewis' entrance in the Missouri whenever he wishes."[20] Calvo changed his mind after hearing from General Wilkinson. Calvo sent an overland express with Wilkinson's warnings to General Nemesio Salcedo, commandant of the Interior Provinces located in Chihuahua, and declared, "The only means which presents itself is to arrest Captain Merry Weather and his party, which cannot help but pass through the [Indian] nations neighboring New Mexico."[21]

General Salcedo received the message in early May and directed New Mexico Governor Fernando de Chacón to seek help from the Indians of the Plains in turning back Lewis and Clark and to send Spanish troops to arrest the Corps of Discovery. Governor Chacón was encouraged to solicit Pedro Vial for assistance because Vial had earlier traveled the region.[22] Vial was a native of France who had performed several exploring expeditions on the northern frontier of New Spain, including opening a route between Santa Fe and San Antonio, another route between Santa Fe and Natchitoches, and a route across the Great Plains from Santa Fe to St. Louis and back.[23] From 1804 to 1806, four expeditions were sent from Santa Fe to try to find and arrest Lewis and Clark, without success. The fourth of those was led by Lieutenant Melgares. In February 1807 another expedition was sent to bring in Pike and his party, which they did.

In August 1804, Pedro Vial, José Jarvet, and fifty men headed north from Santa Fe. Jarvet had earlier served as a translator with the Pawnee Indians.[24] A month later, on the Platte River in present Nebraska, they met up with Pawnees, who had earlier become trading partners with New Spain (perhaps in the early 1780s). The Spanish did not find Lewis and Clark but urged the Pawnees not to trade with the U.S. and to turn back anyone coming from the United States. Pawnee Chief Sharitarish (White Wolf), whom Pike would meet in 1806, welcomed the Spanish and encouraged the trade. A dozen Pawnees, several of whom had been to Santa Fe before, accompanied Vial and party back to Santa Fe, where they arrived in early November.[25] The attempts to bind the Pawnees closer to Spain appeared to be succeeding.

In 1805 a new governor arrived in Santa Fe, Joaquín del Real Alencaster, and he was also directed by General Salcedo to send troops to find "Captain Merry" or persuade the Indians to seek and capture Lewis and Clark. Alencaster was especially charged with seeking better relations with the Indian tribes, particularly the Pawnee, to prevent U.S. intrusions. Vial, Jarvet, and fifty-two men were sent to pursue those missions. Jarvet and Vial were directed to remain with the Pawnees through the coming winter and watch for Lewis and Clark as well as cement relations with the tribes. Jarvet was to accompany the chiefs to Santa Fe in the spring while Vial remained to move closer to the Missouri River, seek information about Lewis and Clark, and arrest them if possible. The party, joined by others making a total of just over one hundred men (including five recent migrants from the U.S. who were to proceed to Missouri as spies and later report to Santa Fe), was attacked by Indians (later confirmed to be Skidi Pawnee) near the junction of the Purgatory and Arkansas Rivers. The Spaniards lost most of their supplies and had one man wounded. Unable to continue, the expedition returned to Santa Fe. Vial recommended the establishment of a fort on the Arkansas River.[26]

Spanish officials believed the U.S. was winning influence with some of the Plains tribes and had probably encouraged those who attacked Vial's party. The Pawnees did not come to Santa Fe in the autumn of 1805 to trade as they had been doing in previous years, and this too was interpreted as the growing influence of the U.S. Another expedition from Santa Fe set out under the leadership of Vial and Jarvet in April 1806. Within a month they were back because many of their troops had deserted. Vial was now discredited.[27]

Then another threat from the United States was perceived by Spain. A U.S. expedition planned by William Dunbar and led by Thomas Freeman and Captain Richard Sparks with twenty-two men was sent by President Jefferson to explore up the Red River to its source. They carried a Spanish passport issued by Calvo, who insisted that some Spanish subjects accompany them, including a planted spy, Tomás Power. General Salcedo, however, notified Calvo that he would not honor the passport and would not permit the U.S. explorers to enter Spanish territory. Also, orders from Spain reached Salcedo in February 1806, urging him again to stop Lewis and Clark and turn back other attempts to intrude on Spanish territory. This was considered more urgent because of information that U.S. Vice-President Aaron Burr had designs on Spanish territory. Salcedo notified Governor Alencaster in Santa Fe. Also in February 1806, U.S. troops took possession of the Spanish outpost at Los Adaes in Texas, located only fourteen miles from Natchitoches in Louisiana. This was almost an act of war against Spain by the U.S.[28] Clearly, tensions were increasing between the U.S. and Spain in the region where Lieutenant Pike would soon venture.

The fourth expedition sent from New Mexico to stop "Captain Merry" was led by Lieutenant Melgares in 1806. It was, according to one historian, "the largest Spanish force ever sent onto the Great Plains."[29] Melgares, with sixty additional soldiers, had been sent by General Salcedo from the presidio of San Fernando de Carrizal some seventy-five miles south of El Paso to Santa Fe at Governor Alencaster's request, to help deal with the Indians who had stopped Vial and Jarvet from reaching the Plains. Melgares carried with him orders to turn back the Freeman–Sparks expedition on the Red River, if that had not already been accomplished by other troops from Texas, and then proceed northward to attempt to intercept Lewis and Clark and meet with several Plains tribes (particularly the Pawnees, Omahas, and Kansas) to seek closer ties with them and urge them to reject overtures from the United States. Melgares set out from Santa Fe on June 15, 1806, with one hundred five soldiers, four hundred New Mexican militia, one hundred Indian allies, and more than two thousand horses and mules. The size of this force was designed especially to impress the Pawnees, whose loyalty to Spain seemed to be wavering, and to secure their cooperation against U.S. citizens.[30]

According to Pike, who later appended information about the Spanish expedition to his journal, Melgares was from an aristocratic family in Spain, who was a career army officer and "had distinguished himself in several long expeditions against the Appaches and other Indian nations." Pike noted, "he was a man of immense fortune, and generous in its disposal, almost to profusion; possessed a liberal education, high sense of honor, and a disposition formed for military enterprise."[31]

Melgares was born in 1775 in Villa Carabaca, Murcia, Spain, and received an education and was trained as a military officer.[32] He was a man whom Pike clearly admired. Pike was of similar background (although not wealthy), born in New Jersey in 1779, son of a career army officer and himself a career officer. Pike mistakenly believed that Melgares had been sent out to search for him rather than for Lewis and Clark.[33]

At Santa Fe the Spanish expedition was provided equipment and supplies for six months. The large force traveled down the Red River but did not meet up with the Freeman–Sparks expedition which had been turned back by troops from Spanish Nacogdoches, led by garrison commander Francisco Viana by order of General Salcedo. Melgares did meet some bands of the Comanches, who were still aligned with Spain, and held council with them.[34] Melgares then headed northeast when— according to Pike who disparaged the Spanish militia by stating "it is extraordinary with what subordination they act" — approximately one-third of his force signed a petition requesting that they proceed no farther and go back home. Melgares reacted quickly and harshly, as Pike reported.

He halted immediately, and caused his dragoons to erect a gallows, then beat to arms. The troops fell in: he separated the *petitioners* from the others, then took the man who had presented the petition, tied him up, and gave him fifty lashes, and threatened to put to death on the gallows erected any man who should dare to grumble. This effectually silenced them, and quelled the rising spirit of sedition.[35]

When they reached the Arkansas River, Melgares left two hundred forty of his men with many worn-out horses in a camp southwest of present Larned, Kansas. He took the remaining troops and proceeded to the Pawnee village on the Republican River southwest of present Guide Rock, Nebraska, where he met with leaders of the Republican and Grand Pawnees, "held councils with the two nations, and presented them the flags, medals, &c. which were destined for them."[36] Pike saw those gifts when he visited the same village later. Melgares, Pike wrote, "did not proceed on to the execution of his mission with the Pawnee Mahaws and Kans, as he represented to me, from the poverty of their horses, and the discontent of his own men, but as I conceive, from the suspicion and discontent which began to arise between the Spaniards and the Indians." The Pawnees opposed Melgares's plans to proceed to the Missouri River, or so Chief Sharitarish told Pike. The Spanish troops returned to the Arkansas, picked up the remaining soldiers, and continued upstream until they left the river to return to Santa Fe, where they arrived October 1, 1806.[37]

They brought with them the 10-year-old, half-Pawnee son of José Jarvet, and two Frenchmen (Andrés Sulier and Henrique Visonot) whom they had met at the Pawnee village. Jarvet's son was sent to live with his father, and the Frenchmen were sent to meet General Salcedo in Chihuahua.[38] The Melgares expedition, as with the three previous attempts to find Lewis and Clark, had failed in that mission. He may not have accomplished his mission to the Indians either. His experiences and observations, however, would prove valuable to Pike and his reports.

Warren Cook, who has written the best account of the Melgares expedition, offered a cogent evaluation: "The 'apprehension' of Captain Merry, one suspects, was at least one purpose of the huge Spanish force that advanced northward toward the Missouri but was hamstrung by horse thieves and stalemated by determined Pawnee opposition." At the same time, Governor "Alencaster wanted to awe the Plains Indians, and Melgares's force was well suited for that purpose." On the other hand, "It was too unwieldy for a surprise attack on Lewis and Clark. . . . It was overkill, in the modern sense, and that proved a part of Melgares's undoing." As it turned out, "His force was too big to travel swiftly, live off the land, keep from offending Indian allies, and succeed in its hypothetical objective." Cook concluded,

> With 240 of his men in one spot and 360 in another, his lines of supply were nonexistent, and it would have been difficult for him to push on to the Missouri, fend off the Pawnee, and remain there for a protracted time until Merry's problematical return. Vial's previous expeditions had not led him to expect Pawnee opposition.[39]

How effective Melgares's appeal had been to the Pawnees would be tested a few weeks later by Lieutenant Pike.

Pike's second expedition, 1806–1807, begun almost immediately after completion of his first expedition to find the source of the Mississippi River (1805–1806), was designed to accomplish several goals, including the return of fifty-one Osage Indians to their villages in present western Missouri, accompany a delegation of Pawnees to their villages and seek their friendship and their aid in contacting the Comanches, work out a peace agreement between the Kansa and Osage tribes, and make contact with the Comanches and try to arrange for peace with them. Pike was also to locate the headwaters of the Arkansas and Red Rivers. General Wilkinson's son, Lieutenant James B. Wilkinson, was to accompany Pike partway and then lead a small detachment down the Arkansas River. Part of his mission was to see if the Arkansas were navigable. In addition, Pike was to report on natural resources, lay of the land, Indians met along the way, and anything else of interest to the U.S. Upon completion, he was to follow the Red River to the post at Natchitoches in Louisiana, where his expedition would end.

On July 15, 1806, Pike and his party left Fort Bellefontaine near St. Louis with the Osages they were escorting to their villages, and a few Pawnees. With Pike were twenty-three men, including Lieutenant Wilkinson, Dr. John Hamilton Robinson (a civilian surgeon who may have been a spy for General Wilkinson), interpreter Antoine François "Baronet" Vásquez (called Baroney by Pike), one sergeant, two corporals, sixteen privates (one of whom deserted), and a volunteer (George Henry) who went as far as the Osage villages. They wore lightweight summer uniforms and expected to complete the expedition by late fall, which would have been impossible considering the distances and the several missions assigned to the expedition. They would suffer terribly during the coming winter without adequate clothing.

Pike fulfilled his assignments regarding Indians with the return of the Osages to their village in western Missouri, arranging a meeting between the Osages and Kansas which led to more peaceful relations between those two tribes, and visiting the Pawnees at their village on the Republican River. The Pawnees were being courted by the Spanish and Anglo-Americans but made no firm commitments to either. Pike faced a tense situation when he requested that the Pawnees lower the Spanish flag recently presented to them by Melgares and raise the flag of the United States, but this was done. Pike wisely told the Pawnees to keep the Spanish flag so they could hoist it if Spanish troops returned.[40]

Chief Sharitarish may have prevented Melgares from going farther east to the Missouri River, and he tried to prevent Pike from going farther west into the land of the Comanches, enemies of the Pawnees. Pike threatened to fight to the death if the Pawnees obstructed his party's advance, and he was permitted to push on, following the route of Melgares to the Arkansas River. Pike, it should be noted, was assisted by Indian guides from his outset in Missouri until he reached the Arkansas River. There, near present Great Bend, Kansas, on October 28, Lieutenant Wilkinson took five of the soldiers and two Osages and attempted to navigate down the river to Arkansas Post in hastily-built skin canoes. They had a very difficult trip and some of the men deserted. Pike and the remaining fifteen men, including interpreter Baroney, Dr. Robinson, and thirteen enlisted men, followed the Spanish trace up the Arkansas. Pike never met up with the Comanches as specifically ordered by General Wilkinson (although he mentioned seeing many Comanche campsites in his journal), but that may have been to his benefit since they were powerful, had ties to Spain, and were enemies of the Pawnees Pike had visited.

Pike's mission changed as he marched farther up the Arkansas to the mountains. His primary goal was now exploration, seeking the headwaters of the Arkansas and Red Rivers, both considered important in settling the boundary of the Louisiana Purchase (as in fact they turned out to be). This assignment seemed fairly easy, since the mouth of each river where it entered the Mississippi was well known. It was assumed, mistakenly as Pike and many other explorers were to learn, that the headwaters of both rivers would be found in the western mountains. What was not understood is that the Red River does not rise in the Rocky Mountains (its sources are on the plains of Texas) and that an attempt to move from the source of the Arkansas south through the mountains would lead not to the Red River but to other tributaries of the Arkansas and, farther south and west, to the drainage of the Rio Grande to the Gulf of Mexico, not to the Mississippi.

Pike kept track of the "Spanish trace" left by Melgares and troops, and could easily have followed their tracks to Santa Fe had that been his goal. Actually, Pike carried with him a map showing a route from the Pawnee village to Santa Fe, provided to him soon after he began the expedition by three men at La Charrette village on the Missouri River west of St. Charles.[41] Santa Fe was not his destination. Pike continued toward the Rocky Mountains, entering present Colorado on November 11, 1806, and took time to attempt to climb the mountain he called Grand Peak (later named Pikes Peak in his honor), which he first sighted on November 15, noting it "appeared like a small blue cloud."[42] Pike tried to ascend the Grand Peak with three companions from November 24 to 27, without success (although they did climb another peak nearby, Mount Rosa).

The expedition pushed on. After much struggle in winter weather, Pike and his companions reached a point near the source of the Arkansas, and in mid-December while wandering around lost also found the headwaters of the South Platte River. Their suffering intensified as the snow accumulated and they searched to the south for the source of the Red River. They believed they had found it when they arrived at the Rio Grande on January 30, 1807, and in early February they built a small stockade on a tributary, the Conejos River, in which to survive the rest of the winter. On February 7 Dr. Robinson left to go to Santa Fe, where his arrival led to the dispatch of troops to bring in Pike and his few soldiers. On February 26 José Jarvet and Pedro Vial, in advance of a platoon of soldiers, made first contact with Pike at his stockade. They were immediately followed by fifty Spanish dragoons and fifty mounted militiamen, led by Lieutenant Ignatio Saltelo, who took the explorers to Santa Fe to meet Governor Alencaster.[43]

On March 3 Pike was in Santa Fe. After meetings with Governor Alencaster, Pike and seven of his party were escorted on toward Chihuahua and General Salcedo the following day. At Albuquerque on March 7, Dr. Robinson rejoined Pike and explained that he had recently been placed under the charge of Lieutenant Melgares. Robinson informed Pike that Melgares had led the Spanish troops to the Pawnees, and told Pike that he would find Melgares to be "a gentleman, a soldier and one of the most gallant men you ever knew."[44] The next day, March 8, they met up with Melgares at the village of San Fernandez. Pike wrote, "he received me with the most manly frankness and the politeness of a man of the world." He continued,

> Malgares finding I did not feel myself at ease took every means in his power to banish my reserve, which made it impossible on my part not to endeavor to appear cheerful; we conversed [in French] *as well as we could* and in two hours were as well acquainted as some people would be in the same number of months.[45]

Pike described his new acquaintance with admiration. "Malgares possessing none of the haughty Castillian pride, but much of the urbanity of a Frenchman; and I will add my feeble testimony to his loyalty, by declaring that he was one of the few officers or citizens whom I found, who was loyal to their king." Pike was honored when Melgares told him his private possessions, including his papers, would not be confiscated or abused by him or his troops. That evening Lieutenant Melgares hosted a fandango for his new guest at San Fernandez.[46] Pike was a guest of honor during at least five fandangos while detained in Spanish territory, an indication that he was treated more as a respected visitor than a prisoner.

From March 9 to 21, on the road to El Paso del Norte, Pike rode daily in company with Melgares, visiting while they traveled and in camp each evening. After laying over a day at El Paso, the party, accompanied by an escort of dragoons, continued on to Chihuahua City, arriving there April 2. There, Melgares introduced Pike to General Salcedo who examined Pike's papers and confiscated some of them. While Pike remained a guest of the government in Chihuahua until April 28, he had almost daily visits with Melgares, met the lieutenant's wife and her parents (her father, Alberto Maynez, was a captain in the army), visited with several government officials, and continued to gather information that was useful to his reports. Lieutenant Melgares also accompanied Pike when they left Chihuahua to go across Texas and return to the United States at Natchitoches in Louisiana. On May 6, at a point beyond Guajoquilla (now Jiménez) where Captain Mariano Varela replaced Lieutenant Melgares as commander of the party, Pike and Melgares parted. Pike wrote, "Our friend Malgares accompanied us a few miles, to whom we bad[e] an eternal adieu, if war does not bring us together in the field of battle opposed as the most deadly enemies, when our hearts acknowledge the greatest friendship."[47] The two enemies had truly become friends.

Pike's party continued across Texas and arrived at Natchitoches on July 1, 1807,[48] where his original orders directed him to conclude his expedition. His journal of the expedition was first published in 1810, bringing information about the Great Plains, Rocky Mountains, and northern New Spain into public view. When published, Pike attached appendices which provided detailed reports on the route he traveled, brief summaries of the Indians of the plains, and a lengthy appendix about New Spain.

His report on the Plains contained praise for the Arkansas River as a route of travel, with abundant game and only scattered Indian tribes to obstruct passage. He thought this route could become the best overland road to the Pacific Ocean.[49] On the other hand, he compared the Great Plains to a desert, declaring "these vast plains of the western hemisphere, may become in time equally celebrated as the sandy desarts of Africa."[50] Pike said this might serve "one great advantage to the United States, viz: The restriction of our population to some certain limits, and thereby a continuation of the union." This would also "leave the prairies incapable of cultivation to the wandering and uncivilized aborigines of the country."[51] When these views were reinforced later by the Stephen H. Long expedition (1820-1821), which labeled a portion of the Plains the "Great American Desert," the U. S. Congress decided to move eastern tribes into the region. The lands west of Missouri were not opened to settlement until the passage of the Kansas–Nebraska Act in 1854. For good or ill, Pike was partly responsible for that delay.

The appendix on New Spain was more detailed and, in the long run, more important than what he wrote about the Plains. Pike included information about the geography, economy, government, population, society, and culture of the internal provinces, especially New Mexico, Biscay (Nueva Vizcaya, now the states of Chihuahua and Durango), and Coahuila. It seems clear that much of what Pike wrote about travel across the Plains to New Mexico, about the economy of Northern Mexico, as well as about the geography and culture or the region, came in large part from his conversations with Melgares, as well as his own observations.

From Melgares, Pike gained information about several plains tribes of Indians, including tribes Pike never met, such as the Comanches. He learned much about the military organization of New Spain, and Melgares explained in some detail how he had engaged Indians in battle. They discussed their respective trips across the Plains, and Pike gathered geographical information from Melgares about places he, Pike, had not seen. In all, it is impossible to determine how much of the information Pike presented in his journal and reports was enhanced by his numerous conversations with Melgares, but it appears to be considerable. Since Pike also had opportunities to visit with other army officers and government officials, even he may not have known how much of his report on New Spain came from Melgares. Pike, with the assistance of Melgares, helped the United States win the contest for control of the Louisiana Purchase, sealed by treaty in 1819.

Pike's observations, plus information gleaned from Melgares, made it clear that New Mexico was far removed from the source of supplies coming up El Camino Real from Mexico City, and his descriptions of a trip across the Plains demonstrated to enterprising merchants in the U.S. how close they were to northern New Spain and that profits could be made by taking commodities to New Mexico. Some were willing to risk arrest and confiscation of merchandise, part of Spanish policy to keep outsiders from trading with the empire. The following portion of Pike's 1810 report inspired enterprising merchants to attempt to open trade between the United States and northern New Spain, especially after the war for Mexico's independence began under Padre Miguel Hidalgo y Costilla in 1810, a revolution which, incidentally, Facundo Melgares helped crush the following year as part of the royalist army.[52]

Pike wrote in 1810,

New Mexico carries on a trade direct with Mexico through Biscay, also with Senora and Sinaloa: it sends out about 30,000 sheep annually, tobacco, dressed deer and cabrie [pronghorn] skins, some fur, buffalo robes, salt, and wrought copper vessels of superior quality. It receives in return, from Biscay and Mexico, dry goods, confectionary, arms, iron, steel, ammunition, and some choice European wines and liquors, and from Senora and Sinaloa, gold, silver, and cheese. The following articles sell as stated (in this province), which will shew the cheapness of provisions and the extreme dearness of imported goods:

Flour sells, per hundred at	2 dollars
Salt, per mule-load	5
Sheep, each	1
Beeves, each	5
Wine del Passo, per barrel	15
Horses, each	11
Mules, each	30
Superfine cloths, per yard	25
Fine cloths, per yard	20
Linen, per yard	4

and all other dry goods in proportion.

The journey with loaded mules from Santa Fe to Mexico, and returning to Santa Fe, takes five months.[53]

That quotation from Pike's report on New Spain was undoubtedly read or known by every trader who set out from the U.S. to New Mexico, beginning with the Robert McKnight and James Baird party in 1812[54] through William Becknell's successful trading venture in 1821, and including fur-trade ventures of Auguste P. Chouteau and Jules de Mun in 1815–1816 and again in 1817 when they were arrested by Spanish troops. Two years later, it should be noted, Luis de Mun (brother of Jules and an officer in the U.S. Army) wrote a detailed report on New Mexico, relying mostly on Pike's publication with additional information from his brother.[55] He described three possible routes through New Mexico's mountains, including one through San Miguel del Vado and Glorieta Pass, which later became the route of the Santa Fe Trail. David Meriwether reached Santa Fe in 1819. A trading venture led by Thomas James and John McKnight reached Santa Fe a few weeks after Becknell in 1821. The fur-trapping expedition of Hugh Glenn and Jacob Fowler followed the Arkansas into present Colorado in 1821, and Glenn entered New Mexico early in 1822. News traveled fast that Mexico was independent and traders were welcome.

It is safe to conclude that everyone who traveled across the Plains to the Southwest, including other explorers such as Stephen Long, knew of Pike's expedition, whether from reading the reports, talking with someone who had read the reports, or even talking with soldiers who were on that expedition. Pike, with the help of Melgares and others in New Spain, provided the solid information that stimulated attempts to open trade, which became successful when Mexico won independence from Spain in 1821 and the restrictions on trade with foreigners were removed. When Becknell's small party arrived in New Mexico in 1821 with a pack train of trade items, they were welcomed at Santa Fe by Governor Facundo Melgares who respected Americans, in part, because of his friendship with Pike. Becknell quickly sold his commodities at great profit and returned to Missouri where he outfitted the first wagons for a trading trip to Santa Fe in 1822, and many others followed.

The Pike expedition of 1806–1807, the Melgares expedition that preceded it, and Pike's published reports of both helped set in motion a series of events that ultimately resulted in the annexation of Texas in 1845 and the war with Mexico, 1846–1848, which brought the entire Southwest—more than half of Mexico—into the United States. President Jefferson and General Wilkinson could never have dreamed that the Pike expedition of a few soldiers would bear such fruit for a growing nation. Wilkinson considered the expedition a failure because Pike had not met with the Comanches nor found the source of the Red River. Even today, unfortunately, Zebulon Montgomery Pike does not receive the recognition he deserves (being known primarily for the mountain that bears his name), and very few people have ever heard of Facundo Melgares, two enemies who became friends and changed the course of history of North America.

Leo Oliva, Ph.D., is a retired professor of American History and presently serves as the editor of *Wagon Tracks*, the publication of the Santa Fe Trail Association, and recently served as assistant to the editor of *Kansas History* to prepare a special edition on Zebulon Pike's expedition. Dr. Oliva is the author of more than thirty articles and of twelve frontier military history books, including his most recent, *Fort Harker: Defending the Journey West*.

Notes

1. Pike, First U.S. Infantry, was promoted from lieutenant to captain during his expedition, effective August 12, 1806, which he did not learn until his return to the United States the following year. Thus he was referred to as "Lieutenant Pike" during his entire expedition. To avoid confusion, that rank will be used throughout this article, although he was officially Captain Pike during most of his expedition.

2. Donald A. Nuttall, The American Threat to New Mexico, 1804-1821 (M.A. Thesis, San Diego State College, 1959), 17; see also Henry Folmer, *Franco-Spanish Rivalry in North America, 1524-1763* (Glendale: The Arthur H. Clark Company, 1953) and A. P. Nasatir, ed., *Before Lewis and Clark: Documents Illustrating the History of the Missouri, 1785-1804*, 2 vols. (1952; reprint, Lincoln: University of Nebraska Press, 1990).

3. See Abraham P. Nasatir, *Borderland in Retreat: From Louisiana to the Far Southwest* (Albuquerque: University of New Mexico Press, 1976) and Charles L. Kenner, *A History of New Mexican–Plains Indian Relations* (Norman: University of Oklahoma Press, 1969), 66-68.

4. Nasatir, *Borderland in Retreat*, 136-137.

5. Warren L. Cook, *Flood Tide of Empire: Spain and the Pacific Northwest, 1543-1819* (New Haven: Yale University Press, 1973), 450, 491, 516.

6. Nasatir, *Before Lewis and Clark*, I:2, 17, 19, 50; Kenner, *History of New Mexican–Plains Indian Relations*, 52-58.

7. Nuttall, American Threat to New Mexico, 12.

8. See Cook, *Flood Tide of Empire*, 255-267.

9. Carondelet, quoted in James Alexander Robertson, ed., *Louisiana Under the Rule of Spain, France, and the United States, 1785-1807*, 2 vols. (Cleveland: The Arthur H. Clark Company, 1911), I:294, 298, 300, 301-345.

10. Cook, *Flood Tide of Empire*, 269-270.

11. Carondelet, quoted in Nasatir, *Before Lewis and Clark*, II:440.

12. Cook, *Flood Tide of Empire*, 442-444.

13. Donald Jackson, ed., *The Journals of Zebulon Montgomery Pike, with Letters and Related Documents*, 2 vols. (Norman: University of Oklahoma Press, 1966), II:300-301.

14. Nuttall, American Threat to New Mexico, v, wrote: "From the time of the first French arrivals, foreign intrusions into New Mexico were opposed by the Spaniards. They were not only in violation of Spain's restrictive colonial policies but were looked upon as a threat to the province's security. This Spanish anxiety attained its apogee during the period under consideration [1804-1821]. Following the acquisition of Louisiana by the United States, Spain grew increasingly apprehensive of that expanding nation's designs on the land of her American empire. One of the principal manifestations of this phobia was the anticipation of an American invasion of New Mexico. The threat was illusory, but it was very much a reality to the Spaniards, and, as such, exerted considerable influence upon New Mexico in the ensuing years. Reaction to the American menace became, in fact, one of the salient features of the province's existence."

15. Wilkinson, quoted in Robertson, *Louisiana Under Spain, France and the United States*, II:341, 342.

16. Ibid., II:337-341.

17. Ibid., II:345.

18. Ibid., II:342-343.

19. Cook, *Flood Tide of Empire*, 453-454.

20. Nasatir, *Before Lewis and Clark*, II:725.

21. Ibid., II:731; Cook, *Flood Tide of Empire*, 455.

22. Ibid., 456-458.

23. Noel M. Loomis & Abraham P. Nasatir, *Pedro Vial and the Roads to Santa Fe* (Norman: University of Oklahoma Press, 1966), 262-287, 316-415.

24. Ruth Steinberg, "José Jarvet, Spanish Scout and Historical Enigma," *New Mexico Historical Review*, 67 (July 1992): 232.

25. Cook, *Flood Tide of Empire*, 462-465.

26. Ibid., 465-469.

27. Ibid., 470-472.

28. Ibid., 472-476.

29. Ibid., 477.

30. Ibid.

31. Jackson, *Journals*, I:324.

32. Arthur Gomez, "Royalist in Transition: Facundo Melgares, the Last Spanish Governor of New Mexico, 1818-1822," *New Mexico Historical Review*, 68 (October 1993): 372.

33. Cook, *Flood Tide of Empire*, 479-480.

34. Ibid., 480; Jackson, *Journals*, I:323-324.

35. Ibid., II:57-58. It is interesting to note that Pike had a similar experience with one of his soldiers and reacted in a similar fashion. On January 24, 1807, while tramping through heavy snow in the mountains, Private John Brown began to complain, as Pike noted, ibid., I:372-373, he "presumed to make use of language which was seditious and mutinous." Pike let it pass until they were in camp that evening, when he reprimanded Brown: ". . . it was the height of ingratitude in you, to let an expression escape which was indicative of discontent. . . . But your duty as a soldier called on your obedience to your officer, and a prohibition of such language, which for this time, I will pardon, but assure you, should it ever be repeated, by instant *death*, I will revenge your ingratitude and punish your disobedience." Pike recorded no further disciplinary problems.

36. Ibid., I:325.

37. Ibid., I:325, 329.

38. Steinberg, "José Jarvet," 245-246; Loomis & Nasatir, *Pedro Vial*, 455.

39. Cook, *Flood Tide of Empire*, 482-483. Isaac Joslin Cox, "Opening the Santa Fe Trail," *Missouri Historical Review*, 25 (October 1930): 52, wrote of Melgares: "His force was really too large for effective scouting and exploration. Mutiny in the ranks retarded his movements, which were still further hampered by the raids of Indians on his live stock."

40. Jackson, *Journals*, I:328-329.

41. Lowell M. Schake, *La Charrette: Village Gateway to the American West* (Lincoln: iUniverse, 2003), 23-25.

42. Jackson, *Journals*, I:345.

43. See Pike's journal in ibid., I:331-385, for details of the expedition from the Pawnee village to the arrival of the Spanish troops. The identity of Jarvet and Vial is provided by Steinberg, "José Jarvet," 246.

44. Jackson, *Journals*, I:404.

45. Ibid., I:405.

46. Ibid., I:405-406.

47. Ibid., I:425.

48. Ibid., I:447.

49. Ibid., II:25.

50. Ibid., II:27.

51. Ibid., II:28.

52. Gomez, "Royalist in Transition," 378-379.

53. Jackson, *Journals*, II: 50-51.

54. Frank B. Golley, "James Baird, Early Santa Fe Trader," *The Bulletin of the Missouri Historical Society*, 15 (April 1959): 179, states that the 1812 party used Pike's publication "as their guide book."

55. Loomis & Nasatir, *Pedro Vial*, 257.

"Pike Entering Santa Fe," also known as "A Spanish Escort," by Frederic Remington, was published in *Collier's Weekly* on June 16, 1906, as a full-color, full-page spread.

Zebulon Pike & American Popular Culture, or, Has Pike Peaked?

Michael L. Olsen

With his death at the Battle of York in 1813, Brigadier General Zebulon Montgomery Pike entered the pantheon of genuine American military heroes. As with many of those heroes, however, his heritage and his exploits largely have been forgotten. Had Pikes Peak, heralded today in Colorado as "America's Mountain," not been named for him, he might be as little-remembered as General James Miller, Commodore Joshua Barney, or Captain Lewis Warrington, and other heroes of the War of 1812.[1]

Even when Americans do remember Pike, they have mistaken impressions of his achievements. He did not discover the source of the Mississippi River, although he came close, and his journey to Leech Lake, Minnesota, in the winter of 1805–1806 is a saga of endurance against great odds. Nor did he climb Pikes Peak, although he made a valiant effort to do so. His Southwest Expedition in 1806–1807 should be known as one of the most arduous yet productive in the annals of American exploration, but even at the time it was overshadowed by the feats of Meriwether Lewis and William Clark, as it has been again recently during the bicentennial celebration of the Lewis and Clark Expedition.

On the other hand, most histories of American expansion, especially collections issued periodically touting "America's great explorers," do include accounts of Pike, his men, and their sufferings. These accounts most often cover his search for the sources of the Arkansas and Red Rivers. Pike's involvement in the schemes of Aaron Burr and General James Wilkinson also receives periodic attention, particularly among academic historians.

As might be expected, Americans have eulogized and commemorated Pike most frequently in the quarter-century after his death, both in connection with memories of the War of 1812 and during the patriotic fervor surrounding the Mexican War in the late 1840s and early 1850s. Somewhat ironically, but understandably, he was entirely forgotten in the decades following the Civil War. Americans then had other heroes and preoccupations. With the approach of the 1906 centennial of his Southwest Expedition, Pike was once more remembered with celebratory festivals, new monuments, and a variety of memorabilia. Two of the four novels based on his western explorations also appeared at this time.[2]

During September 1906 Colorado Springs, in the shadow of Pikes Peak, hosted a week-long, lavish celebration of the one-hundredth anniversary of Pike's Southwest Expedition. The nationally promoted centennial event encouraged travelers to come by train from near and far. *From Special Collections, Pikes Peak Library District.*

During the remainder of the twentieth century an occasional historic site, or a new dam on the Ohio and Mississippi Rivers, or a state park in Iowa, would be dedicated to the memory of Pike and his deeds. The city of Colorado Springs, Colorado, in the shadow of Pikes Peak, celebrated the sesquicentennial of his western journey in 1956, although not as lavishly as it had for his 1906 centennial. It is interesting that Pike has lived on most notably in the pages of juvenile literature. Many of these books present his boyhood and youth in somewhat fanciful detail and hold him up as an example to be emulated.

Now that two hundred years have passed since Pike ascended to his place in American history, and given the relatively checkered career of his heritage, has Pike's reputation peaked? If so, when was it at full tide and when did it begin to ebb? Must it now be said of Pike, as expressed in the well-known words of a popular World War I song immortalized by General Douglas MacArthur, "old soldiers never die, they only fade away?"[3]

Pike's most enduring legacy perhaps rests in the places named for him in the land that was becoming America. Between 1814 and 1833 the residents of no fewer than sixteen counties and towns chose to call themselves after the hero of the Battle of York. His name, for two decades at least, readily came to mind as Americans moved west. Counties named for Pike march chronologically and geographically west from the Appalachians to the Mississippi: Pennsylvania (1814); Mississippi and Ohio (1815); Indiana (1817); Missouri (1818); Alabama, Illinois, and Kentucky (1821); Georgia (1822); and Arkansas (1833).

Towns named for Pike today range in size from mere hamlets to prosperous county seats. Some of them are Piketon, Ohio (1815); Zebulon, Kentucky (1821); Pikeville, Kentucky (1821); Zebulon, Georgia (1822); and Pikeville, Tennessee (1830). The town fathers of present Murfreesboro, the seat of Pike County, Arkansas, named their town "Zebulon" in 1833 but then changed the name in 1836. Zebulon, Georgia, also is the seat of that state's Pike County. A state historical marker there reads, "It was named for Zebulon Montgomery Pike (1779–1813), leader, in 1805 of an expedition to trace the Mississippi River to its source. Later he explored the interior of Louisiana. Made brigadier general in 1813, he was killed at Toronto, Canada, while commanding American forces there." Names can be deceiving, however. Neither of the towns of Zebulon nor Pikeville—both in North Carolina—was named for Zebulon Pike.[4]

Steamboats were another quintessentially nineteenth century phenomenon linked to the westward expansion of the United States. And here too, the public amply commemorated Pike in the decades immediately following his death. In fact, it is claimed that the *Zebulon Pike* was the first steamboat to dock in St. Louis, in 1817. Built at the Fulton shipyard in Cincinnati, it also was the first western steamboat designed for passenger service. Subsequently at least half a dozen boats bearing the name *Pike* or *General Pike* plied the Ohio and the Mississippi.

The first vessel named for Pike, however, was a United States warship constructed by the New York shipbuilder Henry Eckford at Sackets Harbor, New York. Eckford began building her on April 9, 1813, just weeks before Pike's death. She was launched on June 12, 1813, having survived a fire during a British foray on the town. She served in various engagements on Lake Ontario, most notably against the *Royal George*. Laid up at Sackets Harbor at the end of the war, she was sold in 1825. Today, somewhat fittingly since Pike was a career army officer, the only ship bearing his name is the LT 805 *General Zebulon Pike*, a United States Army *Greene* class large coastal tugboat launched in 1994.[5]

Pike received other typical nineteenth-century accolades in addition to counties, towns, and steamboats adopting his name. Still extant are at least one "mourning memo memorial," a monody eulogizing him, and a raft of hagiographic biographies.

The "mourning memorial" is a watercolor painting in the classic style of the time. It depicts two women dressed in black pining at a grave marker. A weeping willow tree overhangs the tombstone, and an angel hovers in the distance holding a banner that reads, "Wreaths of laurel over his tomb entwine." This piece was painted sometime between 1813 and 1825.[6]

Nathaniel Hill Wright published an early poem eulogizing Pike in 1814. Entitled "Monody, on the Death of Brigadier-General Zebulon Montgomery Pike: Who Fell at the Battle of

York, Upper Canada, April 27, 1813," it was republished with a collection of Wright's works, *The Fall of Palmyra: and Other Poems*, in 1817. Like "mourning memorials," monodies were a popular form of collective grieving for public figures. The term itself is both literary and musical. It can be applied to an ode spoken by a single actor in ancient Greek drama, to a piece of music with a single melodic line, or to a poem in which a "speaker" mourns a death. Nathaniel Wright, a New Hampshire native and Dartmouth College graduate, practiced law in Hamilton County, Ohio, and was "one of a club of young men of literary proclivities, who contributed articles to the newspapers of Cincinnati."[7]

Wright himself is the speaker in his monody, which he dedicated to Pike's widow, Clarissa. In an introduction, he wrote, "I am aware that an apology is due for my presumption, in dedicating to you, without permission, this feeble tribute to the memory and virtues of your departed husband." He further set the laudatory and somber tone of the poem by noting, again in his introduction,

> The memory of a hero is always dear to his countrymen—and the recollection of the exulted principles of honor, the undaunted heroism, and the milder virtues, which shone forth in their native lustre, in the character of General Pike—will ever be cherished by a grateful people. The tears of a nation spring afresh at his remembrance, and flow in holy sympathy with the tears of those who were "Dearer than life to him."[8]

The poem opens at "The Battleground, near York." It is evening and, "Sweet sleep the brave, who for their country die! / Around their urn the whisp'ring breeze shall sigh." Wright had no doubt that in the future, "On that dear spot shall thousands, yet unborn, / Retire to shed the willing tear, and mourn!" He invoked first the heavens, "Spirit of Sympathy! from Heaven descend! / A Nation Weeps!— Columbia mourns a friend!" and called as witnesses "the patriot dead" of the Revolution and others from the recently concluded conflict with Britain.

Pike's leadership, inspiration, and valor on the battlefield are enshrined in stanzas typical of the entire work:

Unmov'd, the gallant chief beholds the scene,
And mid the battle's carnage smiles serene!
His noble soul glows with a patriot fire,
His cheering words each noble soul inspire;
The humblest warrior, bent on deeds of fame,
Feels the glad impulse thrill thro'out his frame
Whilst, the bright Eagle hov'ring o'er their heads,
From rank to rank th'infusive ardor spreads.

The details of Pike's death are then recounted. A British magazine explodes and "hurls the pond'rous stones," mortally wounding Pike. Reflecting opinion at the time, Wright characterized the explosion as British treachery, appending the footnote, "The inhuman conduct of the enemy, here alluded to, must be fresh in the recollection of the public, and need not be recapitulated." Pike is then carried aboard a ship—"the proud ship its precious freight receives," and the captured British flag is placed beneath his head—"the well earn'd banner now is spread, / A glorious pillow for a soldier's head!" In conclusion, Wright called for monuments to Pike's memory, "Shall not THY COUNTRY some memorial raise? / Some grateful tribute of A NATION'S praise? / Yes! let thy name the marble proudly tell, / Who liv'd in honor and in glory fell."

While monuments to Pike do dot America today, Wright would probably be distressed at how few of them celebrate his patriotism and sacrifice and mourn anew at how Pike has been forgotten as a fallen war hero.

Numerous biographies of Pike appeared in the decades following his death. They usually came bound in volumes also featuring the lives of other heroes of the War of 1812. Examples include R. Thomas's *The Glory of America, Comprising Memoirs of the Lives and Glorious Exploits of Some of the Distinguished Officers Engaged in the Late War with Great Britain;* James Renwick's *Lives of Count Rumford, Zebulon Montgomery Pike, and Samuel Gorton;* Charles Jacobs Peterson's *The Military Heroes of the War of 1812, with a Narrative of the War;* and John S. Jenkins, who wrote *Jackson and the Generals of the War of 1812* and then reworked it as *Daring Deeds of American Generals* and as *The Lives of Distinguished American Generals in the Last War with Great Britain.* These studies appeared in a bewildering number of editions and sometimes with a variation in title. The interest of Americans in these lives evidently remained high, or at least was actively sought by publishers.[9]

One of the earliest and most effusively titled of the biographies was John M. Niles's *The Life of Oliver Hazard Perry, with an Appendix, Comprising a Biographical Memoir of the Late Captain James Lawrence; with Brief Sketches of the Most Prominent Events in the Lives of Commodores Bainbridge, Decatur, Porter and Macdonough. A List of the Officers of the Navy. To Which Is Added, a Biography of General Pike, and a View of the Leading Events in the Life of General Harrison.* At least there could be no doubt in a buyer's mind as to what he or she was purchasing. Niles, a lawyer and newspaper publisher, founded the *Hartford Times* and also published the Connecticut *Gazetteer* and Rhode Island's *The Independent Whig.* He represented Connecticut in the U.S. Senate for various terms in the 1830s and 1840s and served briefly as postmaster general in 1840.[10]

Niles's tribute to Pike is as florid as its title. Cast in the mold of Parson Weems's biography of George Washington, it seeks to instruct as well as praise. For example, of Pike's early years Niles wrote, "From his youth he sedulously cultivated in himself a generous spirit of chivalry, . . . the chivalry of the ancient school of European honor." On the other hand, modern readers might find Niles not too wide of the mark when he said of Pike, "His conduct towards the Indians was marked with equal good sense, firmness, and humanity," and concerning the western expedition, "In the course of this long, toilsome, and perilous march, Pike displayed a degree of personal heroism and hardihood, united with a sagacity which, had they been exerted on some wide theatre of action, would have done honour to the most renown general."

Like Nathaniel Wright, Niles commanded the highblown rhetoric of the day to enjoin future generations to remember and revere Pike, imploring,

Gallant Spirit! Thy country will not forget thee; thou shalt have a noble memory. When a greatful nation confers upon the heroes of Niagara and Erie the laurels they have so nobly earned, she will bid them remember that those laurels were first gathered on the shores of York; and were watered by the blood of a hero; and hereafter, when our children and children's children shall read the story of patriots and heroes who have gallantly fallen in the arms of victory, when their eyes glisten, and their young hearts throb wildly at the kindling theme, they will close the volume which tells of Epaminondas, of Sydney, or of Wolfe, and proudly exclaim, "And we too had our Montgomery and our Pike."[11]

John Jenkins's biography is reflective of all the others that appeared in the 1840s and 1850s. Coming thirty years later than Niles's work, it is equally laudatory but less emotional, more factual, and demonstrates the inevitable loosing of bonds with the passage of time and the older generations. Jenkins began, "This gallant officer . . . was bred in a camp, lived a soldier's life, and died a soldier's death." Pike's poor education—a distress to Pike himself and the bane of readers of his journals—is acknowledged, although Jenkins added, "He possessed an inquiring mind, habits of investigation and reflection, and was a nice observer of men and things." Of Pike's army career, Jenkins observed, "His whole soul was in his profession . . . He panted for action, for glory and fame." He characterized Pike as "active in temperament, enthusiastic, ambitious to excel, and, perhaps, too fond of innovations," and then continued on to recount a story of Pike "drilling his men with snow shoes, in anticipation of a winter campaign in Canada."

In considering Pike's death, Jenkins quoted extensively from the letter Pike wrote to his father the day before he embarked for Canada, a letter that contained the somewhat prophetic phrase, "If success attends my steps, honor and glory await my name; if defeat, still shall it be said that we died like brave men, and conferred honor, even in death, on the American name." Jenkins remarked, "The hero's wish was gratified. . . . He desired no higher, or greater distinction, in life, than to serve his country in the tented field—he asked no nobler death than that which awaited him, in the hour of his proud triumph." Conspicuously missing from Jenkins's account, given the earlier effusions of

Wright and Niles, is the assertion that in the future Americans will make pilgrimages to Pike's grave.[12]

From this point—in the nineteenth century at least— almost nothing more is heard of Pike. He disappeared from the cultural landscape, with one exception. Through popular usage, especially among the fur trappers, traders, miners, and tourists who came to Colorado over the ensuing decades, Pike became associated with "his" mountain, Pikes Peak. No clear evidence points to if or when it was so officially designated, although John C. Frémont, on his maps and in his reports of his explorations in the Rockies in 1842 and 1844, consistently used the name. The twentieth century, however, witnessed a renewed interest in Pike, sparked in part by the 1906 anniversary of his Southwest Expedition. But unlike the accolades he received in the nineteenth century, Pike was now remembered almost exclusively for his explorations.[13]

States and localities erected a number of monuments to mark Pike's impact on the opening of the American West. Kansas can lay claim to the dedication of one of the first such sites along Pike's western route, although as it turned out the wrong locale was chosen.

In late September 1806, Pike and his men held a grand council with the Pawnees at their village. Noting the Spanish flag flying over the village, Pike demanded that it be taken down and a U.S. flag raised in its place. For some eager Kansans, this became the first U.S. flag flown in Kansas. In 1901, at the supposed site in Republic County, a twenty-six-foot-tall granite monolith was placed to mark the event. Today it is generally acknowledged that the Pawnee village Pike visited actually lay farther north, across the Kansas–Nebraska border, near Guide Rock. Nebraska Highway Marker 47 now directs interested travelers to the proper site.

A second Kansas monument to Pike is situated near the town of Delphos. Raised in 1962 by the Ottawa County Historical Society, it commemorates Pike's passage up the Solomon River valley on his way to meet with the Pawnees.[14]

Colorado hosts perhaps the greatest number of Pike monuments. In Colorado Springs, the week-long, lavish celebration of the one-hundredth anniversary of Pike's trek through Colorado, presided over by then U.S. Vice President Charles Fairbanks, spurred the dedication of various memorials. Two of the most prominent include a ten-foot-tall, seventeen-ton boulder set up in the city's Antlers Park and an impressive bronze plaque securely affixed at the summit of Pikes Peak. Each is suitably inscribed. In 1936 the State Historical Society of Colorado reconstructed the stockade that Pike and his men built near present Sanford. It was there that Spanish troops found Pike and from which he and his men departed for Santa Fe on February 27, 1807. The city of Pueblo also has honored Pike, creating Pike Plaza as part of its new Historic Arkansas Riverwalk in 2002. The plaza features a plaque dedicated to Pike by the Daughters of the American Revolution, an "interpretive" contemporary sculpture of Pike, and a series of medallions quoting selections from his journal.[15]

The most poignant of all Pike markers may be that commissioned in 1934 by the National Society of the United States Daughters of 1812. It stands near the spot where Pike lost his life, at Historic Fort York in Toronto, Ontario, Canada. It must be one of the few memorials in the world to an enemy combatant on the soil of the injured country. Placed "by permission of the mayor and council of the City of Toronto," it reads, "To the glory of God and in memory of Brigadier General Zebulon Montgomery Pike and of the officers, soldiers and men of the Army and Navy of the United States of America who were killed during the attack on York, April 27, 1813." Here is where any tears for Pike might most appropriately be shed — not least because the exact location of his mortal remains is unclear. It is certain that he is buried in the military cemetery at Sackets Harbor, New York, and investigations are under way to attempt to pinpoint which grave is his, but the only marker there is a modest granite monument carrying a small bronze cannon, placed in a far corner. The original wooden monument on the grave had largely deteriorated by 1860 and later disappeared.[16]

Besides monuments, Pike also has been remembered in the twentieth century with various place-names, although not counties and towns, as he was in the nineteenth century. In the 1930s Iowans marked his voyage up the Mississippi River with the creation of Pikes Peak State Park near McGregor in 1935 and with the completion of the Zebulon Pike Lock and Dam at Dubuque in 1937. In Minnesota, Fort Snelling State Park boasts a Pike Island, and Morrison County is home to Zebulon Pike Lake. In Colorado, the U.S. Forest Service established Pike National Forest in 1907. Near New Orleans, Louisiana, Fort Pike State Historic Site comprises the extant ruins of fortifications constructed and named for Pike in 1826. Officially abandoned in 1890, it was placed on the National Register of Historic Places in 1972. The Army Corps of Engineers completed Pike Island Locks and Dam on the Ohio River, near Wheeling, West Virginia, in 1963, replacing older corps structures built between 1912 and 1916.[17]

As previously noted, Pike lives on perhaps most vibrantly in literature. Four novels and more than a dozen juvenile accounts of his life and adventures have appeared since 1900. The novels all reflect romantic notions of the American West at the time they were published. The juveniles are of varying content and merit. The first novel to appear was Robert Ames Bennet's *A Volunteer with Pike, the True Narrative of One Dr. John Robinson and of His Love for the Fair Señorita Vallois,* published in 1909. It is loosely based on the life of Dr. John Robinson who accompanied Pike on his expedition to the Southwest, attached as a civilian physician. Historically, Robinson's ostensible reason for enduring the hardships of the journey was that he carried the claims of one William Morrison, an Illinois businessman, against Baptiste La Lande, who had disappeared with Morrison's goods and was rumored to be in Santa Fe. In reality, General James Wilkinson sent him to spy on the Spanish as part of the plot Wilkinson and Aaron Burr were hatching to create their own empire. A decade later Robinson would join the Mexican army in the revolt against Spanish rule. Eventually, he settled in Natchez, Mississippi, and opened a medical practice.[18]

Approximately one third of this novel touches on Pike and his expedition. When it does so it is relatively accurate and informative. Otherwise, it is highly romanticized. The story opens in Washington, D.C., where Robinson has gone to entreat President Jefferson for an appointment to go west with Pike. There he meets Alisandra Vallois, the "fair señorita" of the title. In the course of the book he voyages down the Ohio with the señorita and her uncle; obtains permission to accompany Pike, although he is only mildly interested in the Burr–Wilkinson conspiracy; slogs over the Sangre de Cristos hoping to reach Chihuahua, where Alisandra is living with her family; arrives in Chihuahua; fights a duel with a rival for Alisandra's hand; is escorted to Natchitoches when Pike is returned there; attempts to make his way with the pirate Jean Lafitte to Vera Cruz, Mexico, where, he has learned from a secret message, Alisandra will be awaiting him—she having eluded her family's attempts to marry her off elsewhere; and is captured by a British warship which just happens to be carrying Señorita Vallois, who naturally has had a few adventures of her own. Love conquers all. Married by the captain of the warship, the pair transfers to a merchant vessel that then, in the words of the novel's final sentence, "puts into one of the many mouths of the Mississippi, and, ascending in charge of a pilot, landed us at New Orleans, the happiest couple in all the wide world."[19]

Far better than Bennet is Edwin L. Sabin's *Lost With Lieutenant Pike*, published in 1919. Sabin was a prolific author of both fiction and nonfiction, drawing on western events and themes. His *Kit Carson Days* is still in print. He closely adheres to Pike's journals in writing this novel, although he introduces a young boy, a captive of the Pawnees, as his protagonist. The book's lengthy subtitle effectively sums up the plot:

> How from the Pawnee village the boy named Scar Head marched with the young American chief [Pike] clear into the snowy mountains; how in the dead of winter they searched for the lost river and thought that they had found it; and how the Spanish soldiery came upon them and took them down to Santa Fé of New Mexico, where another surprise awaited them.

The surprise is that Scar Head actually is Jack Pursley, son of Kentucky fur trapper James Pursley. Here Sabin ingeniously grafts his plot onto the presence in Santa Fe of the historical Kentuckian James Purcell, whom Pike called "Pursley" in his journal. Purcell, a fur trapper, trader, and sometime gold prospector, was one of the first Americans to enter New Mexico, going there in 1805 to trade and staying on for nineteen years, making his living as a carpenter. Sabin's premise is plausible within the confines of his plot, and the story is very entertaining.[20]

The only other two novels incorporating Pike's career are Arthur Carhart's *Drum up the Dawn*, published in 1937, and Richard Woodley's *Zebulon Pike – Pioneer Destiny*, which appeared in 1982. Carhart was a dedicated conservationist who wrote widely from the 1930s to the 1950s on a variety of environmental topics but also tried his hand at fiction. His novel is concerned primarily with the fate of William Meek, one of Pike's most trusted and supportive men. Meek did not return to the United States with Pike, having killed his fellow soldier and friend, Theodore Miller, in Chihuahua. The Spanish held him there until 1820. Woodley's *Pioneer Destiny* is one of a number of fictional works in the publisher's *American Explorers Series*. For action it adheres closely to Pike's journal, reading much like the journal with dialogue added. In the usual vein of such action-packed Westerns, a romantic element is introduced, with General Wilkinson attempting to seduce Clarissa, Pike's wife, and Pike falling for the inevitable raven-haired señorita in Santa Fe. None of the novels with Pike as the hero follows his career to its end by using his role in the War of 1812 and his death as part of its plot.[21]

The juvenile accounts of Pike's life have a curious publishing history. Only two appeared before 1950, *The Boy's Story of Zebulon Pike, Explorer of the Great Southwest*, which despite its title also considers Pike's Mississippi River explorations, and *As The Crow Flies*, which dramatizes Pike's relationship with the Indians on the upper Mississippi. Of the others, six have publication dates in the 1950s and 1960s. Then there is a gap of two decades, with six more available since 1990. Most of the earlier volumes follow the pattern of Augusta Stevenson's *Zeb Pike, Boy Traveler* (1950) in that they simplify and dramatize Pike's boyhood, depicting the hardships of his frontier existence as preparation for his later deeds. Several also portray his death in the solemn tones of the nineteenth century.

All of the most recent books aimed at elementary and secondary school students focus exclusively on Pike's explorations, with emphasis on the Southwest Expedition. His death is treated almost as a footnote to his exploits. All but one are part of publishers' series featuring *Legendary Heroes of the Wild West*, *The World's Great Explorers*, or *Exploring the West*, for example. Most are solidly researched and handsomely illustrated. Through them, for the first time in popular literature as opposed to the academic realm, Pike is firmly placed in the first rank of American explorers. In this instance, at least, his reputation has never stood higher.[22]

Pike's heritage has also been promoted in other popular, although somewhat ephemeral or fugitive, forms. A variety of medals depicting Pike have been struck, beginning in 1906 in conjunction with the one-hundredth anniversary celebrations of the Southwest Expedition. The Franklin Mint, Danbury Mint, and International Geographical Union followed suit, with most examples being offered in the 1970s. In 1984 a well-scripted and -produced documentary video entitled *Zebulon Pike and the Blue Mountain* was released. It highlights Pike's path in Colorado, and it won a Certificate of Commendation from the American Association for State and Local History. Pike aficionados and children of all ages today can even go "geocaching" for Pike, via an Internet Web site directing users to points in Colorado Springs, Colorado. But the most unique popular artifact of Pike has to be the June 1941 issue of *True Comics*. It carried a feature entitled *Frontier Fighters: Zebulon Pike* — a full color, seven-page account of Pike's two expeditions in classic comic book format. It is interesting that this was only the second issue of *True Comics* and why Pike's story was chosen is not known. Daniel Boone was featured as a "frontier fighter" in the following August issue and that was the end of the series, such as it was.[23]

As the country celebrates the two-hundredth anniversary of Pike's Southwest Expedition, it is evident that Pike's place in American popular culture is secure. It might astonish his nineteenth-century admirers that he is remembered more for his explorations up the Mississippi and to the Southwest than for his death in battle. Old soldiers truly do fade away and in that sense Pike "peaked" long ago. For most Americans today, Pike's memory and reputation are irrevocably tied to the mountain bearing his name. Somewhat ironically, Pike secured his fame not with his heroic death but when, on November 15, 1806, he spotted a "small blue cloud" — Pikes Peak — on the western horizon. For the tens of thousands of tourists who ascend Pikes Peak annually and who gaze east to the Great Plains and west to the serrated ranks of the Rockies, Pike is and remains one of the great explorers of the American West.

Michael L. Olsen, Ph.D., has been a history professor for more than thirty years. He earned his Ph.D. from the University of Washington. He moved to Colorado Springs, Colorado, after a thirty-year tenure at New Mexico Highlands University, Las Vegas, New Mexico. His major research interest is in the social and ethnic history of the Santa Fe Trail, and he has published extensively on trail history. He is a member of the Pikes Peak Regional History Symposium Steering Committee, the Pike Commission of Santa Fe Trail Association, and the Pikes Peak Posse of the Westerners.

Notes

The author thanks Jessy Randall, archivist at Colorado College's Tutt Library, the staff at the Interlibrary Loan Division — Pikes Peak Library District, and librarians at Pikes Peak Community College, all in Colorado Springs, for aid in obtaining many Pike items. The author thanks Neil Argo for the information he provided, the Pueblo City–County Library for the loan copy of the documentary video *Zebulon Pike and the Blue Mountain*, and Ken Purvis, senior program officer, Historic Fort York, for the information and photograph he provided concerning the Pike memorial.

1. All of the preliminary research for this article, and much of the subsequent development of that research, was conducted via the Internet. In fact, before the advent of this modern intelligence network, an analysis of Pike's place in American culture would have been difficult and expensive, and have taken years to complete. Now, with the stroke of a key, every entry concerning Pike in the Library of Congress can be noted, and memorials to Pike as far-flung as Toronto, the San Luis Valley of Colorado, and southern Louisiana can be viewed and visited. Ten U.S. counties named for Pike all have Web sites. Even the minutes of the November 17, 2003, meeting of the Board of Trustees of Sackets Harbor, New York, concerning

current investigations into the location of Zebulon Pike's grave can be accessed online. All such URL citations were current as of March 15, 2006.

2. Pike novels are discussed and cited later in this article. The Kansas celebration of 1906 received extensive coverage in "One Hundred Years Under the Flag. The Centennial Celebration of Pike's Pawnee Village," *Kansas Historical Collections, 1907–1908* 10 (1908): 15–159. See also Amanda Laugesen, "Making a Unique Heritage: Historical Celebrations in Kansas, 1900–1918," *Kansas History: A Journal of the Central Plains* 21 (Winter 1998–1999): 234–55.

3. E. D. Hirsch, et al., eds., *The New Dictionary of Cultural Literacy*, 3d ed., 2002, accessed at http://www.bartleby.com/59/3/oldsoldiersn.html. General MacArthur paraphrased the lyrics in his famous speech to a joint session of Congress on April 19, 1951.

4. As noted, many of these entities maintain Web sites. For Murfreesboro history, see http://www.rootsweb.com/~arpcahs/pikehistory.htm. For the Pike County, Georgia, historical marker, see http://www.cviog.uga.edu/Projects/gainfo/courthouses/pikeCH.htm.

5. For steamboats, see the Lewis and Clark Journey of Discovery Web site at http://www.nps.gov/jeff/LewisClark2/Circa1804/WestwardExpansion/EarlyExplorers/ZebulonPike.htm; http://members.tripod.com /~Write4801/riverboats/p.html. For the warship *General Pike*, see *Dictionary of American Naval Fighting Ships*, Department of the Navy Web site at www.hazegray.org/danfs/sail/gen_pike.htm. For information about the army's tugboat, *see* http://www.hazegray.org/worldnav/usa/army.htm.

6. http://www.p4a.com/itemsummary/93747.htm.

7. Nathaniel Hill Wright, *The Fall of Palmyra: and Other Poems* (Middlebury, Vt.: William Slade, 1817), 73–89; Wright, *Monody, on the Death of Brigadier General Zebulon Montgomery Pike and Other Poems* (Middlebury, Vt.: Slade and Ferguson, 1814). See also *American Heritage College Dictionary*, 4th ed. (Boston: Houghton Mifflin Co., 2002), 899; William Turner Coggeshall, *The Poets and Poetry of the West: With Biographical and Critical Notices* (Columbus, Ohio: Follett, Foster and Co., 1860), 113, at http://www.wvu.edu/~lawfac/jelkins/lp-2001/wright_n.thml.

8. Wright, *The Fall of Palmyra*, 77–78. All subsequent quotations from Wright's monody are from this source.

9. R. Thomas, *The Glory of America, Comprising Memoirs of the Lives and Glorious Exploits of Some of the Distinguished Officers Engaged in the Late War with Great Britain* (New York: E. Strong, 1834). Other editions

include New York: E. Strong, 1836, 1837, 1843, 1845; Philadelphia: Leary and Getz, 1833, 1836; Hartford: Sumner and Goodman, 1847; Hartford: A. C. Goodman, 1850. James Renwick, *Lives of Count Rumford, Zebulon Montgomery Pike, and Samuel Gorton* (Boston: C. C. Little and J. Brown, 1845); Little and Brown published a subsequent edition in 1848. Charles Jacobs Peterson, *The Military Heroes of the War of 1812, with a Narrative of the War* (Philadelphia: W. A. Leary, 1848); other editions include, Philadelphia: W. A. Leary, 1849, 1850; Philadelphia: J. B. Smith and Co., 1848, 1858, 1859. John S. Jenkins, *Jackson and the Generals of the War of 1812* (Philadelphia: J. L. Gihon, 1854); a subsequent edition is Philadelphia: J. B. Smith and Co., 1856. John S. Jenkins, *Daring Deeds of American Generals* (New York: A. A. Kelley, 1856); other editions are New York: A. A. Kelley, 1857, 1858. John S. Jenkins, *The Lives of Distinguished American Generals in the Last War with Great Britain* (Auburn, N.Y.: Derby, Miller and Co., 1849); subsequent editions are 1850, 1851.

10. John M. Niles, *The Life of Oliver Hazard Perry, with an Appendix, Comprising a Biographical Memoir of the Late Captain James Lawrence; with Brief Sketches of the Most Prominent Events in the Lives of Commodores Bainbridge, Decatur, Porter and Macdonough. A List of the Officers of the Navy. To Which Is Added, a Biography of General Pike, and a View of the Leading Events in the Life of General Harrison* (Hartford: William S. Marsh, 1820); a second edition is Hartford: O. D. Cooke, 1821. See also the Miller Center of Public Affairs, University of Virginia, http://www.americanpresident.org/history/martinvanburen/cabinet/PostmasterGeneral/JohnMNiles/h_index.shtml.

11. Niles, *Life of Oliver Hazard Perry*, 318, 322, 326, 337.

12. Jenkins, *Lives of Distinguished American Generals* (1851), 323, 324, 328, 329, 336–37.

13. The apostrophe in "Pike's" was removed at the instigation of the U.S. Bureau on Geographic Names after 1891, and the Colorado State Legislature in 1978 passed a law requiring the spelling "Pikes Peak." See W. Eugene Hollon, *The Lost Pathfinder, Zebulon Montgomery Pike* (Norman: University of Oklahoma Press, 1949), 128; *Wikipedia*, "Pikes Peak," at http://www.answers.com/topic/pikes-peak; U.S. Geological Survey at http://interactive2.usgs.gov/faq/list_faq_by_category/get_questions_for_category.asp?category_id=33.

14. The 1901 marker was integrated into Kansas's Pawnee Indian Museum State Historic Site until 2005, when it was largely destroyed by a tornado. See http://kansasphototour.com/pawnee.htm. For the controversy concerning the site of the village, see Anne M. Platoff, "The Pike–Pawnee Flag Incident: Reexamining a Vexillological Legend," *Raven: A Journal of Vexillology* 6 (1999): 1–8, at http://

aplatoff.home.mindspring.com/flags /pikepawnee.html. The text of the Nebraska marker can be read at http://www.nebraskahistory. org/publish/markers/texts/republican_pawnee_village.htm. Information on and photographs of the Delphos marker are at http:// www.kansasphototour.com/pikemon.htm.
    15. For the 1906 festivities in Colorado Springs, which had hilarious and sometimes ludicrous moments, *see* Nancy E. and Edwin A. Bathke, "The Pike Celebration Centennial 1906," in this book, pages 243-262. Views of Pike's stockade are at http://members.tripod.com/ %7Emr_sedivy/colorado14.html. Pueblo Riverwalk information is at http://www.puebloharp.com; http://sangres.com/places/pueblo / riverwalk. htm; Peyton Abbot, "Pueblo's New Monument to Zebulon M. Pike," *Wagon Tracks: Santa Fe Trail Association Quarterly* 17 (August 2003): 23.
    16. The Daughters of 1812 maintain a Web site at http://www. usdaughters1812. org. For information on Pike's grave, present and past, see "Finding Pike: Fort Drum archaeologist searches for general's remains," at http://www.drum.army.mil/sites/postnews/ blizzard/blizzard_archives/news.asp?id=9&issuedate=10-9-2003; "Village of Sackets Harbor Mayor's Report, Monthly Board Meeting," November 17, 2003; Benson J. Lossing, *Pictorial Field-Book of the War of 1812* (New York: Harper and Brothers, 1868), at http://freepages. history.rootsweb.com/~wcarr1/Lossing2/Contents.html (select ch. 28). Lossing visited Pike's grave in 1855 and again in 1860. His account includes a description and engraving of the deteriorating monument.
    17. For Iowa, see http://www.iowadnr.com/parks/state_park_ list/pikes_peak.html; http://www.dubuquechamber.com/visit/ attractions. cfm?Page=AT&Cat=10. For Minnesota, see http://brass612. tripod.com/pike.html, http://www.dnr.state.mn.us/lakefind/index. html. For Pike National Forest, see Maxine Benson, *1001 Colorado Place Names* (Lawrence: University Press of Kansas, 1994), 168. For Fort Pike State Historic Site, see http://www.crt.state.la.us/crt/parks/fortpike/ fortpike.htm. For Pike Island Locks and Dam, *see* http://www.lrp.usace. army.mil/nav/pike.htm.
    18. Leroy R. Hafen, *Colorado and Its People: A Narrative and Topical History of the Centennial State*, 4 vols. (New York: Lewis Historical Publishing Co., 1948), 1:54, 2:388.
    19. Robert Ames Bennet, *A Volunteer with Pike: The True Narrative of One Dr. John Robinson and of His Love for the Fair Señorita Vallois* (Chicago: A. C. McClurg and Co., 1909), 453.
    20. The book was published under two titles, *Lost with Lieutenant Pike* (Philadelphia: J. B. Lippencott, 1919); and *With Lieutenant Pike*

(Philadelphia: J. B. Lippencott, 1919). For information on Sabin, *see* http://www.lib.uiowa.edu/spec-coll/Bai/jordan2.htm. For Purcell's story, see Hafen, *Colorado and Its People*, 1:63, 65.

21. A precise glimpse of Pike's men and their lives is Donald Jackson, "Zebulon Pike's Damned Rascals," *Occasional Papers No. 1* (Colorado Springs: Pikes Peak Posse of the Westerners, 1979); Arthur Carhart, *Drum up the Dawn* (New York: Dodd, Mead and Co., 1937); Richard Woodley, *Zebulon Pike, Pioneer Destiny,* (Wayne, Pa.: Banbury Books, 1982).

22. The following are ranked in order of first publication date: Mary Gay Humphries, ed. *The Boy's Story of Zebulon Pike, Explorer of the Great Southwest* (New York: Charles Scribner's Sons, 1911); Cornelia Meigs, *As The Crow Flies* (New York: Macmillan Co., 1927); Faith Yingling Knoop, *Zebulon Pike* (Evanston, Ill.: Row, Peterson and Co., 1950); Augusta Stevenson, *Zeb Pike, Boy Traveler* (Indianapolis: The Bobbs-Merrill Co., 1953) (part of the publisher's "Childhood of Famous Americans" series); Nina Brown Baker, *Pike of Pike's Peak* (New York: Harcourt, Brace and Co., 1953); Leonard Wibberly, *Zebulon Pike: Soldier and Explorer* (New York: Funk and Wagnalls Co., 1961); Howard Stanley Aronson, *Zeb Pike* (San Antonio: Naylor Co., 1963); Bern Keating, *Zebulon Pike: Young America's Frontier Scout* (New York: H. P. Putnam's Sons, 1965); Susan Sinnot, *Zebulon Pike* (Chicago: Childrens Press, 1990) (part of the publisher's "The World's Great Explorers" series); Jared Stallones, *Zebulon Pike and the Explorers of the American Southwest* (New York: Chelsea House, 1992) ("World Explorers" Series); William R. Sanford and Carl R. Green, *Zebulon Pike, Explorer of the Southwest* (Springfield, N.J.: Enslow, 1996) ("Legendary Heroes of the Wild West" series); Charles W. Maynard, *Zebulon Pike, Soldier-Explorer of the American Southwest* (New York: Rosen Publishing Group, 2003); Barbara Witteman, *Zebulon Pike: Soldier and Explorer* (Mankato, Minn.: Capstone Press, 2003) ("Let Freedom Ring—Exploring the West" series); Patricia Calvert, *Zebulon Pike, Lost in the Rockies* (New York: Marshall Cavendish, 2005) ("Great Explorations" series).

23. For the 1906 commemorative medal, see Bathke, "The Pike Celebration," in this book. A number of the medals can be viewed on line; see especially http://www.skyrunner.com/story/pp_medals.htm. The difficult-to-find documentary video was produced by John Henry Johnson and narrated by Burgess Meredith, with musical score by Neil Argo. The geocaching site is at http://www.geocaching.com/track/track_detail.asp?ID=10682. The *True Comics* issue is available on line at http://digital.lib.msu.edu/collections/index.cfm?action=view&TitleID=57&Format=gif.

Pike lives on most vibrantly in literature. Four novels have appeared since 1900, the first being Robert Ames Bennet's *A Volunteer with Pike, the True Narrative of One Dr. John Robinson and of His Love for the Fair Señorita Vallois*, published in 1909. This illustration shows Pike leading the ascent of "The Grand Peak!" while Robinson calls out, "we'll name it for you." *From Special Collections, Pikes Peak Library District.*

Marketing the Mountain:
Pikes Peak in the Popular Imagination

Leah Davis Witherow

Shortly after the death of her husband, grieving young widow and mother Gladys Bueler was faced with a dilemma. Her 11-year-old son Bill had a cold and had to be left at home alone while she went off to work and her 13-year-old daughter Barbara went to school. It was a decision she felt badly about as she drove to her job in downtown New Orleans. Her day was about to get worse when she noticed a new "No Parking Day or Night" sign in the vacant lot where she parked every day. Something inside of Gladys broke and she decided that she and her family needed a fresh start. She drove home in tears to find Bill looking at an atlas. In desperation she asked, "Bill, find us someplace to move." Bill paged through the atlas and finally stopped on Colorado. He exclaimed, "Here's Colorado Springs, it's got Pikes Peak. Let's move there!" "All right, let's do!" she replied. Three weeks later Gladys and her two children were bound for Colorado Springs and Pikes Peak. The year was 1942.[1]

Why Colorado? Why Pikes Peak? Because by 1942 Pikes Peak was instantly recognizable, not just to the Beuler family but to people from around the world. It was an American icon, one of the geographic features that defined America's unique identity much like the Grand Canyon and Niagara Falls. For over one hundred years, images and written descriptions of Pikes Peak had captured the imaginations of Americans who were eager for a glimpse of the curious topography that lay west of the Mississippi River.

For generations, civic boosters, promoters and entrepreneurs cemented the legendary status of the mountain by relentlessly marketing Pikes Peak to suit the needs and values of each new era. Pikes Peak became a "must-see" on any western vacation or tour. "To really experience America and its history you have to go see the Grand Canyon and you need to go to the summit of Pikes Peak," commented Michele Carvell, a local resident and tourism expert.[2]

By the twentieth century, Pikes Peak represented the history of the American West combined with a good dose of imagination and adventure—in other words, a perfect place to start a new life.[3]

Today over six million people from around the globe visit the Pikes Peak region yearly and five hundred thousand make a pilgrimage up Pikes Peak to take in the view that inspired Katharine Lee Bates' "America the Beautiful."[4] The mountain never climbed by Zebulon Pike, but named for him, has served as Colorado Springs' greatest marketing asset from its founding date in 1871 to the present. As a result, the places (Colorado Springs and Manitou Springs) and the products (mineral water, malt liquor, toys, beer, automobiles, tires, and nail polish are a few examples) associated with America's Mountain have always been highly desirable. Playing a central role in the development of the region, Pikes Peak provides a thread linking the historical past with the present. Tourism, long an important part of the local economy, now generates one billion dollars in income per year.

Pikes Peak appears massive. In reality it is 14,115 feet tall, a respectable height for the Rocky Mountains but in Colorado alone there are over fifty mountains over 14,000 feet.[5] Historically, the mountain may have appeared higher than others due to its unique geographical position on the Front Range. Pikes Peak stands to the east of the main ranges of the Rocky Mountains and as such it has served as a guide for travelers heading west along the Great Plains. Whether traveling by foot, horseback, wagon, railroad or automobile, the mountain made a powerful first impression upon many weary travelers. Pikes Peak's imposing shape and eastern location have meant that over time the mountain that lent its name to a region grew in reputation to become known as "America's Mountain."

On November 15, 1806, when Zebulon Pike first spotted "America's Most Famous Mountain," he called it by a very different name. As he and his men stood on a hill near Las Animas, Colorado, they gave "Three cheers to the Mexican Mountains!"[6] Pike's attempt, and ultimate failure, to climb what he described as the "Grand Peak" was well documented in his 1810 published journal. His written description of the mountain that would later bear his name was perhaps the first printed in the English language—but certainly not the last nor the most elaborate.

Following in Pike's footsteps came other explorers, scientists, artists, geographers, and eventually commercial photographers and travel journalists who sought out Pikes Peak as a destination. Time and time again they described the mountain as an awe-inspiring example of America's unique scenic beauty. Travelogues such as *Crest of the Continent* and *Beyond the Mississippi* as well as the illustrated weeklies such as *Frank Leslie's* and *Harper's* provided a flurry of Pikes Peak images created by artist Thomas Moran and many others. These skillful prints and photographs inspired a generation of Americans to see the West with their own eyes.

One such thrill seeker was Julia Archibald Holmes. She, her husband James and several companions reached the summit of Pikes Peak on August 5, 1858. Interested in comfort, she wore a calico dress reaching just below her knees with matching pants known as "reform dress" or "bloomers." She shocked her fellow members of the gold-seeking Lawrence Party with her radical attire and ideas about equality as they moved west along the trail to the Pikes Peak region. Her vivid description of the multiple-day ascent up the mountain was widely published in newspapers that fall. "In all probability I am the first woman who has ever stood upon the summit of this mountain and gazed upon this wondrous scene . . ."[7] For Julia as for countless others, Pikes Peak represented a personal challenge.

By the mid-nineteenth century Pikes Peak was so well known that its name was used to describe the entire region during the 1859 Colorado Gold Rush.[8] Representing the dashed hopes of those seeking instant fortunes, perhaps no other image is so closely associated with the mountain as W. M. Cary's "Pikes Peak or Bust—Busted By Gosh!" Published in a variety of formats over the ensuing decades, the iconic "Busted" image represented the thousands of hopeful "Pikes Peakers" who returned home empty handed and worse for wear. The familiar image of the wagon combined with the slogan "Pikes Peak or Bust!" proved to be so popular that it is still in use today.

Over a decade later, General William Jackson Palmer founded the resort town of Colorado Springs seven miles east of Pikes Peak. In the 1870s tourism was limited primarily to the wealthy. Travel for the sake of viewing scenery of a sublime or picturesque

This iconic "Pikes Peak or Bust" image by artist W. M. Carey may have discouraged many hopeful gold seekers, ca. 1860. *Courtesy of Starsmore Center for Local History at the Colorado Springs Pioneers Museum.*

nature was extremely fashionable among the upper class.[9] In an impressive effort to market the fledgling town to tourists from the East Coast and abroad, local promoters likened Colorado Springs to the famous resorts of Europe.[10] Civic leaders and business owners lured wealthy travelers and invalids west by bragging about our "pure mountain air" and Alpine-like views. Scores of pamphlets and viewbooks published by local hotels, tourist attractions and civic boosters extolled the curative effects of our climate and mountain scenery. Pikes Peak was advertised as the "nearest thing to Switzerland to be found in America."[11]

Later promotional efforts linked Colorado Springs with the "Wild West," but in 1883 civic boosters publicly stated that although our region held many scenic wonders it was not a wilderness. With a population of thirteen thousand, "many of whom are wealthy and as public-spirited as any in the East," Colorado Springs was a first class destination with Pikes Peak as a stunning backdrop.[12]

A group of local business owners formed an Advertising Committee, later known as the Board of Trade and eventually the Chamber of Commerce. Pooling their advertising dollars, they hired an ambitious secretary, George Rex Buckman, who sent submissions to hundreds of periodicals yearly. Images of Pikes Peak accompanied by romantic and exciting stories frequently appeared in the pages of illustrated weeklies as well as newspapers across the country and Europe. An interesting result of this publicity was the dramatically different versions of Pikes Peak that appeared. Illustrated by artists in England or Germany who had never seen the mountain in person, Pikes Peak often looked more like a part of the Alps than the Rockies.

Pikes Peak appears highly stylized in this undated Thomas Moran print. *Courtesy of Starsmore Center for Local History at the Colorado Springs Pioneers Museum.*

Perhaps the boldest marketing strategy initiated by early civic boosters was the successful effort to locate a branch of the United States Signal Service atop Pikes Peak. Civic leaders and businessmen realized the marketing potential of the highest weather station in the world and launched an ambitious lobbying effort. In the nineteenth century weather reports were avidly read by Americans fascinated by the latest forecasting technology, and Pikes Peak represented a unique opportunity to view storms and other meteorological phenomenon. Citizens in Colorado Springs frequently received reports from the Signal

Corps soldiers stationed at the summit house via an extensive telegraph system. News from the Peak filled local and national papers and added to the allure of the mountain.[13]

Unfortunately, not all the news arriving from the Signal Service Station was of a scientific nature. In 1875 John Timothy O'Keefe was posted by the U.S. Army atop Pikes Peak. A year later O'Keefe reported that one night while transmitting telegraphic reports to Washington D.C. he was startled by a piercing scream from his wife. She rushed into the room crying, "O, the rats! The rats!"[14]

Apparently vast numbers of giant mountain rats were attacking the poor woman. Acting quickly, O'Keefe immediately encircled his wife with a scroll of zinc plating which prevented the rats from climbing up her clothing. He placed each of his legs in a joint of stovepipe and began to fight a ferocious battle for his life.

In the midst of the swarm, Mrs. O'Keefe hurled an electric wire through the air to encircle herself and her husband. Luckily, the wire was hanging near a heavily charged battery and instantly the dark room was showered with a brilliant electric light. The rats touching the wire met instant death while the others ran off blinded. Sadly, the bedroom door had been left ajar and the rats had devoured the O'Keefe's infant daughter Erin. The grieving parents buried her tiny body on the side of Pikes Peak.

Mourners at the Pikes Peak gravesite of infant Erin O'Keefe, 1875. *Courtesy of Starsmore Center for Local History at the Colorado Springs Pioneers Museum.*

Fortunately, none of the above story is true. However, the "Famous Pikes Peak Rat Story" was printed in newspapers across the globe including London, Paris and Cairo. Tourists flocked to the summit house to pay their respects to the grieving parents only to find an unmarried John O'Keefe. The enterprising sergeant happily sold photographs of an anonymous baby from Colorado Springs to gullible visitors for fifty cents each.[15]

By making travel across the continent affordable, railroads democratized the "American Vacation." During the late nineteenth century tourism became not just a pastime for the wealthy but also for the rapidly expanding middle class. The creative marketing of unique attractions such as Pikes Peak combined with the glamour of travel by rail enticed many vacationers west. Viewbooks extolling the grand scenery of the Pikes Peak region observable from the comfort of a train car were distributed throughout the country.[16]

Railroad companies and hotels often found opportunities to jointly promote the Pikes Peak Region. In the April 11, 1891, edition of the *Colorado Springs Gazette*, the "hotel-men of Colorado Springs" are described as strategizing the "advantages of the place." They planned to travel throughout the country giving stereopticon lectures about Pikes Peak, the scenic beauty of the region and the inherent health benefits of our mountain climate. The hotel managers and owners stated confidently that the railroads would provide free transportation for the physician and publicist chosen to deliver marketing literature across the nation.[17] Postcards produced by various Colorado Springs hotels proved a reliable method of advertising.

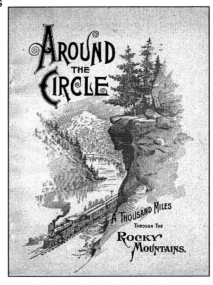

Viewbook published by the Denver & Rio Grande Railway, ca. 1890. *Courtesy of Starsmore Center for Local History at the Colorado Springs Pioneers Museum.*

The spring of 1893 found the hotel owners, railroad promoters and civic boosters of Colorado Springs attempting to lure tourists west from the Chicago World's Fair. That summer, a bright young professor of English from Wellesley College named Katharine Lee Bates visited the fair on her way to teach at Colorado College. One day she and a group of colleagues took a day off to travel to the top of Pikes Peak. Upon reaching the summit Miss Bates declared the stunning view worth the tiring trip.[18] After returning to her hotel in Colorado Springs, she penned the lines of a poem, which later became the beloved anthem "America the Beautiful." Grateful citizens of Colorado Springs later acknowledged her inadvertent efforts to popularize Pikes Peak by placing a plaque in her honor in Shove Chapel at Colorado College as well as a matching memorial in Boston.[19]

At the turn of the century, clever promotional campaigns linked sightseeing in the west to a patriotic rite of passage. The marketing slogan "See America First" encouraged Americans not to go abroad for travel but to stay home instead. Coined in 1905 by a publicist in Salt Lake City, "See America First" boosters urged tourists to "See Europe if you will—but see America first."[20] The catchphrase caught on as Pikes Peak and other famous landmarks were seen as literal expressions of the democratic spirit of the American people. Pikes Peak was no longer just a beautiful mountain but instead represented the basis of a new national pride.

Cover illustration from E. T. Tomlinson's "See America First" manifesto—*Four Boys on Pikes Peak*, published in 1912. *Courtesy of Starsmore Center for Local History at the Colorado Springs Pioneers Museum.*

The Preface to *Four Boys on Pikes Peak*, a work of juvenile literature authored by E. T. Tomlinson in 1912, perfectly illustrates the values and patriotic notions that proponents of "See America First" were working to instill in Americans:

Few places in America combine more romantic, historical, and scenic interests than does Pike's Peak. The name is familiar to all, but how few comparatively have seen its cloud-capped summit or have climbed its rugged slopes. And yet it is within the reach of many. Whatever advantages may arise from the study of the history of other lands or from travel in foreign countries, certainly none of these ought to prevent American boys and girls from becoming well informed concerning the glories of the land they claim as their own. The four boys whose experiences are related in this story believed in seeing their own country first. If the readers of this tale shall be inspired to learn more and see more of America, then its highest purpose will have been accomplished.[21]

Although the formal "See America First" movement eventually came to an end, the persuasive language and imagery that accompanied the countless promotions persisted in the minds of Americans throughout the century.

Zalmon Simmons rode to the summit of Pikes Peak on a mule in 1888. Zalmon, the inventor and founder of the Simmons Beautyrest Mattress Company, made the trip in part to inspect another of his inventions, an insulator for the telegraph wires running to the Army Signal Station atop Pikes Peak. Upon arrival he found the views incredible, but the trip miserable. Simmons later vowed that the next time he reached the summit it would be in the "greatest comfort science can provide."[22] He partnered with John Hulbert, a Civil War veteran from Michigan, to organize the Manitou and Pike's Peak Railway Company. Hulbert served as the chief promoter of the railway and its first president while Simmons functioned as the majority stockholder and owner.

The pair proved successful at attracting investors and railway construction began in 1889. For their dangerous work on the Cog Road the laborers were paid twenty-five cents an hour and six men lost their lives in construction accidents. In 1890 the first three engines arrived from the Baldwin Locomotive Works in Philadelphia. They were named "Pikes Peak," "Manitou," and "John Hulbert." On June 30, 1891, the first passenger train carrying a church choir from Denver made its way to the summit of Pikes Peak. Ironically, a group of dignitaries had been scheduled to officially open the road for publicity purposes but were earlier that day forced to turn back by a rock slide blocking the rail at twelve thousand feet.[23]

The Manitou and Pikes Peak Cog Railway has carried well over a million people to the summit of Pikes Peak. Due to steep mountainous terrain, the use of a cog wheel that meshes into a special rack rail is necessary. This system allows the railway cars on Pikes Peak to climb twenty-five percent grades, while standard railroads typically ascend four to six percent grades.

Reaching a top speed of nine miles per hour, the 8.9 mile trip to the summit has been thrilling passengers for over a century.[24]

Tourists formerly resigned to riding on the back of a mule or burro to glimpse the view from the summit could now relax in relative luxury and marvel at the Cog's cutting edge technology. Today the Manitou and Pikes Peak Cog Railway continues to offer a unique and memorable Pikes Peak experience that visitors seek to commemorate through photographs and souvenirs. Although burros and

Sublime scenery captured in "A Burro Party, Pikes Peak," by artist Charles Graham, for *Harper's Weekly*, ca. 1885. *Courtesy of Starsmore Center for Local History at the Colorado Springs Pioneers Museum.*

mules no longer carry people to the top of Pikes Peak, images of them appear on everything from t-shirts to ashtrays and convey nostalgia for the past that is part of the Pikes Peak mystique.

In the late nineteenth century the people of Colorado Springs were seeking new ways to commemorate the life of Zebulon M. Pike. Pike's journals had been republished in 1889 under the title *Exploratory Travels in North America* and interest in "frontier history" was on the rise. On November 27, 1896, a public meeting was held to discuss the formation of a Zebulon M. Pike Monument Association.[25] Interested citizens began planning for the eventual placement of a permanent memorial to Pike in Colorado Springs. Unfortunately, due to difficulties they faced in fundraising and a lack of congressional support, only a plaster monument to the explorer was erected. Over time the statue disintegrated and was removed but interest in Pike continued to build until 1906.

The Pike Expedition Centennial Celebration was enormously exciting and popular with both locals and tourists. It lasted for over a week and included military maneuvers, parades, rodeos,

Crowds celebrating the very temporary statue of Zebulon Montgomery Pike in front of the Antlers Hotel in Colorado Springs, August 1, 1901. *Courtesy of Starsmore Center for Local History at the Colorado Springs Pioneers Museum.*

dances, concerts, celebrity appearances and an encampment of Native Americans. To kick off the event, churches in Colorado Springs held special services on Sunday, September 23, dedicated to the outstanding moral character of Zebulon Montgomery Pike. Each subsequent day centered around a theme such as Pioneer Day, Historical Day, and Pike Day. On Thursday, September 27, over ten thousand people attended a ceremony in Antlers Park and sang "Ode to Colorado" as an enormous granite boulder dedicated to Pike was unveiled.[26]

The leading men and women of Colorado Springs who organized the commemoration realized the inherent marketing potential of the centennial event and subsequently scheduled the festivities to fall on the shoulder of the tourist season to maximize potential visitors. In addition to advertising efforts by the Centennial Committee and promotions by local businesses, several major railroads offered reduced price fares to entice visitors to our region. A roundtrip ticket from Chicago was reduced to $25 while those arriving from Omaha paid $15.[27]

By all accounts the 1906 Centennial Celebration was a smashing success. Colorado Springs received a remarkable amount of national press and acclaim. Although President Theodore Roosevelt was unable to attend the events, he sent Vice President Fairbanks in his stead. Additionally, numerous congressmen and foreign diplomats were special guests and delighted in viewing a Colorado Springs swathed in yellow and white bunting, a brand new courthouse illuminated with electric lights covering its exterior, and the volunteer firefighters who carried lighted torches to race down Cascade Avenue.[28] Organizers minted a series of medals that were widely circulated. In subsequent years, local boosters have continued to seek opportunities to celebrate Zebulon M. Pike and Pikes Peak at anniversaries ranging from the Rush to the Rockies Centennial in 1959 or the one hundred year anniversary of Colorado statehood in 1976.

The first automobile driven to the top of Pikes Peak was a steam powered Locomobile in 1901.[29] The arduous but exciting trip took sixteen hours to complete. It was just a taste of things to come. The mass production of automobiles in the early twentieth century revolutionized the tourist industry. Auto tourism made travel even more convenient and affordable to middle-class Americans. Without the time constraints placed on them by fixed railroad schedules and routes, tourists now had freedom of movement. The automobile proved to be a thrilling way to travel that allowed an intimacy with nature that could not be found by peering out the window of a train. Although early cars broke down frequently and required almost constant maintenance, America fell in love with automobile travel and took to the roads in droves.

In 1916 the Pikes Peak Auto Highway opened to usher in the modern era of automobile tourism in the region. An engineering marvel for its day, it was the brainchild of marketing guru Spencer Penrose. The nineteen-mile road cost $400,000 to build and required extensive use of draft animals, manpower and explosives to carve a road suitable for automobile traffic up the

mountain. To recoup his investment and that of his stockholders, Penrose charged a fifty cent toll.[30] Anticipating the reluctance some tourists might have to paying the cost to reach the summit, Penrose launched an extensive marketing campaign. A 1916 promotional brochure urges, "Cost should not be considered. It would be foolish to allow the question of cost to deter one from making what is, and forever will be, the World's Most Wonderful Trip!"[31] Local newspapers predicted up to five thousand automobile tourists would arrive in the month of August alone and urged business owners to prepare for them.

The exciting and unique tourist experience offered by the Pikes Peak Auto Highway thrilled visitors in the early twentieth century and continues to do so today.

Colorful pamphlet published in 1916 to celebrate the opening of the Pikes Peak Auto Highway. *Courtesy of Starsmore Center for Local History at the Colorado Springs Pioneers Museum.*

Acknowledging that all drivers and their automobiles might not be suitable for the challenging drive up Pikes Peak, enterprising entrepreneurs outfitted fleets of automobile touring cars to whisk visitors up and down the mountain. At the tender young age of fourteen, Robert K. Brown of Colorado Springs began working as a tourist driver on the Peak making several trips a day during the summer months. His passengers must have been delighted at the trip up the mountain and yet relieved to return down safely when they learned his age! Fleet drivers were known to make the trip as thrilling as possible in order to receive large tips at the end of the drive from grateful passengers.[32]

To generate further excitement and publicity for the Pikes Peak Auto Highway and the soon-to-be-opened Broadmoor Hotel, Spencer Penrose created the first annual Penrose Trophy. Putting up the $2,000 prize money himself, the Hill Climb Contest up Pikes Peak garnered so much national attention that articles about it appeared on the front pages of six hundred fifty different newspapers. Now known as the Pikes Peak International Hill Climb or the "Race to the Clouds," it is the second oldest race

The winner of the annual "Princess Power" contest poses with the Penrose Trophy at the Pikes Peak Hill Climb, ca. 1932. *Photograph by Stewarts Commercial Photographers, from Special Collections, Pikes Peak Library District.*

in the United States next to the Indianapolis 500.[33] Every July, automobiles, trucks and motorcycles speed around one hundred fifty-six corners to the summit, a total distance of 12.4 miles.[34] The race is legendary and draws an international audience, with racers and fans coming from as far away as Germany, Japan and Dubai. The Hill Climb has had a significant impact on local tourism and perhaps even more importantly, has added another fascinating layer of interest to "America's Mountain."

David Bachoroski has driven to the top of Pikes Peak at least three thousand five hundred times. Why? Bachoroski managed the secret General Motors Pikes Peak High Altitude Vehicle Test Headquarters in Manitou Springs.[35]

David has always loved cars. Before legal driving age, he borrowed his brother's car at age fifteen to enter a hill climb contest and won! In high school he worked part-time at the GM facility. At the age of twenty, David left Colorado behind and headed to Detroit. He showed up at the General Motors Proving Ground and asked for a job testing cars. The track manager was impressed with his driving skills but nevertheless requested a permission letter from David's parents before hiring him. Two years later and missing the mountains, David transferred back to Manitou Springs and was promoted to manager within a few months.

Opened in 1954, the General Motors operation in Manitou used the Pikes Peak Auto Highway to test both new vehicles and new components. The information collected by test drivers on the Peak significantly influenced many of the modern brake and safety systems such as Anti-Lock Brakes that we rely on today. The average test car would cost over $200,000 and was a hand-built prototype shipped from Detroit by tractor trailer. For that reason, safety was extremely important to Bachoroski and his employees. He credits extensive preparation as the key to avoiding any test driver fatalities or serious accidents.

Although the location and purpose of the Pikes Peak High Altitude Vehicle Test Headquarters was kept secret from competitors, tourists on the way up the mountain often could not help but notice the cars that David and his employees were driving. Directed to drive at tourist speed to replicate "real-world conditions," the cars were camouflaged to obscure the make and model. Even though they often placed signs indicating a brake test was in progress, alarmed tourists would call local police to alert them of smoking cars or burning tires. David Bachoroski still drives up Pikes Peak even though he retired from the business several years ago. He confidently states that Pikes Peak Auto Highway is the "safest road in the world." We'll take his word on it.[36]

In 1922, a group of friends decided to climb Pikes Peak on New Year's Eve in bitterly cold weather. The five men, Ed and Fred Morath, Harry Standley, Willis Magee, and Fred Barr, shot off red flares and started a bonfire that caught the attention of people for miles around. After making it home safely, the group decided to make the hike an annual event and invite one man to join them each year, thus the name AdAmAn. These founding members of the club are now lovingly remembered as the "Frozen Five." The early hikes were not known for their safety or comfort. Lacking fancy climbing clothes or gear, the men wrapped newspapers around their legs and wore leather motorcycle caps to keep warm. On the 1925 climb, Barr and two other members suffered from severe frostbite when the temperature dropped to 32 degrees below zero.[37]

A difficult climb up a snowy Pikes Peak for the AdAmAn Club, ca. 1925. *Photograph by Harry L. Standley, Courtesy of Starsmore Center for Local History at the Colorado Springs Pioneers Museum.*

Today the club hikes up Barr Trail and stops overnight at Barr Camp on December 30. The group climbs again the next day and arrives at the summit around three in the afternoon on New Year's Eve. Each year the club's newest member leads the hike, and at nine in the evening sets off five fireworks in remembrance of the "Frozen Five." At the stroke of midnight, the club begins the real fireworks show. People from all over the state are able to see the display, and the event has become an important New Year's Eve tradition for many Colorado residents.

There are typically about thirty to forty people who make the rigorous two-day trip each year, with nearly half of them being guests of the club. To become a member, a person has to make six to seven successful climbs as a guest. Club membership is exclusive and is determined by secret ballot. Most new members have family ties to the club and to Colorado Springs. Sue Graham became the first female member of the club in 1997 after making ten climbs as a guest. Both her husband and her father-in-law were already AdAmAn members.

Since the first climb in 1922, the AdAmAn Club has not missed a single year. Occasionally the weather is too inclement for fireworks, but the group still makes it to the top of Pikes Peak. The AdAmAn Club tradition is a fascinating and unique piece of local history. Their exploits have garnered Pikes Peak attention from people around the world. For many years the climbers carried radio equipment that allowed them to broadcast details of their thrilling Pikes Peak ascent to eager listeners. An excellent archive of photographs, papers, and films record the yearly climbs and document the role the AdAmAn Club has played in popularizing Pikes Peak and contributing to the legacy of "America's Mountain."

For many years the Colorado Springs Chamber of Commerce functioned as the greatest promoter of Pikes Peak regional tourism. Operating as a membership organization, the chamber collected dues from local business owners each year that paid for the production and distribution of promotional advertising. The Chamber distributed literally millions of pamphlets, booklets and beautiful brochures as well as films and photographs.

The Chamber operated a publicity bureau that sent out weekly press releases to newspapers across the country, which were frequently featured as articles with accompanying illustrations. They hired local photographer Harry L. Standley to create a series of photographs depicting the favorable climate and scenic beauty of Colorado Springs. The Chamber then sent the glossy publications to hundreds of organizations around the country. A Chamber committee solicited convention travel, marketing Colorado Springs as the "The Convention City," while utilizing the seemingly timeless imagery and slogan, "Pikes Peak or Bust."[38]

When the automobile revolutionized travel in the early twentieth century, the Chamber of Commerce "shifted gears." They began to promote Pikes Peak and Colorado Springs as being accessible to automobiles and used the catchphrase "A Motorist's Mecca" in their advertisements and free travel maps. Of course, tourists needed to get to Colorado Springs in order to see Pikes Peak and other area attractions. As a result, the Chamber of Commerce launched an ambitious lobbying campaign for new road construction with local civic leaders and their state and national legislators. At the time, roads were not funded or maintained by either state or federal governments, and as a result, local organizations were extremely involved in what became known as the "Good Roads Movement."[39]

For many years the Pikes Peak Ocean to Ocean Highway remained the focus of local road improvement and publicity projects. Not a single highway but instead a connected network of roads from New York to Oregon, the Pikes Peak Ocean to Ocean Highway was seen as pivotal to tourism and the local economy. Civic boosters and business owners organized a series of "Automobile Sociability Tours" to publicize the road in 1914.[40] Traveling by convoy over rough and often impassable roads, they created a large amount of press coverage as Americans across the country read avidly of their journeys. The members of the sociability tours acted as ambassadors of our region and were treated as celebrities wherever they traveled.

The Pikes Peak Marathon, billed as "America's Ultimate Challenge," represents a distinct market for local tourism and the promotion of Pikes Peak. The marathon course which runs up the mountain and then back down again is legendary and among the most challenging in the world. In August of each year runners, their families, friends and fans from all over the world converge in Manitou Springs. The instant recognition of Pikes Peak as a marketing tool has led to a variety of corporate sponsorships and advertisements for products such as beer, running shoes and athletic wear.

Before the marathon officially began in 1956, other competitive races were held on Pikes Peak. In 1936, twenty-five men and two women raced up the mountain as a part of the celebration marking the transition of the formerly private Pikes Peak Highway to a public road owned and operated by the City of Colorado Springs. On July 4, 1938, the Junior Chamber of Commerce sponsored a 12.5 mile race called the "Pikes Peak Vertical Mile" for its elevation gain.[41]

In June 1956, a Florida physician named Dr. Arne Suominen issued a challenge to cigarette smokers. As a former marathon champion from Finland, Dr. Suominen was eager to prove the negative physical effects associated with smoking. Fourteen runners started the race with only three being smokers. Monte Wolford, a non-smoking competitive bodybuilder won the race with the time of five hours, thirty-nine minutes, and fifty-eight seconds.[42] Today, elite runners the likes of world-class competitor and Manitou Springs resident Matt Carpenter run the race in a little over two hours. The Pikes Peak Marathon is so popular that in 2006 race officials stopped taking runner registrations after only twenty-three hours. Marathon runners, like hikers, get to know Pikes Peak in an intimate, personal way that tourists who never venture off the highway might not.[43]

In addition to attracting visitors and athletes, Pikes Peak has promoted products ranging from automobile tires to scissors. Its popularity can be gauged by the sheer number of times it has been utilized and the variety of products it has appeared on. Perhaps the most elegant application of Pikes Peak is the "Pikes Peak Ring" from Zerbe Jewelers. The downtown Colorado Springs jewelry store has sold several rings to soldiers heading off on distant assignments eager to have a beautiful memento of their hometown.

Examples of not-so-elegant Pikes Peak products are beer, malt liquor and mineral water bottled in Michigan. Pikes Peak has even been marketed to the young at heart. Hot Wheels collectible toy cars, OPI brand nail polish called "Pikes Peak-A-

Boo Purple" and the limited edition Crayola "Pikes Peak Purple" official state crayons represent modern and fun-loving uses of all the time-worn clichés regarding Pikes Peak. Both as a tourist attraction and as a marketing tool for consumer products, the fame of Pikes Peak has meant that "America's Mountain" — the myth, the idea, the ideal — is here to stay.

Pikes Peak has captured our imaginations. It has come to symbolize a region, a state, the nation, and perhaps more importantly, the ideals that Americans have embedded in their imagined West. As a landmark, an icon or a breathtaking backdrop, it has meaning that resonates within people. Traveling to or living near Pikes Peak has proven to be a transformative experience for

Two of the "famous" Pikes Peak beverages available — both brewed in Pueblo, Colorado. *Courtesy of Starsmore Center for Local History at the Colorado Springs Pioneers Museum.*

many. Pikes Peak is "America's Mountain" and the proof is in the nail polish!

Leah Davis Witherow is the archivist at the Colorado Springs Pioneers Museum. She has a Master of Arts in history from the University of Colorado, Colorado Springs, where she has taught courses in material culture, public history and Colorado history. She is a graduate of the Modern Archives Institute at the National Archives, former president of the Society of Rocky Mountain Archivists, and has achieved archival certification through the Academy of Certified Archivists. She is a frequent speaker for archival and museum organizations.

Notes

1. Interview with Gladys Beuler, January 22, 1994, Voices and Visions Collection, Starsmore Center for Local History, Colorado Springs Pioneers Museum, Colorado Springs, Colorado.

2. Interview with Michele Carvell, January, 2006, Starsmore Center for Local History.

3. David M. Wrobel and Patrick T. Long, eds., *Seeing and Being Seen: Tourism in the American West* (Lawrence, Published for the Center of the American West, University of Colorado at Boulder by the University Press of Kansas, 2001), 105.

4. "Experience Colorado Springs at Pikes Peak," Convention and Visitors Bureau website, January 2006, http://www.experiencecoloradosprings.com.

5. *Colorado Springs Gazette*, January 1, 2006, 30.

6. Donald Jackson, ed., *The Journals of Zebulon Montgomery Pike: With Letters and Related Documents* (Norman: University of Oklahoma Press, 1966), 345.

7. Agnes Wright Spring, ed., *A Bloomer Girl on Pikes Peak 1858: Julia Archibald Holmes, First White Woman to Climb Pike's Peak* (Denver: Western History Department, Denver Public Library, 1949), 39.

8. *Nebraska City News*, May 28, 1859, 3.

9. Wrobel and Long, *Seeing and Being Seen*, 43-46.

10. Anne Farrar Hyde, *An American Vision: Far Western Landscape and National Culture, 1820-1920* (New York: New York University Press, 1990), 147-183.

11. J. P.Treat, *The Famous Pike's Peak Region, a Veritable Paradise for Students of Geology, Botany, Mineralogy and Birds* (Colorado Springs Chamber of Commerce, undated pamphlet), Pikes Peak Library District, Special Collections Department, Colorado Springs, Colorado.

12. *Colorado Springs Gazette*, April 20, 1893, 5.

13. Phyllis Smith, *Weather Pioneers: The Signal Corps Station at Pikes Peak* (Athens: Ohio University Press, 1993), 28.

14. Judge Eliphalet Price, "The Famous Pikes Peak Rat Story," Price Collection, Starsmore Center for Local History.

15. Smith, *Weather Pioneers*, 62-67.

16. John F. Sears, *Sacred Places: American Tourist Attractions in the Nineteenth Century* (New York: Oxford University Press, 1989), 9-10.

17. *Colorado Springs Gazette*, April 11, 1891, 7.

18. Dorothy Burgess, *Dream and Deed: The Story of Katharine Lee Bates* (Norman: University of Oklahoma Press, 1952), 101-106.

19. *Pikes Peak Reader*, April 1972, 2.

20. Marguerite S. Shaffer, *See America First: Tourism and National*

Identity, 1880-1940 (Washington: Smithsonian Institution Press, 2001), 26-39.

21. E. T. Tomlinson, *Four Boys on Pikes Peak* (New York: D. Appleton and Company, 1912), preface.

22. The Manitou and Pike's Peak Railway website, January 2006, http://www.cograilway.com.

23. Ibid.

24. Ibid.

25. *Colorado Springs Gazette*, November 28, 1896, 5.

26. Ed and Nancy Bathke, *The Pike Celebration, 1906*, Papers of the Historical Society of the Pikes Peak Region, Starsmore Center for Local History.

27. *Colorado Springs Gazette*, May 4, 1906, 5.

28. Bathke, *The Pike Celebration*, 1-24.

29. Pikes Peak Vertical File, Collections of the Starsmore Center for Local History.

30. Thomas J. Noel and Cathleen M. Norman, *A Pikes Peak Partnership: the Penroses and the Tutts* (Boulder: University Press of Colorado, 2000), 84-88.

31. Pikes Peak Highway Brochure, 1916, Collections of the Starsmore Center for Local History.

32. Author's conversation with William K. Brown, December 30, 2005.

33. Noel and Norman, *Pikes Peak Partnership*, 85-86.

34. Pikes Peak International Hill Climb website, January 2006, http://www.ppihc.com.

35. Interview with David Bachoroski, April 4, 2006, Starsmore Center for Local History.

36. Ibid.

37. James Bates, *The First Fifty Years of AdAmAn: 1923–1973* (Colorado Springs: AdAmAn Club, 1973), preface.

38. Chamber of Commerce Vertical File, Collections of the Starsmore Center for Local History.

39. Richard H. Jackson and Mark W. Jackson, "The Lincoln Highway: The First Transcontinental Highway and the American West," *Journal of the West*, vol. 42, No. 2, Spring 2003, 57.

40. Chamber of Commerce Vertical File.

41. Hal Walter, *America's Ultimate Challenge: the Pikes Peak Marathon* (Colorado Springs: Triple Crown of Running Club, 1995).

42. Ibid.

43. Author's conversation with Matt Carpenter, April 2006.

The Pike Centennial Celebration 1906

Edwin A. & Nancy E. Bathke

Just twelve miles due west of the center of the city of Colorado Springs, towering over it by more than 8,000 feet, reposes that grand peak, Pikes Peak. This mountain was so remarkable that it was known to all the Indian nations for hundreds of miles around, and was spoken of with admiration by early travelers into the region, such as the Spanish from New Mexico. But the first man to describe the mountain in print and to draw a map of it was Lieutenant Zebulon Montgomery Pike.

Lieutenant Pike was the leader of a small band of soldiers with the mission of mapping the Red and Arkansas Rivers, exploring for President Thomas Jefferson a portion of the vast Louisiana Purchase that this country had acquired from France three years earlier. On November 15, 1806, Pike's party obtained its first view of the peak from near the present site of the city of Las Animas, and they "gave three cheers to the Mexican Mountains." Pike's interest in the Peak is shown by his decision to explore it, which was not part of his instructions. Probably he hoped to gain knowledge of the rivers he was exploring from such a vantage point. Poorly prepared and stymied by bad weather, he abandoned his attempt to scale the "High Peak" on November 27.

Zebulon Pike certainly fits the role of "All-American Hero." He attained the rank of general by the age of thirty-four. He died a hero's death in his successful assault on York (now Toronto), when, on being told that the fort was captured, he closed his eyes with the remark "I die content."

Herein, then, lies the raw material worthy of celebration and patriotic display: the thrilling story of Western exploration, the grandeur of America's most famous mountain, and the heroic military career of its discoverer. But much more is required for a truly great celebration. Two other basic requirements are the organized planning with an adequate amount of time to carry out details, and a competent, dedicated individual to mastermind the mammoth undertaking. As we examine the records of the Pike Centennial Celebration in 1906, we will see just what goes into the development of such a celebration.

The primary sources of information for this paper are the Special Collections Department of the Pikes Peak Library District, for four scrapbooks of clippings and printed artifacts prepared by the centennial committee and two bound volumes of onionskin carbons of committee correspondence, and the Colorado Springs Pioneers Museum collection of photocopies of U.S. Mint correspondence and other data compiled by Clark Yowell in 1956. Newspapers provided an excellent historical source for public events, but these other sources produced a normally unattainable insight into the planning and behind-the-scenes activities of these events.

To begin with, foresighted individuals initiated their efforts of commemorating Pike in 1896, ten years before the centenary date. On November 27, exactly ninety years to the day that Zebulon Pike gave up on his Peak climbing attempt, a public meeting was held to organize the Zebulon Montgomery Pike Monument Association. Newspaper accounts hailed the cause, using the quotation, "monuments not only mark but make civilization." The Association was incorporated on December 4, 1896. By-laws provided for a limit of five hundred members, each paying a membership fee of $10, and for an unlimited number of associate members at $1 each. The first officers were John Campbell, president; Horace G. Lunt, vice-president; Joel Addison Hayes, treasurer; and George Rex Buckman, secretary. Thirty-five directors of the corporation were named. General William Jackson Palmer was an original director, although he was out of town during the organizational meeting. The purpose of the Association was the erection of a monument of Pike "of heroic size and in enduring bronze" and to "preserve, perpetuate, and forever maintain said monument and historical data." The Zebulon Pike Chapter of the Daughters of the American Revolution (DAR) offered $100 towards the monument, requesting that this sum be placed at the head of an eventual subscription list.

Judge Horace G. Lunt is credited with the idea of striking a commemorative medal to raise funds. He wrote to Colorado Senator Edward D. Wolcott, suggesting, "if this medal could be struck from some old cannon its historic value would be enhanced." Further correspondence revealed insurmountable difficulties: a joint resolution of both houses of Congress was required to appropriate a condemned cannon; both the War Department and the Navy Department replied that bronze cannons were scarce and it was impossible for them to supply any.

Initial good intentions stagnated, and lack of finances and lack of public interest lulled the Association into a state of dormancy.

The most significant manifestation of Pike commemorative activity prior to the centennial took place in front of the Antlers Hotel on August 1, 1901, the date of the twenty-fifth anniversary of Colorado statehood. Providing a worthy background, the new Antlers, number one hotel of Colorado Springs, had just been completed that year, replacing the first Antlers which had burned spectacularly in 1898. General William Jackson Palmer, on one of his rare public appearances, delivered the dedicatory address for the "staff statue" of Pike. The statue was twelve feet in height and on a pedestal eight feet high. Its description in the quartocentennial issue of *Facts* magazine follows:

> Pike is depicted in the attitude of climbing a mountain, his right foot on a rock and his right arm extended upward as if pointing to the distant heights. His left hand clasps the hilt of his sword and his hat rests on his arm.

On the front of the base was the inscription: "Lieutenant Zebulon Montgomery Pike, 'The desert shall rejoice and blossom like the rose.'" On the left end was a line from his diary: "A mountain to our right which appeared like a small blue cloud." This magnificent pose of Pike appears prominently in photographs of activities taken in front of the Antlers during the next few years. But the statue was a plaster cast, representing future intentions, and it soon disintegrated, a victim of natural weathering.

In conjunction with the dedication ceremonies at the Antlers, a "Banquet to the Editors of Colorado by the Citizens of Colorado Springs" was held on August 2. Joining toastmaster Wolfe Londoner in presenting toasts were Vice President Theodore Roosevelt, Senator Henry M. Teller, Thomas Walsh, and William Byers. Guests dined on mountain trout à l'Antlers, tenderloin of beef à la Washington, punch à la Pike, chaud-froid of chicken à la Roosevelt, and Gilpin ice cream, amid other delicacies.

After these initial efforts at commemorating Pike, a distinguished personality was needed to manage a successful centennial celebration. This man was Henry Russell Wray. Wray, a native of Pennsylvania, came to Colorado Springs in 1893. He was active in the Mining Exchange, and was the editor of the Colorado Springs *Gazette* for many years. He had been the secretary of the local Chamber of Commerce since 1903. Early in 1905 he began working towards the centennial celebration.

About this time rumors and letters to newspapers referred to the grave of General Pike in Lawrenceburg, Indiana. Wray initiated official inquiries. Authenticated records of the War Department revealed that Zebulon M. Pike was buried within the stockade of Madison Barracks, at Sackets Harbor, New York. The location of his burial site, hitherto unknown to the general populace, and photos of his grave marker, received prominent attention in publicity releases for the approaching centennial. Apparently, the grave in Lawrenceburg, Indiana, was that of Pike's father.

Later, the War Department was not nearly so accurate in responding to a request for Pike-related information. The picture they sent of "General Zebulon Pike" was of a "Pike with a long grey beard" and "looking like Longfellow." After being notified that they had inadvertently sent a picture of Zebulon Montgomery Pike's father, the department located the now well-known painting by Charles Willson Peale in Philadelphia, and this oil rendition of Pike became the official view used in all centennial matters.

Newspaper accounts of Wray's centennial plans prompted Judge Horace G. Lunt to come forth with data on the forgotten Zebulon Montgomery Pike Monument Association. In June 1905, Judge Lunt detailed a letter to Wray how he and Rex Buckman had started the project, how they were unsuccessful in getting a bill through Congress to strike a medal, and that they were not successful in getting much else done.

Wray, in a letter to Thomas J. Fisher on June 29, stated:

If we are to have a bronze monument of Pike to be unveiled on the centennial anniversary of the discovery of the Peak, we should do something at once, for it will take a year to model and cast such a monument, and we have but 16 months until Nov. 15, 1906.

He also wrote to Colorado Congressman Franklin E. Brooks on that same date, mentioning the medal idea of 1896, and requesting Brooks to look into resubmitting a bill in Congress.

By the end of the year 1905, the necessary organization for the celebration had begun to take shape. Impetus was probably provided by the Denver newspaper's coverage of the suggestion of Charles R. Dudley, librarian of the Denver Public Library, and Secretary of the State Historical Society. He had suggested to Governor Jesse F. McDonald that a proclamation set aside Nov. 26 and 27, 1906, as Colorado holidays. The part of his suggestion that wasn't favorably received locally was that Mr. Dudley seemed to be thinking of the Pike Centennial celebration as a Denver affair. Committees were formed; one typewritten page listed twenty-five committees with their chairman and estimated expenses required for the celebration. (The date of this page is unknown, but it appears to be from the latter days of the celebration.)

For the following year papers would carry daily articles pertaining to publicity, proposed activities, and events of the centennial. Plans were laid for the striking of the commemorative medals, for the monument to Pike, for church services, banquets, parades, addresses by politicians and pioneers, and numerous other activities.

Henry Russell Wray had been concerned with a statue commemorating Pike for some time. In December 1904 he had written to T. J. Fisher of Colorado Springs, inquiring about a statue he knew of in the studio of Charles J. Pike, noted New York sculptor and grandnephew of Zebulon M. Pike. As mentioned earlier, in June 1905, Wray was already concerned about the short time span remaining before the centenary date. The general consensus of opinion held among those responsible for celebration plans is aptly stated in a letter from Judge Lunt to Wray dated January 30, 1906. He mentions writing to Palmer about the statue, and the possibility of erecting "a plain, heroic granite shaft, with proper inscription." Just who should be credited with first suggesting a granite monument is not known exactly. However, in this January letter Lunt writes of talking to Palmer on the telephone that morning, and that it was Palmer's wishes that

> . . . no statue should be erected unless it was by a master hand, and that there certainly ought to be a competition

before any statue was selected. He did not believe that a statue would do justice to the situation; that the Peak was always before us, and that *it* was really a sufficient monument. He thought that a fine granite block or slab with suitable inscription was the best and most suitable object to be erected—much better he felt, than a statue.

At first a boulder from the top of Cheyenne Mountain was suggested for the monument, since it was popularly thought that Pike had reached that summit in his unsuccessful attempt to climb Pikes Peak. For this reason, a plan to construct a cog incline to the top of Cheyenne Mountain was also proposed. However, the impending centennial prompted wide reading and thorough studying of Pike's journals. It became obvious that Pike could not have advanced as far north as Cheyenne Mountain, and this settled the matter of selecting a boulder from that site.

The next suggestion, worded dramatically, was of selecting a great boulder from the very summit of that grand peak. However, Clinton W. Sells, president of the Manitou and Pikes Peak Railway, declined a contract for moving a "monster stone." Quoting him, "if a rock weighing several tons were placed on a car of the Cog Road, gravity would send the car through Manitou at several miles per minute, leaving a path of kindling wood—former residences—in its wake." Moving the boulder from the summit of the Peak was termed a problem rivaling the Panama Canal, the most masterful construction project of that era. The next plan called for rolling the boulder down the side of the mountain. It wouldn't be attempted unless everyone in the three cities at the base of the peak had life insurance policies taken out.

Another ingenious plan proposed lifting a boulder from the peak with a balloon, and dropping it in Monument Valley Park. As farfetched as this plan may appear, the *Gazette* on March 30 told of the famous French aeronaut Count Henri de la Vaulx, who was visiting this country and was interested in a balloon race from Pikes Peak to New York.

In May a boulder was selected, its location being about fifteen feet from the Colorado Springs and Cripple Creek "Short Line" tracks near milepost 15, on the southern slopes of Pikes Peak. An interesting speculation was that since the boulder was on a direct line between Pueblo and the top of the Peak, Pike himself may have seen the very boulder used as a monument to him one hundred years later. Wray wrote to Superintendent James B. Flaherty of the Short Line on May 18, thanking him for the boulder-hunting trip, and saying that he would borrow a derrick from the Colorado Midland to load the boulder on a railroad car. The boulder, ten feet long and four to five feet thick, was finally determined to weigh 33,870 pounds, almost seventeen tons. The Midland derrick was too small, having only a one-ton capacity, so the Denver and Rio Grande was contracted next. Eventually the boulder was brought down the railroad to the Rio Grande yards in the city.

The boulder was to be skidded to Antlers Park. A crew of four horses and twelve men moved it two feet in three hours, a little more slowly than expected. Yet, a couple evenings later a frantic call was received by the police that the boulder was being stolen. Two men were placed under arrest, and the boulder lay in an irrigation ditch. A $100 reward was posted for the arrest of anyone attempting to remove the boulder.

In February Wray began correspondence about the tablets to be mounted on the boulder. In April he sent letters asking for bids and designs to Winslow Brothers, Chicago; the Henry Bonnard Bronze Works, New York; and the Gorham Company, New York. Prices were sought on the four tablets to be mounted on the boulder, and on the four- by seven-foot plaque to be installed in a christening ceremony atop the Peak. In a letter to Zalmon G. Simmons on May 25, Wray provides the details on awarding the bid on the tablets. Winslow Brothers of Chicago was chosen, having bid $545 for the large tablet and $410 for the four small tablets, delivered in Colorado Springs. Gorham had bid $900 for the total, but its prices were F.O.B. Providence, Rhode Island. The Henry Bonnard Bronze Works submitted impressive elaborate designs, but its price was $1,800, and the decision was made on the basis of cost. Another letter to Winslow Brothers acknowledging receipt of the four bronze tablets was dated September 1.

The required steps to be taken in striking the commemorative medals slowly but steadily were carried forth. On January 24, 1906, Congressman Franklin E. Brooks introduced Bill #13085 calling for an appropriation of $10,000 to finance striking of "not to exceed 100,000" medallions in the U.S. Mint at Denver.

On January 27 Brooks wrote to Judge Lunt that $5,000 would make fifty thousand medals, half silver, the size of a quarter, and half bronze, the size of a dollar. A month to six weeks would be required to make the design and die. Although the work could be done more quickly at Denver, it would be low relief. The Philadelphia Mint had a regular medal press, which, except for small jeweler presses, was the only one in the country. However, Philadelphia had a contract of several months' duration for Portland Fair medals, and was not through with the World's Fair medals, so that it would be late summer before it could complete the Pike medals.

On February 1, Brooks introduced a rewritten bill, H. R. 13783, which did not call for an appropriation, and which did not specify a mint at which the work was to be done. Since the U.S. Mint was to be reimbursed for its expenses, this bill passed the House on March 9. Passage in the Senate occurred early in May.

Wray answered an offer of the American Railway Supply Company, New York, on March 20, turning down its offer to manufacture commemorative medals since the government was to make one hundred thousand. In his correspondence with Brooks on March 28, he asked if the stamp proposition was dead. Commemorative stamps had first been issued by this country in 1893 for the Columbian Exposition, and since that date, in conjunction with the Trans-Mississippi Exposition, the Pan-American Exposition, and the Louisiana Purchase Exposition. As all stamp collectors are aware, the Pike Centennial was not honored with a commemorative postage stamp.

Correspondence from Wray to Brooks on April 25 indicates that by that date the ultimate size of the medal, that of a twenty-dollar gold piece, had been selected. Photographs of Pikes Peak from Colorado Springs were submitted to the mint for the design. Several designers were requested to submit drawings, including Charles Pike, and local artist Carl G. Lotave. But the beautiful final product may well be the work of the accomplished Mint Chief Engraver Charles E. Barber. U.S. Mint correspondence includes letters from Barber, stating "sketches [are] prepared for the proposed medal," and on a later date, "I am now ready to execute your order . . ."

Artistic license on the photographs provided for the medal is implied in a letter dated May 21 from Wray to Brooks:

"... hardly think the Cameron Cone makes any difference and will not be noticeable to any except the extremely critical and knowing observer." We leave it to possessors of the commemorative medals whether nature has been faulted or the cause of artistry served.

On May 28, Wray wrote to Brooks that the leaden cast of the medal had been received. Local newspapers reported the first of the medals, totaling one hundred twenty-five, were received on June 16. On June 29, Wray asked Brooks if a gold medal could be struck as a golf tournament prize. Apparently this was not feasible, because no further mention of this is found. Quantities of the medallions were slow in coming, and a July 17 letter laid the delay to the fact that the mint had to have the gilt plating done by an outside plater instead of at the mint facilities. Then, mint records show that two thousand bronze and one thousand silver medals were shipped on July 21. Four hundred and fifty silver were shipped August 17, and one thousand five hundred bronze on August 30. The remainder of the mintage was shipped during the second week in September. Mint records reveal that six thousand five hundred bronze were made (of which two hundred fifty were gold plated), and four thousand four hundred fifty silver medals were made. Perhaps the somewhat-tardy delivery rate contributed to the small number of medals minted. Likewise, sales must have been slower than anticipated, because newspaper releases in the days prior to the week-long celebration called for pushing sale of the medals. Wray wrote Simon Guggenheim on September 6 that they were hoping to realize $5,000 from the sale of the medals. Statistics can easily show this to have been too optimistic. We have the advantage of historical viewpoint in knowing that approximately four thousand two hundred of the medals were in the First National Bank vaults until 1955. Hence the total sales in 1906 were less than seven thousand medals.

The face of the Pike Centennial medal. *Courtesy of Edwin and Nancy Bathke.*

By Act of Congress, the centennial committee was required to reimburse the U.S. Mint for the cost of the medals.

These costs were seven cents each for the bronze medals and forty-five cents each for the silver medals, plus additional sums for gilding, ribbon, and bars. The sale prices of the medals in 1906 were bronze, fifty cents, and silver, one dollar. The profit being less than fifty cents per medal and the sales totaling less than seven thousand, the proceeds toward the centennial expenses could hardly have exceeded $3,000.

Reverse of the Pike medal, displaying Pikes Peak. *Courtesy of Edwin and Nancy Bathke.*

The first twenty-five each of the bronze, the silver, and the gold-plated medals were to be numbered. Newspaper accounts early in the summer told of plans to auction these highly prized sets for large sums, set number one hopefully bringing in $1,000. We don't know just when the auction plan was abandoned, but on August 4, Wray wrote letters distributing the first six sets. Set number one was given to Palmer, number two to Z. G. Simmons, number three to Judge Lunt, number four to Representative Brooks, number five to Thomas Walsh, and number six to Governor Jesse McDonald. The disposal of the remaining nineteen numbered sets is not recorded.

As will be noted later, Simmons, the mattress king from Wisconsin who was responsible for building the Pikes Peak Cog Road, Palmer, and Walsh, were the three principal benefactors of the celebration, without whose financial support the centennial would never have materialized. General Palmer, Governor McDonald, and Representative Brooks were the Directors-General of the centennial.

Other souvenirs besides the official medal were available. One newspaper advertisement cautioned buyers to get the genuine medal since an imitation was on the market. Van Briggle was manufacturing square plaques of Garden of the Gods red clay for the centennial. One such plaque was a bust of Pike. We have been unable to find any of these, and would be interested in hearing from anyone with information on these medallion plaques. Souvenir spoons were issued, and one was advertised in the newspapers as *the* spoon with the statue of Pike in the bowl.

U.S. Army troops were to play a prominent role in the centennial celebration. From the beginning, plans for the participation of ten thousand troops were widely publicized and mentioned repeatedly in newspaper releases. Secretary of War William H. Taft was to attend. Maneuvers were to be held, the first ever involving all three army branches together—the infantry, the artillery, and the cavalry—and the first ever conducted in the mountains. The culminating event to this spectacular was to be a public maneuver in which the troops would storm Cheyenne Mountain.

In order to allow more troops to attend, and since annual maneuvers were held at Fort Riley, Kansas, the first week in September, the original dates set for the Pike Centennial were changed from September 9-15, to September 23-29. This change in date was done the first of March, before any appreciable advance publicity had been released or arrangements made. A secondary but equally good reason was that the earlier dates conflicted with the Colorado State Fair in Pueblo.

When definite orders to move troops were actually carried out, the number appearing was appreciably less, just one thousand five hundred. But this, it was opportunely pointed out, was a very good number of troops to have in attendance: one thousand five hundred troops was the size of the force with which Pike led his assault on York.

All three branches of the army were represented: six hundred men from the 29th Infantry Regiment, consisting of two battalions and the headquarters band; six troops of the 5th Cavalry and one troop from the 10th Cavalry, together totaling eight hundred men; and one hundred men comprising the 12th Battalion of artillery. Their encampment southwest of the Broadmoor was named Camp Pike. The troops marched in parades nearly every day, the band performed daily, many people visited Camp Pike, and public drills and maneuvers were held; the U.S. Army contributed substantially to the activities of the centennial.

Complementing the troops' appearance were American Indians. Original plans called for the attendance of Indians from each tribe that Pike had come in contact with when exploring the region: the Kiowa, Sioux, Arapaho, and Ute. Wray conducted correspondence with Indian Commissioner Francis E. Luepp in Washington, D.C., obtaining permission to use all the Indians he wanted, and on May 14, seven arrived from Santa Clara, New Mexico, to participate in the celebration. They were keenly disappointed that the centennial was not already in progress, but hoped to find work in town and stay until festivities did start. In a letter on April 27, Wray mentioned that it was essential that the Indians be kept away from the temptation of liquor. Too many Indians could be hard to handle, and while the publicity advertised ten thousand army troops, the number of Indians expected was only about forty or fifty. Due to expenses in bringing Indians to Colorado Springs, economy dictated inviting only Utes, who could conveniently be brought by the Denver and Rio Grande train from Durango.

In an age when the railroad was the primary mode of transportation, conventions and other public gatherings sought special rail rates for their attendees. The Pike Centennial celebration received rates which were considerably more favorable than usual, probably because of the large crowds expected to attend. Round-trip fares from Chicago were $25, from St. Louis $21, from Kansas City or Omaha $15, and similar rates were granted from other points in the nation.

The local railroad also provided invaluable services to the centennial. The most noteworthy act was that of bringing the Pike boulder from the south slopes of the Peak, by the Colorado Springs and Cripple Creek District Short Line. The Cog Road transported all participants to the Peak christening ceremony on the summit Wednesday. The Pennsylvania Railroad had offered half freight rates for Department of War relics from Washington, D.C., to Chicago. The Rock Island Line offered free passage of up to three boxcars of relics and exhibits from Chicago to Colorado Springs. Unfortunately, due to the short period of time to prepare the exhibits and the short period of exhibition at the centennial, the feature was cancelled.

Original plans considered the use of railroads for bringing Indians and thousands of army troops to the celebration. Clippings and correspondence do not reveal if any special considerations were actually received from the railroads. The cavalry troops rode their mounts from maneuvers at Dale Creek, Wyoming. The Utes, living on the reservation at Ignacio, no doubt rode the Denver and Rio Grande from Durango. Charles Craig, chairman of the centennial committee for Indians, was granted a budget of $2,000 which may have been primarily used for transportation costs.

The success of the centennial not only was due to the managing abilities of Henry Russell Wray, but also dependent upon obtaining the vital funding for expenses of the celebration. The problems encountered were summarized early in September in a letter from Wray to Simon Guggenheim. He stated how Colorado Springs businesses had contributed $32,000 to the San Francisco earthquake disaster, and $50,000 to pay off the YMCA mortgage, besides subscribing to the Elks and Typographical Union conventions, so "by the time subscriptions for the centennial were (sought), there was not much left to draw from." Furthermore, the tourist season had not been up to expectations. Zalmon G. Simmons had contributed $5,000, Thomas Walsh $1,000, and General Palmer, $1,000. They had hoped to realize $5,000 from the sale of medallions, and a campaign to raise $5,000 was dubious. This situation brought Wray to seek financial assistance from Guggenheim. A few days later Wray again wrote to Guggenheim, thanking him for his contribution; however, the amount of Guggenheim's generosity is not recorded.

Local merchants' contributions did total $2,800 to $3,000, and the three major philanthropists donated $7,000. The City of Colorado Springs and the County of El Paso each contributed at least $1,250, and, as mentioned earlier, the sale of the medals could not have yielded as much as $3,000. This indicates receipts on the order of $15,000. Irving Howbert was quoted as saying the program was to cost $15,000 to $20,000, and "would have cost $50,000 but for the careful economy of the committee in charge." Grand plans set up in the spring of 1906 underwent repeated economic cutbacks in the few weeks prior to the celebration. It appears that careful husbanding of resources permitted carrying to fruition the major planned activities of the centennial while at the same time avoiding any overwhelming debt at its completion.

Howbert also estimated that the centennial could bring $500,000 worth of business to the city. To bring tourists to Colorado Springs would require proper publicity. Stories and pictures were regularly distributed to newspapers across the country. Records stated that one particular four-paragraph release appeared in "818 newspapers in Michigan, Kansas, Nebraska, and Iowa." All railroads in the region printed centennial folders. Large color posters were distributed. One letter by Wray, to Paul Goerke, who owned Balanced Rock, indicates the broad scope of the publicity operation. Wray sought a photograph of German Prince Hohenlohe at Balanced Rock for use in foreign publicity.

Not only advance publicity but the recording of centennial activities were conscientiously conducted. The U.S. Clipping Bureau of Chicago was hired in March at a monthly fee to provide news clippings pertaining to Pike. This proved to be expensive, averaging twenty-five cents per clipping, and quite unsatisfactory, since articles in major newspapers were being missed. The U.S. Clipping Bureau was notified that it could continue only on the basis as other clipping services, $5.00 per hundred items. Whether an agreement was reached is not known, but other clipping services were also used. The important point to us, however, is that these clippings plus other material produced the invaluable scrapbooks responsible for the majority of information for this paper.

The poetic accolades to Pike and the centennial were many. Charles Pike composed the verse for "Ode to Colorado." Maud McFerran Price's "Colorado" received wide usage. Poetry appeared frequently in the newspapers. At General Palmer's request, Wray extended an invitation to William E. Pabor, prolific poet and publicist of the Colorado Springs Town Company, both to attend the celebration and to compose a commemorative ode for the centennial. But Pabor, retired, in poor health, living at Pabor Lake, Florida, had to decline on both accounts.

Numerous nationally important personages were invited to the centennial. President Theodore Roosevelt, who had attended the quartocentennial state celebration in Colorado Springs in 1901, and who had enjoyed other visits to Colorado, was unable to attend. Vice President Charles Fairbanks and his wife Cornelia were the featured guests of the festivities. The vice president and all the members of the presidential cabinet had been invited by Thomas Walsh to stay at Wolhurst, the Walsh mansion at Littleton. There were a few early acceptances, but except for some members of their families, cabinet officials were unable to attend. Secretary of War Taft had to cancel his plans to attend because of an insurrection in Cuba. Four U.S. Senators: Henry Teller of Colorado, Francis Warren of Wyoming, Chester Long of Kansas, and Nathan Scott of

West Virginia; three representatives, and some foreign diplomats were present. Charles Pike was the house guest of Wray. William Bell, "the father of Manitou," arrived from England.

Sunday, September 23, the first day of the centennial celebration, the churches of the city honored Pike with appropriate services based on his high moral character, religious life, and patriotism. That evening a commemorative service at the First Presbyterian Church featured several addresses and a recital of "Ode to Pikes Peak," written by Virginia McClurg, set to music and illustrated with stereopticon views.

The highlight on Monday, Military Day, was, of course, the military parade at 10 A.M. Besides the U.S. Army troops, the Grand Army of the Republic, Spanish-American War veterans, and other military groups, the Indians and cowboys also paraded. At the end of the parade an old prairie schooner appeared as a surprise feature. For the finale, the wagon was attacked by the Indians, who, in turn, fled when the cavalry sounded its bugles for the rescue. Patriotic exercises were held that afternoon by the DAR and the Colonial Dames of Colorado.

Tuesday was Pioneer Day. A settlers' program was held in Stratton Park, honoring the oldtimers. Among those speaking were Irving Howbert and Judge Wilbur F. Stone. Three thousand people heard Vice President Fairbanks speak at the Opera House at 10:30 A.M. The Indians, who were camped at the old Boulevard ball park in Ivywild, had to postpone their war dances that evening due to lack of light and firewood; they would perform with cowboys Thursday afternoon.

The major event on Wednesday, Historical Day, was the christening of Pikes Peak. Edward E. Nichols, mayor of Manitou Springs and chairman of the committee on unveiling the bronze tablet on the Peak, Henry R. Wray, and Clinton W. Sells, general manager of the Cog Road, selected the boulder for the plaque on top of the peak, at the highest point overlooking the bottomless pit. The weather was cold, four feet of snow having fallen on the Peak on September 18. The two men working in the snow and cold to hew the rock for placement of the plaque had to make trips down the mountain every few hours to temper their tools. Wednesday's weather was not any better: William F. Slocum, president of the Colorado College, delivered the dedicatory address in a severe snowstorm, witnessed by two hundred army officers and guests, many standing in knee-deep snow. The artillery fired an eleven-gun salute to Pike, and the party returned by cog train, attending lunch at the Cliff House at 2 P.M.

On Thursday, Pike Day, that great boulder was unveiled in Antlers Park, with a crowd of ten thousand people attending. Again, an eleven-gun salute to Pike was fired by the artillery. University of Denver Chancellor Henry Buchtel delivered the principal address. (Wray had invited Palmer to be the speaker, but the publicity-shy general had declined.) Buchtel and Alva Adams were opponents for the Colorado governorship that fall, and both were prominent participants in the centennial activities.

At the boulder ceremony, Rubin Goldmark directed a chorus of one thousand voices in singing "Ode to Colorado," specially written for the centennial, music by Goldmark and words by Charles Pike. The first rehearsal of the chorus ten days previous was attended by less than two hundred; it was hoped that five hundred would turn out for the second rehearsal. But when the

In Antlers Park, west of the rear of the hotel, the seeventeen-ton boulder transported from the southern slopes of Pikes Peak is the park's center piece, commemorating the endeavors of Lieutenant Zebulon Pike. Centennial celebration ceremonies appropriately dedicated the monument. *From Special Collections, Pikes Peak Library District.*

event finally took place, newspaper accounts reported "a thousand voices," the same number as had been publicized all summer.

Following the boulder unveiling in Antlers Park, a banquet was held in the Antlers Hotel. One of the principal speakers, Thomas Walsh, advocated the graduated income tax as the fairest method of distributing wealth.

That evening ten thousand people watched a spectacular fireworks display at Washburn Field on the Colorado College campus; it was termed "probably the largest crowd that ever gathered to witness a public exhibition of any kind in Colorado Springs," and "the most spectacular fireworks in Colorado." Over forty prepared displays were ignited under the supervision of W. C. Paradice, national fireworks expert, and the *Gazette* reported "$2,000 up in smoke" (this is probably a bit exaggerated, since the centennial budget for fireworks was $1,252).

Friday was titled Colorado Day, and Saturday Centennial Day. On these days as well as every other day of the celebration, the army troops marched, drilled or performed some public maneuvers. Concerts were held daily and many evenings as well, by the 29th Infantry Band and the Midland Band. Wild West shows by Guy Parker and his cowboys, and joined by the Indian camp, drew crowds. Men's and women's groups held innumerable banquets, exercises and receptions. The Colorado Bar Association and the Colorado Librarians Association held their annual conventions during the centennial.

The golf tournament was a featured sport attraction of the celebration. The Town and Gown Golf Club had planned on spending $2,500 improving its course for the play. The centennial committee had budgeted $600 for the tourney, and a gold medal plus thirteen cups were to be awarded as prizes. The week-long competition drew one hundred three entrants, and W. Kennon Jewett emerged the victor. The polo tournament had four participating teams: teams from the Cheyenne Mountain Country Club, the Denver Country Club, Sheridan Wyoming, and the 10th Cavalry. After daily play starting the Saturday before the centennial and including exhibition games, the Polo Ranch team of Sheridan, Wyoming defeated the favored 10th Cavalry 8 ¼ to 5, in the annual competition for the Foxhall Keene Cup.

Other sports, such as cricket, shooting matches, and auto races were discussed in planning, but many did not materialize. A football game between Colorado College and the University of Wisconsin was proposed, but on Centennial Day, Saturday, the game was Colorado College 5, Colorado Springs High School 4.

The first grand scheme for auto racing was a race up Pikes Peak. But an immediate assessment declared that $8,000-$10,000 would be required to fix the road and "no machine could attempt the climb unless purposely constructed for work in severe altitude." Centennial Cup auto races from Denver to Colorado Springs and from Colorado Springs to Cripple Creek or Pueblo were considered, but newspaper accounts do not report any of these having been run.

On Saturday morning the army drilled at the base of Cheyenne Mountain (no, they didn't storm the heights). That afternoon the military, Indian and cowboy camps broke up. An evening carnival that Saturday brought down the curtain on the Pike Centennial celebration in 1906.

A great celebration had ended. A worthy subject, — a patriot and a hero — had been duly honored. The men and the organizational efforts necessary to carry celebration plans to their successful completion had come forward. We are fortunate in their having preserved these efforts in scrapbooks and correspondence. Our primary purpose has been to share with you the entertaining stories leading up to the public celebration. But we are often told that history is also to provide us a lesson. Certainly there is one for us here: our predecessors have shown us what it takes to plan and carry out a great centennial celebration.

Edwin A. and Nancy E. Bathke are co-authors of many articles that have been published in regional history journals, including the Denver Westerners Brand Book and the Denver Westerners Roundup magazine. Wisconsin natives, they moved to Colorado in 1960 where Ed later retired as an engineer with Kaman Sciences and Nancy retired from teaching elementary school. By profession, Ed is a mathematician, holding degrees in the subject from the University of Wisconsin, and a Master of Science in Applied Mathematics from the University of Colorado. Nancy earned a Bachelor of Science in Education from the University of Wisconsin, and a Master of Arts from the University of Colorado.

"What, is Not This the Red River?"
Pike Speaks On Pike's Peak, His Life & Times: A Puppet Presentation

Conceived, Written & Performed by
Stephen Collins & Katherine Scott Sturdevant

This is a transcript rather than a script. The presenters used notes and, where quoting, read excerpts from original documents (primarily Zebulon Pike's journals and Clarissa Pike's pension testimonies), but they ad-libbed their own words for spontaneity's sake. Therefore, this printed version comes from oral historian Rick W. Sturdevant's transcription of DVD and audio tapes made of the June 3, 2006, presentation at the Pikes Peak Regional History Symposium, "'To Spare No Pains': Zebulon Montgomery Pike and His 1806-07 Expedition, A Bicentennial Symposium."

About the puppet stage: Stephen Collins uses heavy black curtains hung on PVC pipe. The puppets all appear above the curtains. Kathy Sturdevant interviewed the puppets from a speaker's lectern beside the puppet stage.

About the puppets: Unless otherwise identified, these are two-dimensional, historical portrait puppets. Stephen Collins made each by digitally enlarging an authentic face-forward portrait, cutting a moveable mouth, and mounting the puppet face and torso on a black (thus invisible) stick, operating the mouth mechanically. For both the Zebulon Pike and Aaron Burr puppets, there were no suitable portraits, so the enlargements came from photographed statues. Puppets identified as "cloth puppets" are commercially manufactured and resemble the large, three-dimensional puppets associated with "The Muppets." Every puppet has a unique Stephen Collins voice.

General James Wilkinson, Katharine Lee Bates, General Zebulon Montgomery Pike and Aaron Burr were among the historical portrait puppets given life by Stephen Collins and interviewed by Katherine Scott Sturdevant. *Photograph courtesy of Stephen Collins and Katherine Scott Sturdevant.*

The Play Begins.

CALVIN OTTO: To introduce our presenters, Katherine Scott Sturdevant is Chair of the History Department for Pikes Peak Community College. Her teaching specializations include western, women's, environmental, ethnic, Colorado, and Pikes Peak regional history. She is a well known local and national speaker, an expert oral history interviewer, and author of two books on a scholarly approach to family history.

Stephen Collins is Chair of Speech and Communications at Pikes Peak Community College. His teaching specializations include historical rhetoric, interpersonal and group communication, and resource interpretation. He is a master puppeteer with thirteen years of experience.

Now I'll turn it over to Kathy Sturdevant. Kathy.

KATHY STURDEVANT: First, I think I should make the point, as you may have noticed, that I and my colleague, Stephen Collins, and others on the program today are from PIKE'S PEAK Community College. And, I do not like it without the apostrophe! Usually at an event like this, as a historian, I would propose a paper, and give a talk about that paper — hopefully not read that paper. And, usually, I would talk about some serious subject and try to inject humor in it. But, I also believe in alternative teaching, delivery methods, and sources. And, as Cal mentioned, I'm also an oral historian. So, today, we're going to learn some things about Pike, about his expedition, about Pike's Peak, and even about women's history, interestingly enough, through various learning styles and particularly through oral history.

We have the unusual opportunity today — as an oral historian, this is the opportunity of a lifetime — to interview General Zebulon Pike. General Pike!

[The Pike puppet appears. He is from a photograph of a model for a statue of Pike, courtesy of Carol Kennis, Colorado Springs Pioneers Museum.]

GENERAL ZEBULON MONTGOMERY PIKE: Yes, how are you?

KATHY: I'm fine, General, thank you. You look a little stony today, however.

PIKE: Well, you know.

KATHY: General Pike, let me ask a few starting questions, the way that we would in an oral history interview. Could you tell us your full name?

PIKE: Well, my name is Zebulon Montgomery Pike.

KATHY: OK, and could you tell us when and where you were born?

PIKE: Well, I was born in Somerset County, New Jersey.

KATHY: I'm sorry. And, could you tell us about your parents?

PIKE: Well, my father was Captain Zebulon Pike. He died in 1834.

KATHY: But, you're not dead yet yourself. So, forget that.

PIKE: This oral history stuff is hard.

KATHY: I know. It's a little bit like meeting a medium, but we'll work on it. General Pike, your greatest accomplishment, I think, is the expeditions that you made. Could you tell us a little bit about how your first expedition got started—how you became involved in these activities?

PIKE: Well, yes I could. Soon after the purchase of Louisiana by an enlightened administration, measures were taken to explore the then unknown wilds of our western country—measures founded on principles of scientific pursuits. His excellency Meriwether Lewis, then a captain, was selected by the President of the United States in conjunction with Captain Clark to explore the then unknown sources of the Missouri, and I was chosen to trace the Mississippi to its source.

KATHY: Oh my! Well, how did that go?

PIKE: I made it to Leech Lake.

KATHY: Oh. Why is it called Leech Lake?

PIKE: Don't ask.

KATHY: Oh.

PIKE: I think you get the idea. It sucked. Can I say that on TV?

KATHY: You just did, General Pike. I don't even think there's a tape delay. But then, you're not familiar with television are you?

PIKE: No.

KATHY: Well, the expedition we're really interested in most today is called the Arkansas or Southwest Expedition. Could you tell us a little bit about that? For example, I heard you had an interesting group of soldiers.

PIKE: Boy, howdy, did I! Called them a dam'd set of rascels. Actually, it was nothing but a whole bunch of history docents, and the occasional librarian. Do you have any idea what it's like to go an expedition with a whole bunch of history docents? No wonder we were ill prepared!

KATHY: It sounds as though you would have been well informed along the way.

PIKE: Well, yes, but they never stop informing you!

KATHY: They must have helped you find the restrooms.

PIKE: OK, I'm not going there.

KATHY: Well, along with this group, did you have any particular problems with supplies or clothing for all these rascels?

PIKE: Well, yes. I have to admit we weren't that well prepared. We came with summer uniforms because, frankly, we didn't expect cold weather when we set out on July 15th 1806 from Fort Bellefontaine.

KATHY: And, when you set out, did you really have a plan of what you were going to do and how long it was going to take you?

PIKE: Well, I was told by General James Wilkinson to scout as close as possible to Santa Fe.

KATHY: Why would he want you to go to Santa Fe?

PIKE: No comment. Need to know only.

KATHY: Alright, well at least I won't have to edit the transcript.

PIKE: Yes. Don't ask—don't tell.

KATHY: Alright, General Pike, we need to discuss the experience of discovering our beautiful peak that we've named after you.

PIKE: It's a pretty pathetic name if you ask me. It should have been called Zebulon's Zenith.

KATHY: Oh!

PIKE: Has a catchy sound to it, you know.

KATHY: It does!

PIKE: Zebulon's Zenith.

KATHY: Yes, well, but you didn't name it that. Did you name it Pike's Peak?

PIKE: No, no, I was not nearly that arrogant! Please!

KATHY: Well, we're glad of that. What was it like when you set out to climb it? Or, when you even just saw it?

PIKE: Well, I'll tell you, it was quite the experience. It was November 25th. I'll read to you from my journal, if you permit me to.

KATHY: Oh, please. Think of this, people, we get to hear his own voice reading his journal.

PIKE: "Marched early, with an expectation of ascending the mountain, but was only able to encamp at its base, after passing over many small hills covered with cedars and pitch-pines. Our encampment was on a creek, where we found no water for several miles from the mountain; but near its base, found springs sufficient. Took a meridional observation, and the altitude of the mountain. Killed two buffalo." Missed the docents.

KATHY: Well, at least you didn't hit the docents, like the dog we've heard about.

PIKE: Oops.

KATHY: So, did you take many provisions with you?

PIKE: Uh, no. November 26th: "Expecting to return to our camp the same evening, we left all our blankets and provisions at the foot of the mountain. Killed a deer of a new species, and hung his skin on a tree with some meat. We commenced ascending; found it very difficult, being obliged to climb up rocks, sometimes almost perpendicular; and after marching all day we encamped in a cave, without blankets, victuals, or water. We had a fine clear sky, while it was snowing at the bottom. On the side of the mountain we found only yellow and pitch-pine. Some distance up we found buffalo; higher still the new species of deer, and pheasants."

KATHY: What were the conditions the next day?

PIKE: I'm so glad you asked. November 27th: "Arose hungry, dry, and extremely sore, from the inequality of the rocks on which we had lain all night, but were amply compensated for toil by the sublimity of the prospect below. The unbounded prairie was overhung with clouds, which appeared like the ocean in a storm, wave piled on wave and foaming, while the sky was perfectly clear where we were. Commenced our march up the mountain, and in about one hour arrived at the summit of this chain. Here we found the snow middle-deep; no sign of beast or bird inhabiting this region. The thermometer, which stood at 9° above zero at the foot of the mountain, here fell to 4° below zero. The summit of the Grand Peak, which was entirely bare of vegetation and covered with snow, now appeared at a distance of 15 or 16 miles from us. It was as high again as what we had ascended to its pinical [*sic*]. This, with the condition of my soldiers, who had only lights overalls on, no stockings, and were in every way ill provided to endure the inclemency of the region; the bad prospect of killing anything to subsist on, with the further detention of two or three days which it must occasion, determined us to return. The clouds from below had now ascended the mountain and entirely enveloped the summit, on which rest eternal snows. We descended by a long, deep ravine, with much less difficulty than contemplated."

And, I have to say, it will never, never, never, never, never, never, ever, ever, ever, ever be climbed. Did I say that? Never! Not ever!

KATHY: We understand your feelings about that, General.

PIKE: If I couldn't do it, who could?

KATHY: We'll have to see. One of the things that is obvious in your description is that winter was difficult for you. So, where did you go next, when you couldn't make it up the great peak?

PIKE: Well, we actually went over to Salida. We subsisted on buffalo meat. Um, we had no blankets, because we cut them up for socks. We crowded around a bonfire at night. It was so cold that our horses could walk on the Arkansas River down to the Royal Gorge. The train wasn't running.

KATHY: That's because General Palmer's symposium was last year. Well, General—

PIKE: Dang, my luck is always bad.

KATHY: Uhhh—General, is it true that the next thing you did was cross the Sangre de Cristos?

PIKE: Yes.

KATHY: And, what was it like there?

PIKE: Well, it was hilly—mountain-y. It was cold. It was really cold. I'd have liked to have had that doctor who is here with us.

KATHY: Yes, he was good; he was better than Dr. Robinson, wasn't he?

PIKE: Yes.

KATHY: So, when you got to the other side of the Sangre de Cristos, why did you go and put up a stockade there?

PIKE: Well, it seemed like the thing to do, you know, set up camp—set up a stockade.

KATHY: And raise the American flag over it?

PIKE: Absolutely!

KATHY: Wasn't it in Spanish territory, Sir?

PIKE: [Pause] I know nothing about that.

KATHY: Well, didn't someone come along and tell you it was Spanish territory?

PIKE: Uhhh, the Spanish did. Yes, it was one of those minor technicalities. The Spanish came along and told us we were in Spanish territory. I describe it in my journal as follows: "The commanding officer addressed me as follows: 'Sir, the governor of New Mexico, being informed you had missed your route, ordered me to offer you, in his name, mules, horses, money, or whatever you might stand in need of to conduct you to the head of Red river; as from Santa Fe to where it is sometimes navigable is eight days' journey, and we have guides and the routes to the traders to conduct us.' 'What,' said I, interrupting him 'is not this the Red river?' 'No, Sir! The Rio del Norte.' I immediately ordered my flag to be taken down and rolled up, feeling how sensibly I had committed myself in entering their territory, and conscious that they must have positive orders to take me in."

KATHY: OK, Sir, so didn't you really disobey orders by spending the winter in the area where you were? Didn't you openly commit an act of invasion by raising your flag over your stockade in the San Luis Valley? Didn't all those things cause great suffering amongst your men, and also cause you to be captured by the Spanish?

PIKE: [Long pause] You're as big a pain as those dang history docents, aren't you? I have no comment.

KATHY: I'm sorry, Sir, I sort of slipped. Well, what happened to your papers, then, once you were captured?

PIKE: Well, actually, they were confiscated. General Salcedo desired to assist me in taking out my papers once we were at Santa Fe, "and requested me to explain the nature of each; such as he conceived were relevant to the expedition he caused to be laid on one side, and those which were not of a public nature on the other; the whole either passing through the hands of the general or of Walker, except a few letters from my lady. On taking these up, and saying they were letters from a lady, the general gave proof that, if the ancient Spanish bravery" [Pause, with sound of turning page] Sorry, I had to turn the page.

KATHY: Did you drop your journal? I'm sorry, General.

PIKE: "had degenerated in the nation generally, their gallantry still existed, by bowing; and I put them in my pocket. He then informed me that he would examine the papers, but that in the meanwhile he wished me to make out and present to him a short sketch of my voyage, which might probably satisfactory. This I would have positively refused, had I had an idea that it was his determination to keep the papers."

KATHY: Well, it's sad that some of your papers were lost, but I know that, later, you were able to write the wonderful journal that's helping all of us right now. How were you treated generally?

PIKE: You know, I have to say, no mistreatment. In fact, I was able to see everything. Ha, ha, ha ha! Secretly took notes, um, even after told not to, and I hid them in the men's gun barrels. That was pretty smart, don't you think? I saw missions, forts, and I was able to assess the population in the area.

KATHY: Oh, so by being taken to Santa Fe and all the way into Mexico, you were able to spy on the Spanish?

PIKE: Wha—wha, I never said that. I was an alternative tourist. After all, I had all those docents with me.

KATHY: Well, General, thank you very much for this part of our interview. We hope we'll be able to speak with you again later today.

PIKE: Oh, you're welcome. Thank you very much for having me.

[Pike puppet exits.]

KATHY: Well, we know that there is a controversy about whether Zebulon Pike was involved in spying. We've already heard several opinions about that. Most historians, at least most historians here, who love Pike, and love the peak, and love the name, prefer to think that it was at least spying that was open and legitimate on Spain, and not some kind of counterbalanced spying influenced by a man who was hero to Zebulon Pike: General James Wilkinson. General Wilkinson, of course, was a very well known double agent for both Spain and the United States. So, we don't have too much doubt about what he did. He also seems to have had a fondness, though, for his protégé Zebulon Pike. I'm wondering if we might be able to speak to General Wilkinson.

[Wilkinson puppet, made from a photograph of a painted, color portrait of Wilkinson, appears.]

KATHY: Hi, General.

GENERAL JAMES WILKINSON: How are you?

KATHY: I'm fine, thank you. Now, please, we don't need any hissing from the crowd. General Wilkinson, I apologize for our audience. There are docents in it.

WILKINSON: Oh, that's OK.

KATHY: General Wilkinson, we're all a little concerned about both your activities and your relationship with Zebulon Pike and his activities, but I know that you were worried at the point that he was captured that he might be lost forever. So, what was your response when you finally heard that he was safe?

WILKINSON: Oh, it, it was terrible. I, I, it, it bothered me a great deal. So, you know, I wrote him a letter in April 1807. I said to him, Dear Zebulon, "After having counted you among the dead, I was most agreeably surprised to find, by a letter from general Salcedo . . . that you were in his possession, and that he proposed sending you, with your party, to our frontier post. I lament that you shall lose your papers, but shall rely much on your memory. Although it was unfortunate that you should have missed . . . the object of your enterprise, yet I promise myself that the route over which you have passed will afford some interesting scenes, as well as to the statesman as to the philosopher. You will hear of the scenes in which I have been engaged, and may be informed that the traitors whose infamous designs against the constitution and government of our country I have detected, exposed, and destroyed, are vainly attempting to explain their own conduct by inculpating me. Among other devices, they have asserted that your and Lieutenant Wilkinson's enterprise was a pre-meditated cooperation with Burr . . ." Ughhhh. "the arch-traitor . . . you must be cautious, extremely cautious, . . ."how you breathe a word; because publicity . . ."

KATHY: Oooo, so, General, you feel that you exposed the conspiracy, you were not part of it?

WILKINSON: Ahg, never! Never! Burr, he was just a burr in my side.

KATHY: And so, Zebulon Pike was part of no conspiracy, then?

WILKINSON: No, never! And, I would never conspire with him.

KATHY: In fact, your words sound almost as though, whether or not you were innocent, Pike was?

WILKINSON: How do I answer that?

KATHY: Well, General, you do claim your own innocence.

WILKINSON: Yes, I do. I am innocent. [Voice parodies Richard Nixon.] I am not a crook.

KATHY: Well, General, we appreciate your being here today. Thank you very much.

WILKINSON: You're welcome.

KATHY: You're excused.

WILKINSON: Thank you.

[Wilkinson puppet exits.]

KATHY: Thank goodness. That was very awkward. I have to admit, as a historian, I have my own opinions about General Wilkinson's veracity. But, at least, thank goodness, be still my heart, I only had to interview General Wilkinson and not the arch-conspirator that we all study in American history. Thank goodness I didn't have to interview Aaron Burr.

[Burr puppet, made from an enlarged photograph of a Burr statue, appears.]

VICE-PRESIDENT AARON BURR: Yo, babe!

KATHY: Oh dear!

BURR: How's it going?

KATHY: Mr. Vice President, I didn't know you were here today.

BURR: Well, hey, how could I resist such a hottie as you?

KATHY: Please, Mr. Burr, you're making me very uncomfortable.

BURR: Well, you know, they always said I was a bit of a dandy.

KATHY: Yes, you have a reputation for many things, including flirtation with women. He looks stony, too, don't you think?

BURR: Well, what can I say.

KATHY: Mr. Vice President, is it true that you convinced Thomas Jefferson to make General Wilkinson the governor of Louisiana as part of your plot to acquire territory?

BURR: There was no plot to acquire territory! And, Wilkinson? Well, he's a fine man, perfect to be the governor of northern Louisiana.

KATHY: Well, then, I suppose, Mr. Burr, you're also going to say that you didn't kill the former Secretary of the Treasury Alexander Hamilton in a duel?

BURR: That was perfectly honorable. I protected my honor, and . . . he . . . bit the bullet.

KATHY: What had Hamilton done that caused you to challenge him to a duel?

BURR: Well, he insulted me. That's ground enough right there.

KATHY: I see, so we're very important aren't we, Mr. Burr?

BURR: Well, yes.

KATHY: What is it that you were trying to do after you killed Mr. Hamilton in a duel? What was it you were trying to do as you moved across the frontier of the United States?

BURR: No comment.

KATHY: Oh, an oral historian's and journalist's nightmare! Well, isn't it true that, whatever it was, you were sending coded letters to General Wilkinson about it?

BURR: I know nothing about a ciphered let—let—letter!

KATHY: I said "coded." You said "ciphered."

BURR: I don't like oral history! You're leading me on. I'm pretty sure you're not supposed to do that.

KATHY: That's true, but then you are Aaron Burr. One of the things that, I think, you might have been doing is organizing people to be a little army for yourself to capture the frontier, perhaps for yourself or Spain or France.

BURR: Never!

KATHY: You're not a traitor, Mr. Burr?

BURR: No, I'm not a traitor; I'm this country's greatest patriot! And, if they realized it, well, things would go better.

KATHY: Well, then, you were captured, and you were put before the Supreme Court.

BURR: Yes, yes, but I was acquitted! I was acquitted. I was.

KATHY: Well, it didn't hurt that the chief justice was politically in your favor.

BURR: I know nothing about that. Rumors!

KATHY: Well, what did you do after you were acquitted, Mr. Burr?

BURR: I went on a trip to Europe.

KATHY: That was convenient.

BURR: I wanted to see Europe.

KATHY: And, what did you become when you returned to the United States?

BURR: I returned to New York City, four years later, and I was an attorney.

KATHY: Ahh!

BURR: It's an honorable profession!

KATHY: Don't we have records that suggest that you did try to serve in the War of 1812, but you lost your commission because of bad service?

BURR: I think they messed up the paperwork.

KATHY: I see. Well, Mr. Burr, I appreciate your being interviewed today. I'm sure it will be quotable at least.

BURR: Perhaps we could have dinner later.

KATHY: No, thank you.

BURR: Oh, these historians.

[Burr puppet exits.]

KATHY : One of the things that seems to be on the shoulders of puppetry in today's event is to include some women's history connected with Zebulon Pike, and we have recently, as many of you know, discovered, or rediscovered, a lovely portrait of Mrs. Pike, known as Clara or Clarissa Brown Pike.

[Portrait of Clarissa Pike (not a puppet) rises on black stick.]

KATHY: It's a lovely portrait. Clarissa or Clara was the daughter of General John Brown of Kentucky. He owned a plantation called Sugar Grove. He was the brother of Zebulon Pike's mother. So, Zebulon Pike married his first cousin. In those days it was considered quite acceptable and, perhaps, still should be, now and then. The father, General Brown, was very angry at their relationship, because he didn't want his daughter to marry a low-level enlisted soldier, living in garrison duty at different camps — and it was difficult for her. So, Zeb and Clarissa eloped from Kentucky to Cincinnati, and Brown even refused to communicate with them for a while.

She did live a difficult life in camps with Zeb. At one point in 1803, when they had been married for two years, he wrote she was "low in spirits and should cheer up and try to be lively and laugh at half the world's folly and despise the envy of the balance," because she was "very nervous her situation here is very lonesome as the ladies are by no means sociable" to her. So, she suffered the snobbery that can occur in a military environment. She also suffered, while Pike was away on his expeditions, from the loss of a little son to illness. But, she was overjoyed when she and her daughter were able to meet him when he returned to New Orleans in 1807 after the capture by the Spanish. So, Clarissa — that little portrait — tells us a lot. Thank you for showing her little portrait.

[Clarissa portrait withdraws.]

KATHY: Now, we have to prepare for some oral history, and I can't interview a portrait.

[Cloth hand puppet of a grandmotherly figure in calico and apron, with white hair in an unkempt bun, appears, as Mrs. Clarissa Pike.]

KATHY: Oh!!!

MRS. CLARISSA (BROWN) PIKE: Hello!

KATHY: Hello! Who are you?

MRS. PIKE: Well, I'm Clarissa.

KATHY: Oh, may I shake your hand?

MRS. PIKE: Oh, you may!

[Kathy and puppet shake hands.]

KATHY: It's such a pleasure to meet you.

MRS. PIKE: Oh, it's entirely my pleasure. Goodness me, I certainly was more attractive then, and I was having a better hair day.

KATHY: We like you just fine, ma'am.

MRS. PIKE: Well, thank you. It's a line, but it's alright.

KATHY: Well, no, really, the best oral history is with women of some maturity.

MRS. PIKE: Careful! Careful where you're going there, dearie.

KATHY: I don't know, first I get accosted by Aaron Burr, and now I'm going to be under the watchful eye of Grandma Pike? OK. Well, Mrs. Pike, would you please tell us about a particular period in your life that's very important to today's study, because I know that many of the papers and artifacts that we would have loved to have had about General Pike were lost after his death.

MRS. PIKE: Oh, yes.

KATHY: And no one can tell us about that experience of carrying on after his death and trying to save his artifacts better than you. So, if you would share some of that, we'd be very grateful.

MRS. PIKE: Oh, it was a terrible moment. It was absolutely terrible! [Pause and gasp.] It was actually—it was actually a fire that was in the house. I had—"I had long cherished the hope and pride of living independent on my own resources, however few. . . . It often happens that every hope is disappointed. . . . A consciousness of never having committed injustice, or willfully injured any one, is my greatest consolation under every vicissitude of fortune. In my transactions with the world, I have generally found myself a loser, as respects pecuniary affairs—disqualified by education and habit. . . .Agreeably to your request I will now proceed to relate the destruction of my dwelling. Oh! Even now, when recurring to that dreadful scene for a moment, I think to save some precious memento of departed friends—one memorial of happier days. Alas! They are only dust and ashes—gone forever—with almost every thing valuable I possess. . . ."

KATHY: We're so sorry to hear this happened to you. And, as I understand it, you were very badly burned yourself and barely got out with your life and that of your grandchildren.

MRS. PIKE: Oh, it was terrible! It was terrible! "After taking shelter from the fire and rain, I became aware that I was considerably burnt; but it had not given me any pain. We had no light, nor means of applying any remedy to the burns . . ." Could have used that doctor. "How in a moment we were reduced, objects of pity, and charity—our most pressing necessities were kindly supplied . . . I did not rise for several weeks; and was much debilitated, unable to walk out for some time. . . ."

KATHY: In fact, I understand that, because of the fire, you were reduced to almost nudity.

MRS. PIKE: Thank you for that moment of just destroying the one shred of dignity I had.

KATHY: Oh, I'm so sorry.

[Mrs. Pike puppet exits unexpectedly.]

MRS. PIKE (from offstage): Huhhm!

KATHY: Mrs. Pike?

MRS. PIKE (from offstage): Yes.

KATHY: Clara?

MRS. PIKE (from offstage): Yes.

KATHY: Please come back.

MRS. PIKE (from offstage): Uhhhh!

[Mrs. Pike puppet reappears.]

KATHY: Sometimes oral historians are a little too oral.

MRS. PIKE: Sometimes they flesh it out just a little too much.

KATHY: Well, can you tell us a little bit more about, specifically, the loss of General Pike's records and artifacts?

MRS. PIKE: Oh, yes, that was perhaps the saddest: his legacy. "One by one, each valued loss was recalled to mind, and then I found that every thing was gone" everything!" —house and all it contained, records of more than sixty years, a trunk filled with Gen. Pike's letters, those of all our friends, every manuscript . . . Spanish and French works of the most costly editions, purchased by Gen. Pike of a Spanish officer in Florida. . . . And all that now remains of my husband's writing, is the remnant of a letter on Military Affairs, wafted by the winds, partly burnt, and picked up by a neighbor some distance from the house. Every relic of former days," every relic "I had so carefully preserved —my husband's sword, military coat, and the flag," the flag "which pillowed his head in death . . . his miniature likeness by Trott, gold chain, and his gold watch, which I had given to my grand-son Pike, who unfortunately declined receiving it until his next visit from West Point."

KATHY: Oh, this is so sad. I'm sure we are all very sorry, both that you went through this and to lose these priceless objects about General Pike.

MRS. PIKE: It was a sad time.

[Mrs. Pike puppet exits.]

KATHY: Well, poor Clarissa died herself not long after she recounted these events. But, of course, we still have mysteries about her as well. Perhaps the most delicate, that I didn't want to mention in front of her, is one that was mentioned earlier: that it might have been a motivation of General Wilkinson's to send her husband off on expeditions because he was interested in spending time with the girl in the lovely portrait.

MRS. PIKE (from offstage): Rumors!

KATHY: I'm sorry; I thought you'd left the room. [Pause] Clarissa died in 1847. The words that she shared with us come from petitions for pensions that she made. We have her as one means of having a little bit of women's history in this story, and there might be other means as well. There might be a woman connected with Pikes Peak who was later than Pike himself.

[Katharine Lee Bates puppet appears, an enlarged photograph made into one of the historical portrait puppets.]

PROFESSOR KATHARINE LEE BATES (Singing): "Climb every mountain!"

KATHY: Professor Bates!

BATES: Oh, yes! How are you?

KATHY: It's wonderful to see you.

BATES: Oh, I'm feeling wonderful!

KATHY: Well, that's good. You ready for a good climb?

BATES: You bet!

KATHY: OK. Well, [to audience] this is Katharine Lee Bates.

BATES: Nice to meet everyone.

KATHY: And, of course, she came out here during 1893.

BATES: Yes.

KATHY: To teach summer school, I think?

BATES: Yes. Yes, at Colorado College.

KATHY: Ahh.

BATES: Pikes Peak Community College wasn't open yet. Because that is a classy place; I would have gone there.

KATHY: Yes. And, it would be so much less expensive than Colorado College.

BATES: Yes, and small class sizes.

KATHY: Yes, and great teachers.

BATES: Yes!

KATHY: Especially in history.

BATES: And speech.

KATHY: Well, when you were out here, what kind of tourist attractions did you go to besides Pikes Peak?

BATES: Oh, Cheyenne Canyon, Bear Creek Canyon, Garden of the Gods, the Austin Bluffs.

KATHY: The Austin Bluffs were a tourist attraction?

BATES: Oh, yes! It still is. It depends on what time of the day you go.

KATHY: I see. Actually, when you went to the top of Pikes Peak . . .

BATES: Yes?

KATHY: by what means did you travel?

BATES: By wagon!

KATHY: Ahh!

BATES: It had "Pike's Peak or Bust" on the side.

KATHY: Oh, that's where that comes from.

BATES: Umhuh.

KATHY: I see. Well, you know, many people think that you got to the top of Pikes Peak and you just sat down and wrote some lyrics.

BATES: No, we actually sang. [Singing] "The hills are alive with the sound of music!"

KATHY: I didn't know Rodgers and Hammerstein were with you.

BATES (Singing): La, la la, la—fa la la la. Oh, yes, had a wonderful time up there with them. Hold on a sec.

KATHY: Oh, I think her voice bothered her a little bit.

BATES (Coughing): OK.

KATHY: Well, one of the things that all of you might not know about the song is that you didn't really write it at the top of the mountain.

BATES: Oh, THE song.

KATHY: Yes, that song.

BATES: Technically, I didn't write a song.

KATHY: What did you write?

BATES: I wrote a poem.

KATHY: Ahh, and what place did you write it in?

BATES: What place did I write it in?

KATHY: Did you write it on the top of the mountain?

BATES: Absolutely not! I wrote it the next day.

KATHY: Oh, OK. And, if it was just a poem, how did it become a song?

BATES: Oh, that's a very interesting story. In fact, it was a contest.

KATHY: Ohhh.

BATES: But, pardon me, I can't stand to hear what they were singing at the time, so, if you don't mind, I will leave.

[Bates puppet exits.]

KATHY: Alright, I'll do it. Anybody know what tune "America the Beautiful" was first sung to? [Kathy sings the first stanza of the familiar lyrics but to the tune of "Auld Lang Syne."] Recognize it? What's the tune? Yes, "Auld Land Syne," and it works! It's kind of surprising. And now, if I can remember how it really goes.

KATHY(singing): "Oh beautiful for spacious skies, for amber waves of grain . . ."

[Suddenly a colorful, comical, cloth penguin hand puppet appears.]

PENGUIN (Screaming loudly in screechy voice.): Stop! [Kathy stops, gasping.] Stop, stop, stop stop, stop! No!

KATHY: I'm sorry, was it that bad?

PENGUIN: Plagiarism!

KATHY: Oh!

PENGUIN: Academic dishonesty!

KATHY: Me?

PENGUIN: Aghhh!

KATHY: Don't do that to me. I don't do that to other people. Well, who are you?

PENGUIN: Well, I am Percy the Penguin.

KATHY: OK. What are you doing in the middle of our Zebulon Pike event?

PENGUIN: You mean, what were you doing on my mountain! The penguins were there first.

KATHY: Penguins on Pikes Peak?

PENGUIN: Yeah, and that Zebulon guy, he knew it, and so did she. She stole our song!

KATHY: It's your song?

PENGUIN: Oh, yes. Penguins lived at the top of Pikes Peak for years, and then people started to move in and we just decided to emigrate.

KATHY: Ohhh.

PENGUIN: We went to San Francisco. And, from there, we—we got a steamer. We went down to the Antarctic.

KATHY: Oh.

PENGUIN: But, it was ours!

KATHY: So, penguins started on Pikes Peak.

PENGUIN: Yeah, we had no trouble with the Utes, but no—Zebulon and, then, Katharine Lee Bates and everybody else, they gave us problems. And, it was our song! She took it!

KATHY: Well, if it was your song, how did *you* sing it?

PENGUIN: Oh, we admired and honored its grandeur.

[Singing to the familiar tune of "American the Beautiful."]

[The "Penguin Peak" lyrics are © 2006 Stephen Collins.]

For penguins with no self-esteem
This peak is now our dream
For we can live up in the sky
As if we all could fly. . . .

O, Penguin Peak, O, Penguin Peak
In you we all can trust
We come from many miles around
It's Penguin Peak or bust.

For flightless tiny water fowl
This peak now gives us hope
To stand where only eagles fly,
Our hearts will soar as high.

O, Penguin Peak, O, Penguin Peak
We'll climb you without fail
But if our dreams all come to plan
We'll travel by cog rail.

And, she stole it! She stole the whole thing.

KATHY: Well, that was amazing.

PENGUIN: Thank you. I'm considered one of the better penguin singers.

KATHY: Well, yes, you're an excellent penguin singer. I think, however, we have to take this back to serious historical discussion.

PENGUIN: Hah, fine, we never get any credit.

[Penguin puppet exits.]

KATHY: Well, when we first did this oral history series of interviews at the Pioneers Museum, with a large audience of children as well as adults, we were asked by Carol Kennis of the Pioneers Museum to make sure the next time we did it that we made one thing clear: there weren't really ever any penguins on Pikes Peak.

PENGUIN (from offstage): Were too.

KATHY: Were not.

PENGUIN (from offstage): Were too.

KATHY: Were not.

PENGUIN (from offstage): Were too.

KATHY: Not.

PENGUIN (from offstage): Too.

KATHY: Not. Well, let's go over some important historical facts for a moment. Of course, Pike's report in 1810 is one of his greatest contributions to history, because it made Americans more interested in coming west—for example, for Santa Fe trade. It also helped solidify the notion of the Great American Desert that caused a lot of Americans to wait until later to come to the West. His description of the peak was something that made everyone want to see it, even though, of course, poor Zebulon never really climbed it. The first person we know of, the first recorded person, to climb Pikes Peak—which it was known by as popular usage—was Edward James, a botanist on the Stephen Long Expedition in 18 . . .

PIKE (from offstage): Oh, wait a second, no way—a botanist?

KATHY: Well yes, General, I'm sorry.

[Pike puppet reappears.]

PIKE: Well, OK.

KATHY: That was 1820. But, Zebulon Pike really blazed the Santa Fe Trail in many respects, although William Becknell is given the credit for it. He was using Pike's route; he was using Pike's maps. And, then, the first recorded woman that we know of who climbed Pikes Peak, Julia Anna Archibald Holmes in 1858, was in her Bloomer costume...

PIKE: Ohhhh, wait on—hold the telegraph! A woman climbed it?

KATHY: Yes, Sir.

PIKE: No, no, no no! We've got something mistaken here. *I* couldn't climb it!

KATHY: Well, she wasn't trying in winter, Sir.

PIKE: You had to bring that up.

KATHY: I'm sorry. It must have been the bloomers.

PIKE: What are bloomers?

KATHY: Oh, that's right. That was after your time.

PIKE: I'm going to have to read up on this stuff.

[Pike puppet exits, muttering.]

KATHY: I guess so. And, as we've already heard, Zebulon Pike was known as a poor man's Lewis and Clark—the Lost Pathfinder—Pathfinder and Patriot, after his expedition. He was promoted to major, and then colonel, and then brigadier general. His death was very sad. He was in the War of 1812 at the Battle of Sackets Harbor, when a mine exploded and a heavy rock hit him on the head. As he died, he said, "Push on my brave fellows and avenge our general." And, they did, with vengeance and brought the British flag to put under his head—the one that Clarissa was talking about—and he said, "I die content."

PIKE (from offstage): I may have died content, but I still want to know why my statue is facing east. You know, that's pretty lame if you ask me. Goodness me, I mean, you know, if they name it after me, can't they have my statue at least look at the dang mountain?

BATES (from offstage): You know, I've got the same problem.

KATHY: Well, now!

[Bates puppet reappears.]

BATES: They blocked my view of the mountain. What is going on around here?

KATHY: Now, Professor Bates, we did a petition campaign, and we tried to prevent it altogether, but at least if you stretch your neck, you can look at the mountain.

BATES: Yeah, sure.

[Bates puppet exits.]

KATHY: Oh, and now, we have the same problem with General Pike, but his statue always looked a little sad, and people used to interpret it as he was sad that he didn't make it up the peak. Now, we know he's sad because he has to faced east. When we think of General Pike, though, we also want to think of something along the lines of the holiday we've just passed—Memorial Day—and honor someone with the kind of language that people did after his death. General Pike, would you please reappear so we can honor you? To quote a passage that another wonderful teacher from Pikes Peak Community College, Michael Olsen, who will be speaking later this afternoon, shared with me . . .

[Pike puppet reappears.]

PIKE: Wow.

KATHY: Sorry. "The memory of a hero is always dear to his countrymen—and the recollection of the exulted principles of honor, the undaunted heroism, and the milder virtues, which shown forth in their native luster [*sic*], in the character of General Pike—will ever be cherished by a grateful people. The tears of a nation spring afresh at his remembrance, and flow in holy sympathy with the tears of those who were 'Dearer than life to him.'" Thank you, General Pike.

PIKE: I'm honored. Thank you.

The End.

Stephen Collins is the senior faculty member for Speech and Communication at Pikes Peak Community College. His teaching specializations include historical rhetoric, interpersonal and group communication, and resource interpretation. He is a master puppeteer with thirteen years of experience in directing puppet teams and ministries, from scriptwriting through performance and design, including award-winning presentations.

Katherine Scott Sturdevant is the senior faculty member for History at Pikes Peak Community College. Her teaching specializations include Western, women's, environmental, ethnic, Colorado, and Pikes Peak

Photograph courtesy of Stephen Collins and Katherine Scott Sturdevant.

regional history. She is a well-known local and national speaker, an expert oral history interviewer, the author of two books on the scholarly approach to family history, and has won local, state, and national awards for teaching excellence.

Looming Large:
The Artistic Legacy of Pikes Peak

Melinda Murphy & Katie Davis Gardner

Looming Large, a major art exhibition of images of Pikes Peak, was developed by the staff of the Colorado Springs Pioneers Museum in conjunction with the 2006 bicentennial of Zebulon Montgomery Pike's Southwestern expedition. This ambitious exhibition brought together, for the first time, the works of the area's finest historic and contemporary artists.

Tens of thousands of artists — students, amateurs and professionals alike — have recorded Pikes Peak in many media. Luminaries of the art world, including Samuel Seymour, Thomas Moran and George Caleb Bingham, have visited the Pikes Peak region and have been inspired to capture the mountain's breathtaking beauty from every angle, in every season and at every time of day. Pikes Peak looms over the foothills and eastern plains like a guardian. It is scenic, imposing, and iconic. For these reasons, the Pikes Peak region has been a favorite destination of artists from the nineteenth century to today.

Much of the Peak's fame comes from the fact that it is the grandest thing one encounters heading west from the Mississippi River. Unlike Colorado's other "fourteeners," Pikes Peak stands proudly by itself and serves as a visual landmark for hundreds of miles around. For generations, Pikes Peak has served as both beacon and symbol.

Pike's journey as an explorer for the United States government brought him to the region in 1806–1807 and he was one of the first to write about it for posterity. Lieutenant Pike called the mountain "Grand Peak" or "Highest Peak," never presuming to name it for himself. From southeastern Colorado he saw and recorded it as "a small blue cloud." Although Pike attempted to climb the mountain in late November 1806, poor weather, along with inadequate supplies and equipment, forced him to turn back. The term "Pike's Mountain" first appeared in 1819, six years after Pike's death. It would take decades before Pikes Peak (formerly spelled "Pike's Peak") became the officially recognized name.

The Ute and many other American Indian tribes occupied the land surrounding Pikes Peak long before Pike's arrival. These cultures provide us with the first description of the mountain. The Ute term for the Peak is *Ta-Wa-Ah-Gath*, which translates to "Grandfather mountain — looming large, collecting the sun's rays." The name is appropriately descriptive as this easternmost mountain is the one upon which the sun shines first at dawn. Pikes Peak was, and still is, a sacred mountain to the Utes. Names may have changed but the mountain's aura remains undiminished.

The earliest view of Pikes Peak included here is Samuel Seymour's watercolor "James Peak in the Rain," a delicate ink and watercolor sketch that was created during the artist's assignment to the Stephen H. Long expedition of 1819. Seymour (ca. 1775–ca. 1823), an English landscape and portrait artist, was the first artist to accompany an American exploratory party to the West. Long named the mountain "James Peak" in honor of his botanist, Edwin James, the first American explorer to climb the Peak. Seymour's works originally belonged to the U.S. government, but ultimately ended up in private collections after the publication of the official expedition report. This earliest-known view of Pikes Peak resides at the Museum of Fine Arts in Boston.

Another early depiction of the Peak entitled "Pikes Peak through the Gateway to the Garden of the Gods" was finished in 1880 by the western landscape painter Thomas Moran. Moran and other artists such as Helen Chain, Walter Paris, and William Henry Jackson at various times accompanied the famous U.S. Geological Survey led by Dr. Ferdinand V. Hayden of Philadelphia. The survey, which covered various locations throughout the West, was accomplished between 1867 and 1878, mainly during the summer months. Thomas Moran first accompanied the Hayden expedition in 1871 to Yellowstone and the Grand Tetons. He sketched Yellowstone, the Grand Canyon of the Colorado [River], and other scenic locations on site and finished the oil paintings in his Newark studio, while his famous compatriot, William Henry Jackson, the Survey's official photographer, recorded the same scenes in photographs. The large-scale paintings of Yellowstone and the Grand Canyon of the Colorado were purchased by the U.S. congress in 1874.

By the mid-nineteenth century, word of the West's beauty and temperate climate had reached eastern artists. The Rocky Mountains quickly became a favorite subject for nineteenth-century painters who saw the West as a grandiose and hallowed "last frontier," and Moran, who traveled extensively throughout the West between 1881 and 1911, became one of the country's most renowned painters of the western landscape.

The appeal of the majestic terrain continues to result in outstanding artwork. The exhibition, *Looming Large: The Artistic Legacy of Pikes Peak*, which featured both the earliest and most current images of the mountain, stands as a tribute to those artists who have been moved to record and share Pikes Peak's radiance and grace throughout the past two centuries. Ten of those paintings are illustrated here as examples of the diversity of artistic interpretation, ranging in date from 1820 to 2004, and including both men and women artists who worked in a wide range of styles.

When I saw the view, I felt great joy. All the wonder of America seemed displayed there, with the sea-like expanse.

—Katharine Lee Bates, author of "America the Beautiful"

View of James Peak in the Rain, 1820
Samuel Seymour (ca. 1775–ca. 1823)
Pen, black ink, and watercolor on laid paper
Courtesy of the Museum of Fine Arts, Boston

A landscape and portrait painter, as well as a prominent engraver of his day, Samuel Seymour became the first artist to accompany an American exploration party, the 1819 Stephen H. Long expedition, to the Rocky Mountains. Artwork by Samuel Seymour and fellow artist Titian Peale illustrated the published account of the Long expedition. On June 30, 1820, he produced the first ink and watercolor sketch of the Rockies and James Peak, which today is referred to as Pikes Peak. This tiny, gemlike watercolor was included in the official expedition report to the U.S. government. This rare image is unusual in that some of the foliage Seymour chose to include looks more fern-like and tropical than what is indigenous to the Western landscape, a tendency with artists who are not intimately familiar with the West. In addition to being the first easterner to capture Pikes Peak on paper, Seymour also painted the first image of the Royal Gorge and is also believed to have made the first field drawing of a Plains Indian dance group and the first painting of the interior of a Plain lodge. He also accompanied the second Long expedition to the Upper Missouri River in 1823. In 1832 a selection of Seymour's artworks were exhibited at the first American museum, Charles Willson Peale's Museum in Philadelphia. Seymour worked out of Philadelphia but may have originally been from England. He painted between 1797 and 1823 and his works are now included in collections at Yale University and the New York Public Library.

View of Pike's Peak, 1872
George Caleb Bingham (1811–1879)
Oil on canvas
Courtesy of the Amon Carter Museum, Fort Worth, Texas

George Caleb Bingham was a prominent frontier genre and portrait painter who worked as an art teacher as well as a practicing artist. Although he lived in Boon's Lick region of Missouri from 1819 on, his work is considered equal in stature and similar in style to that of painters from the Hudson River School and the White Mountain Painters in upper New York State, New Hampshire and throughout New England. A self-taught artist, Bingham followed the advice of mentor Chester Harding and copied engravings with homemade pigment while training.

Bingham is best known for his Missouri river scenes such as "The Jolly Flat Boat Men" and the atmospheric series of election-day paintings called "Stump Speaking" and "The Verdict of the People." Having made several trips to Colorado, this painting, "View of Pikes Peak," was created after a honeymoon visit to Colorado in 1872. Another image of Pikes Peak has been lost, but because of his work in the West he is considered to be part of the circle of artists referred to as "The Rocky Mountain School." An article in the 1872 Colorado Springs Gazette *and* El Paso County News *wrote: "We see it stated that Bingham's great picture, Pike's Peak in Summer time is attracting much admiration in St. Louis, where it is considered a superb piece of art. People should come and see the reality for themselves."*

Pikes Peak through the Gateway to the Garden of the Gods, 1880
Thomas Moran (1837–1926)
Oil
Courtesy of Hill Development Company

*Thomas Moran was one of the greatest American painters, albeit having
emigrated from England. Initially apprenticed to a wood engraver
illustrator sketching designs to make block prints, he began to paint on
his own, and first exhibited his oil paintings in 1858. In 1871, he served
as the official artist on the U.S. Geological Survey, consisting of a series of
expeditions to the West led by F.V. Hayden. The U.S. Congress purchased
his large-scale paintings of the Grand Canyon of the Colorado River and
Yellowstone, which boosted his public recognition. Moran traveled widely,
making preliminary sketches* en plein air *and finishing the oil paintings
in his Newark studio. He died in Santa Barbara, California.*

*Moran painted from emotions. He said, "I place no value upon literal
transcriptions from Nature. All my tendencies are toward idealization.
While I desire to tell truly of Nature, I do not wish to realize the scene
literally but to convey its true impression." This sentiment is consistent
with the ideals of the late-nineteenth-century Luminist painters that
included some of the Hudson River School painters of New York State. This
approach also reflects other painters of the "grand manner" such as Albert
Bierstadt who painted the West. In this painting, luminism is expressed in
the way the light reflects off the clouds, the snow on Pikes Peak, and the
rock formations in the foreground.*

Pikes Peak and Colorado Springs in Winter, ca. 1873
Walter Paris, (1842–1906)
Watercolor

Courtesy of the Colorado Springs Pioneers Museum, gift of Joseph F. Humphrey

This depiction of a snowstorm in Colorado Springs was painted from the window of the old Wanless Block where the First National Bank building now stands. This painting is one of the earliest images of Colorado Springs. It has been assigned the circa date of 1873 because of the heavy, deep snowfall from that year, which shows how paintings can sometimes be used as historical documents.

Walter Paris was born in London and studied at the Royal Academy after having been apprenticed to an architect at age fifteen. He worked most of his career as an architect, including the years 1863–1870 when he worked as an architect for the British government in India. Health reasons necessitated a move to Colorado Springs in 1872, and he became the earliest resident artist in town. He sketched and painted numerous views of the newly founded Colorado Springs and surrounding area including commercial buildings and houses downtown. He also painted regional landscapes, and his watercolor images are not only strictly accurate and painstakingly detailed but also some of the most delicate and beautiful. Paris's two small paintings in the Looming Large *exhibition are particularly significant as they show the way that Colorado Springs and Pueblo looked in the mid- to late-nineteenth century. Walter Paris also worked briefly for the U.S. Geological Survey team led by F.V. Hayden, which remained in Colorado until 1876.*

Pikes Peak, ca. 1890
Helen Henderson Chain (1852–1892)
Oil on ivory
Courtesy of the Denver Pubic Library

Helen Henderson Chain was a well-known Colorado painter and art teacher who had studied art in Europe and under famed romantic Hudson River School painter, George Inness, in New York. She was painting in her own studio in Denver, Colorado by 1877, where she opened and taught in an art school. Her detailed yet grandiose paintings of western landscapes place her style within the "Rocky Mountain School," a designation referring to romantic, spiritually infused and ambitious paintings of the western landscape in the vein of the Hudson River School. The Colorado Springs Pioneers Museum houses her "Mountain of the Holy Cross," a masterful companion piece to Thomas Moran's painting of the same subject. The two landscapes were both painted as a result of the Hayden Survey expedition which both artists periodically accompanied. This small oil painting is unique in that it was executed on ivory giving it a radiant iridescence. Pikes Peak emerges from the mountain mist while Gateway Rock and the Garden of the Gods fill the foreground.

Chain also painted in New Mexico, California and Europe, and she and her husband were known for their world travels. They both lost their lives in a shipwreck while on one of their tours.

Untitled (Back of Pikes Peak), 1920–1950
Francis Drexel Smith (1874–1956)
Oil on canvas
Courtesy of the collection of John Hazlehurst

A Chicago native, Francis Drexel Smith first studied at the Art Institute of Chicago. He continued his education at the Broadmoor Art Academy in Colorado Springs, serving on its first board of trustees in 1919, eventually becoming president of the Academy. He continued his work on the board after it became part of the Colorado Springs Fine Arts Center in 1935. He exhibited his work nationally beginning in 1922, and his pieces are in a number of major institutions nationwide. Known as a regional landscape painter, his graphic style is characterized by bold flat plains of color that border on abstraction. He credited the influence of renowned American realist Edward Hopper for his inspiration.

Smith owned a vast art collection and furnished his self-designed arts and crafts-style house with early American antiques inherited from his Philadelphia Drexel relatives. A quiet and shy man of independent means, Frank Smith devoted time to his art and Colorado Springs social activities, particularly to supporting fellow artists who were struggling to make a living at their chosen vocation. He would generously purchase their work "at exorbitant prices" says his grandson, John Hazlehurst, an art historian who has fond memories of his prolific artist ancestor. He remembers that Smith "radiated kindness" and that after he, as a child, told his grandfather about his imaginary dog "King," Smith asked his artist friend Boardman (Mike) Robinson to paint a likeness of King for his grandson. Hazlehurst noted that upon his death Smith's studio was filled with hundreds of works that were distributed to his friends and colleagues. Many artworks remain in private hands in the Pikes Peak region today; however, more of his paintings are beginning to appear on the art market and are commanding significant prices.

Untitled (Pikes Peak Abstraction), 1930s
Tabor Utley (1891–1978)
Watercolor
Courtesy of the Colorado Springs Fine Arts Center, Museum Purchase

A transplant to Colorado Springs due to poor health, artist Tabor Utley often worked in an early- twentieth-century modernist style. Associated with the Broadmoor Art Academy, the forerunner of the Colorado Springs Fine Arts Center, he worked under such artistic mentors as Randall Davey, Ernest Lawson, Ward Lockwood and Boardman Robinson. He also studied in Denver with Robert A. Graham and J. Campbell, and in Paris and Luxembourg. He is known for his WPA-era murals completed in Colorado Springs and other communities, and he and Boardman (Mike) Robinson collaborated on a mural for New York City's Radio City Music Hall. Due to their restoration, the murals in the Colorado Springs City Auditorium have recently received much attention. Utley contributed the section on "The Arts," depicting the music, dance and theater arts in Colorado Springs.

From early in his life Tabor Utley was clearly a "Renaissance man" who was interested and proficient in a variety of artistic outlets including landscape painting, mural work, ceramics and stage design among other things. In this bright watercolor, the unusual perspective of the Peak seems influenced by his stage design work, as the two vertical bands of color on either side of the painting are suggestive of curtains in a theatre. The three-dimensionality of the actual mountain landscape is flattened into a two-dimensional, decorative "symbol" or shape.

Untitled Pikes Peak, ca. 1950
Ethel Magafan (1916–1993)
Oil on board
Courtesy of Mr. and Mrs. Leroy (Louise) Hibbitts

Ethel Magafan was a painter, a muralist, and a member of the National Association of Women Painters and Sculptors. She and her twin sister Jenne were students of artists Frank Mechau, Boardman Robinson, and Peppino Mangravite at the Broadmoor Art Academy and frequently collaborated in their artwork. Ethel also learned lithography under Pikes Peak regional printmaker Lawrence Barrett. During the Depression years, the

twins contributed to painted murals in post offices in Colorado, Nebraska, Arkansas and Oklahoma. Ethel's 1942 tempera mural "A Horse Corral" is still extant at the South Denver Branch Post Office. Jenne died in 1952, however Ethel, whose artistic style continued to grow and change, exhibited her work in galleries in Los Angeles and New York, ultimately living in Woodstock, New York, until her death in 1993. This view of Pikes Peak seems to be from the south near Fountain, Colorado, and is similar in style to other paintings by Charles Ragland Bunnell (1897–1968) and George J. Vander Sluis (1915–1984) whose Pikes Peak paintings were also included in the exhibit Looming Large. *Her works may be found in the Denver Art Museum, the Newark Museum and the Colorado Springs Fine Arts Center.*

View of Pike's Peak, 1977
Walter Blakelock Wilson (living artist, b. 1929)
Acrylic on canvas
Courtesy of the artist

Walter Wilson grew up in upstate New York and received his first painting commission at age 14. He painted portraits throughout his high school and college years, and while in the U.S. Air Force painted murals for the military. This experience and his love of piloting planes inspired his aerial views, and can be seen in his tendency to create slightly "aerial" vantage points, even in his landscapes such as this. This Pikes Peak shows the mountain from the northwest of Colorado Springs, and Wilson good-humoredly acknowledges taking artistic liberty with the landscape having included an imaginary body of water in the work. Rendered in large blocks of color, Wilson's style makes a dramatic comparison to some of the early nineteenth-century landscapes of this region.

Wilson and his wife Patricia settled in Colorado Springs in 1956 and he headed the art department and taught art at the prestigious Fountain Valley School, a position established by the esteemed artist Boardman Robinson. They now reside in Arizona where Walter continues to paint landscapes and portraits. The collection of the Colorado Springs Pioneers Museum includes one of his works depicting scenes and personages from Colorado Springs and Pikes Peak regional history. Wilson's artwork may be viewed at the Colorado Springs Fine Arts Center, and as an artist Wilson is a favorite among regional collectors, represented in over 300 collections.

Pikes Peak, 2004
Tracy Felix (living artist, b. 1957)
Oil on board
Courtesy of the Colorado Springs Pioneers Museum, gift of the Friends

Tracy Felix worked for many years in the Pikes Peak region from his studio in Manitou until moving to Denver in 2004 with his artist wife, Sushe Felix. Felix paints mainly landscapes of mountains and mountain ranges focusing on their geological shapes, crevices, geometric patterns, vegetation, and weather. His whimsical clouds in particular set the emotional tone of his pieces. In "Pikes Peak" Felix's signature style enables his marshmallow-like clouds to cast palpable shadows on the foothills. He generally paints in oil on canvas and the arts and crafts-style hand-carved frames created individually to match each of his pieces have become one of Felix's trademarks. Having painted most of the peaks in Colorado, he can identify mountains from various points of view when researching historical paintings or photographs. He relates, "I was born near the Sangre de Cristos in the San Luis Valley, Colorado, and grew up under the looming summit of Pikes Peak in Colorado Springs. My whole life has been spent hiking and skiing in the mountains that I feel so much a part of. My paintings are all about expressing my love for the Western landscape." His pieces may be found in the collections at the Sangre de Cristo Arts and Conference Center in Pueblo, Colorado, the Denver Art Museum, and the Colorado Springs Fine Arts Center, and in numerous prestigious private collections.

Melinda Murphy is an independent researcher and curator with a Master's Degree in Art, History, Theory & Criticism from the School of the Art Institute of Chicago, a Master's of Arts in Teaching Elementary Education, and a B.A. in Studio Art from the Colorado College. She has worked in a number of museums including the Colorado Springs Fine Arts Center, the Chicago Historical Society and the Art Institute of Chicago, and has taught overseas in Burma. Melinda Murphy curated the *Looming Large* exhibition at the Colorado Springs Pioneers Museum with the assistance of the museum's curator, Katie Davis Gardner.

Katie Davis Gardner is the curator at the Colorado Springs Pioneers Museum, the City's history museum. She holds a Master's Degree in Early American Culture from the Winterthur Program in Early American Culture and the University of Delaware, and a B.A. from the Colorado College in Art History. She has worked in various museums continuously since her junior year in college, including the Colorado Springs Fine Arts Center and the Colorado Historical Society in Denver.

Selected Bibliography

Adams, Alva. *The Louisiana Purchase and its First Explorer, Zebulon Montgomery Pike*, [Colorado Springs, Colo.[: s.n., 1906.

Allen, John Logan, ed. *North American Exploration*, Lincoln and London: University of Nebraska Press, 1997.

————. *Passage Through the Garden: Lewis and Clark and the Image of the American Northwest*, Urbana and London: University of Illinois Press, 1975.

Baker, Nina Brown. *Pike of Pike's Peak*, New York: Harcourt, Brace, 1953.

Benn, Carl. *The Battle of York*, Belleville, Ontario: Mika Publishing, 1984.

Billington, Ray Allen and Martin Ridge. *Westward Expansion: A History of the American Frontier*, New York: MacMillan Publishing, 1982.

Carter, Carrol Joe. *Pike in Colorado*, Fort Collins, Colo.: Old Army Press, 1978.

Carter, Harvey L. *Zebulon Montgomery Pike, Pathfinder and Patriot*, Colorado Springs, Colo.: Printed by the Dentan Printing Co., 1956.

De Witt, Donald, and Zebulon Montgomery Pike. *Pike and Pike's Peak; A Brief Life of Zebulon Montgomery Pike and Extracts from His Journal of Exploration*, [Colorado Springs]: Gowdy-Simmons Press, 1906.

Erickson, Doug, Jeremy Skinner, and Paul Merchant, eds. *Jefferson's Western Explorations: Discoveries Made In Exploring The Missouri, Red River And Washita by Captains Lewis and Clark, Doctor Sibley, and William Dunbar, and compiled by Thomas Freeman*, Glendale: A. H. Clark & Co., 2004.

Goetzmann, William H. *Exploration and Empire: The Explorer and the Scientist in the Winning of the American West*, New York: Knopf, 1966.

Hafen, Leroy R. and Carl Coke Rister. *Western America: The Exploration, Settlement & Development of the Land Beyond the Mississippi*, New York: Prentice-Hall, Inc., 1951.

Harvey, Charles M. *Captain Zebulon M. Pike, Expansionist*, [New York: Putnam], 1906.

————. *The Pike Exploration Centennial*, [N.Y. : American Monthly Review of Reviews, 1906].

Historical Society of the Pikes Peak Region, and Harvey L. Carter, ed. *The Pikes Peak Region, A Sesquicentennial History*, Colorado Springs, Colo.: Dentan Printing Co., 1956.

Hollon, W. Eugene. *The Lost Pathfinder, Zebulon Montgomery Pike. American Exploration and Travel*, [12], Norman: University of Oklahoma Press, 1949.

Martin, George W. *The Flag in Kansas: The One-Hundredth Anniversary of Its First Unfurling to Be Celebrated September 26-29, 1906*, [Republic County?] Kan: s.n, 1906.

Montgomery, M. R. *Jefferson and the Gun-men. How the West was Almost Lost*, New York: Crown Publishers, 2000.

Pike, Zebulon Montgomery. *An Account of Expeditions to the Sources of the Mississippi, and Through the Western Parts of Louisiana, to the Sources of the Arkansaw, Kans, La Platte, and Pierre Jaun Rivers, Performed by Order of the Government of the United States During the Years 1805, 1806, and 1807 And a Tour Through the Interior Parts of New Spain, When Conducted Through These Provinces, by Order of the Captain-General, in the Year 1807*, Philadelphia: C. & A. Conrad & Co, 1810.

————. *Exploratory Travels Through the Western Territories of North America Comprising a Voyage from St. Louis, on the Mississippi, to the Source of That River, and a Journey Through the Interior of Louisiana, and the North-Eastern Provinces of New Spain : Performed in the Years 1805, 1806, 1807, by Order of the Government of the United States*, Denver: W. H. Lawrence, 1889.

Pike, Zebulon Montgomery, and Elliott Coues. *The Expeditions of Zebulon Montgomery Pike, To Headwaters of the Mississippi River, Through Louisiana Territory, and in New Spain, During the Years 1805-6-7*, New York: F. P. Harper, 1895.

Pike, Zebulon Montgomery, Stephen Harding Hart, Archer Butler Hulbert, and Mark L. Gardner. *The Southwestern Journals of Zebulon Pike, 1806-1807*, Albuquerque: University of New Mexico Press, 2006.

———— . *Zebulon Pike's Arkansaw Journal, in Search of the Southern Louisiana Purchase Boundary Line (Interpreted by His Newly Recovered Maps)*, [Colorado Springs]: Stewart Commission of Colorado College, 1932.

Pike, Zebulon Montgomery, and Mary Gay Humphreys. *The Boy's Story of Zebulon M. Pike*, New York: C. Scribner's Sons, 1911.

Pike, Zebulon Montgomery, and Donald Dean Jackson. *The Journals of Zebulon Montgomery Pike, With Letters and Related Documents*, The American Exploration and Travel Series, Norman: University of Oklahoma Press, 1966.

Pike, Zebulon Montgomery, and Milo Milton Quaife. *The Southwestern Expedition of Zebulon M. Pike*, Chicago: R. R. Donnelley & Sons Co., 1925.

Ronda, James P. *Lewis and Clark Among the Indians* (Lincoln: University of Nebraska Press, 1984.)

Sleeper, Howard L. *Concerning Pike of Pike's Peak*, Denver, Colo.: Public Library Bulletin, 1906.

Terrell, John Upton. *Zebulon Pike; the Life and Times of an Adventurer*. New York: Weybright and Talley, 1968.

Wheat, Carl Irving. *Mapping the Trans-Mississippi West*, San Francisco: Institute of Historical Cartography, 1955.

Wibberley, Leonard. *Zebulon Pike, Soldier and Explorer*, New York: Funk & Wagnalls, 1961.

Wilkinson, James, *Memoirs of My Own Times*, Philadelphia: McCardle, 1816.

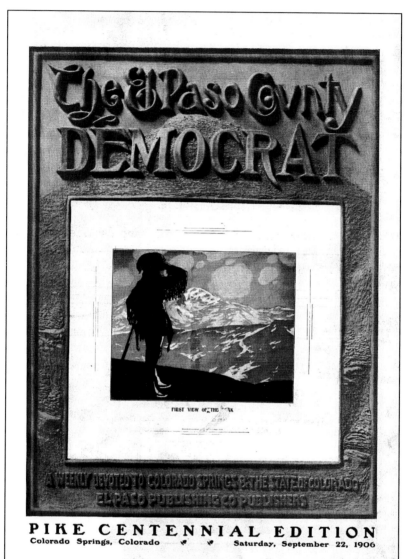

A local paper, *The El Paso County Democrat*, produced a special Pike Centennial Edition in 1906. *From Special Collections, Pikes Peak Library District.*

INDEX

"Aaron Burr, James Wilkinson, Zebulon Pike & the Great Louisiana Conspiracy: A Veteran Prosecutor & Amateur Historian Looks at the Evidence," by John M. Hutchins, 139–172

Abernethy, Thomas, cited, 152

AdAmAn Club, 232–233; fireworks, 233; photo of, 232

Adams, John, 141, 150

Adams-Onís Treaty, 175; map of boundary, 6

Alamosa, Colo., stockade built near, 24, 63

Albuquerque, N. Mex., 187

Alencaster, Joachín del Real (gov. of N. Mex.), 34, 180; dispatches patrols, 42; meets with Robinson, 42; meets with Pike, 187; and Melgares expedition, 182, 184

Allen, John L., 68; "Zebulon Montgomery Pike & American Science," by John L. Allen, 47–68

Ambrose, Stephen, and *Undaunted Courage*, 25

"America the Beautiful," 218, 224, 273

American Alpine Club: analysis of climbing accidents, 101

American Enlightenment, *See* Enlightenment, The

American Flag, 262–263; missing, 120; at Pawnee camp, 21, 32–33, 81–82, 99, 185; in Spanish territory, 42, 43

American imperialism, 71, 80, 175; and Anglo-Americans, 80; and Jefferson, 71–72; and Pike, 15, 72–73; and Spanish territory, 78–80, 84, 176

American Indians. *See* Indians

American Philosophical Society, The, 50, 52

Antlers Hotel: statue dedication, 241; photo of, 227

Antlers Park, 1; monument in, 206, 228, 245, 255; photo of, 254

Anza, Juan Bautista de, 14

Apache Indians, 182

Arkansas River, 22, 24; exploration of, 35; mistaken for Red River, 27, 45; Pike on, 21, 23, 38, 62, 63; and Pike's orders, 56, 90, 91, 117, 184–185; reached by Melgares, 183; as a route of travel, 189; sources passed, 37

Around the Circle, viewbook, illust., 223

Art and artists, 279–292. "The Rocky Mountain School," 283. *See also* Statues

Aurora (newspaper), 149; on Pike's death, 165

Automobile Sociability Tours, 234

Bachoroski, David, 231–232

Ballinger, Joseph (sgt.), 94, 155–157, 162; recruiting Indian allies for Burr, 156

Barber, Charles E., designs Pike Centennial medal, 246

Barr, Fred, 232

Barr Camp, 233

Barr Trail, 233

Bates, Katharine Lee, 224, 271–273;

This plaster model of a proposed statue of Zebulon Pike was dedicated in a great ceremony in front of the Antlers Hotel in 1901. Citizens failed to raise sufficient money to cast the real statue, and this temporary monument eventually disintegrated. Henry Russell Wray described the statue as "a large, pale grasshopper with the colic." *Photograph from Special Collections, Pikes Peak Library District.*